Mometrix
TEST PREPARATION

D0890306

ILTS

Middle Grades Social Science (204) Exam Secrets Study Guide

Dear Future Exam Success Story:

First of all, **THANK YOU** for purchasing Mometrix study materials!

Second, congratulations! You are one of the few determined test-takers who are committed to doing whatever it takes to excel on your exam. **You have come to the right place.** We developed these study materials with one goal in mind: to deliver you the information you need in a format that's concise and easy to use.

In addition to optimizing your guide for the content of the test, we've outlined our recommended steps for breaking down the preparation process into small, attainable goals so you can make sure you stay on track.

We've also analyzed the entire test-taking process, identifying the most common pitfalls and showing how you can overcome them and be ready for any curveball the test throws you.

Standardized testing is one of the biggest obstacles on your road to success, which only increases the importance of doing well in the high-pressure, high-stakes environment of test day. Your results on this test could have a significant impact on your future, and this guide provides the information and practical advice to help you achieve your full potential on test day.

Your success is our success

We would love to hear from you! If you would like to share the story of your exam success or if you have any questions or comments in regard to our products, please contact us at **800-673-8175** or **support@mometrix.com**.

Thanks again for your business and we wish you continued success!

Sincerely,
The Mometrix Test Preparation Team

Need more help? Check out our flashcards at: http://MometrixFlashcards.com/ILTS

Copyright © 2022 by Mometrix Media LLC. All rights reserved.
Written and edited by the Mometrix Exam Secrets Test Prep Team
Printed in the United States of America

TABLE OF CONTENTS

[Handwritten margin notes: "April-May" beside Illinois History; "May-June" beside Geography; "June July" beside Economics/US Government; "July August" beside Psychology, Sociology, and Anthropology]

Introduction

Thank you for purchasing this resource! You have made the choice to prepare yourself for a test that could have a huge impact on your future, and this guide is designed to help you be fully ready for test day. Obviously, it's important to have a solid understanding of the test material, but you also need to be prepared for the unique environment and stressors of the test, so that you can perform to the best of your abilities.

For this purpose, the first section that appears in this guide is the **Secret Keys**. We've devoted countless hours to meticulously researching what works and what doesn't, and we've boiled down our findings to the five most impactful steps you can take to improve your performance on the test. We start at the beginning with study planning and move through the preparation process, all the way to the testing strategies that will help you get the most out of what you know when you're finally sitting in front of the test.

We recommend that you start preparing for your test as far in advance as possible. However, if you've bought this guide as a last-minute study resource and only have a few days before your test, we recommend that you skip over the first two Secret Keys since they address a long-term study plan.

If you struggle with **test anxiety**, we strongly encourage you to check out our recommendations for how you can overcome it. Test anxiety is a formidable foe, but it can be beaten, and we want to make sure you have the tools you need to defeat it.

1

Copyright © Mometrix Media. You have been licensed one copy of this document for personal use only. Any other reproduction or redistribution is strictly prohibited. All rights reserved.

Secret Key #1 – Plan Big, Study Small

There's a lot riding on your performance. If you want to ace this test, you're going to need to keep your skills sharp and the material fresh in your mind. You need a plan that lets you review everything you need to know while still fitting in your schedule. We'll break this strategy down into three categories.

Information Organization

Start with the information you already have: the official test outline. From this, you can make a complete list of all the concepts you need to cover before the test. Organize these concepts into groups that can be studied together, and create a list of any related vocabulary you need to learn so you can brush up on any difficult terms. You'll want to keep this vocabulary list handy once you actually start studying since you may need to add to it along the way.

Time Management

Once you have your set of study concepts, decide how to spread them out over the time you have left before the test. Break your study plan into small, clear goals so you have a manageable task for each day and know exactly what you're doing. Then just focus on one small step at a time. When you manage your time this way, you don't need to spend hours at a time studying. Studying a small block of content for a short period each day helps you retain information better and avoid stressing over how much you have left to do. You can relax knowing that you have a plan to cover everything in time. In order for this strategy to be effective though, you have to start studying early and stick to your schedule. Avoid the exhaustion and futility that comes from last-minute cramming!

Study Environment

The environment you study in has a big impact on your learning. Studying in a coffee shop, while probably more enjoyable, is not likely to be as fruitful as studying in a quiet room. It's important to keep distractions to a minimum. You're only planning to study for a short block of time, so make the most of it. Don't pause to check your phone or get up to find a snack. It's also important to **avoid multitasking**. Research has consistently shown that multitasking will make your studying dramatically less effective. Your study area should also be comfortable and well-lit so you don't have the distraction of straining your eyes or sitting on an uncomfortable chair.

 The time of day you study is also important. You want to be rested and alert. Don't wait until just before bedtime. Study when you'll be most likely to comprehend and remember. Even better, if you know what time of day your test will be, set that time aside for study. That way your brain will be used to working on that subject at that specific time and you'll have a better chance of recalling information.

Finally, it can be helpful to team up with others who are studying for the same test. Your actual studying should be done in as isolated an environment as possible, but the work of organizing the information and setting up the study plan can be divided up. In between study sessions, you can discuss with your teammates the concepts that you're all studying and quiz each other on the details. Just be sure that your teammates are as serious about the test as you are. If you find that your study time is being replaced with social time, you might need to find a new team.

2

Copyright © Mometrix Media. You have been licensed one copy of this document for personal use only. Any other reproduction or redistribution is strictly prohibited. All rights reserved.

Secret Key #2 – Make Your Studying Count

You're devoting a lot of time and effort to preparing for this test, so you want to be absolutely certain it will pay off. This means doing more than just reading the content and hoping you can remember it on test day. It's important to make every minute of study count. There are two main areas you can focus on to make your studying count.

Retention

It doesn't matter how much time you study if you can't remember the material. You need to make sure you are retaining the concepts. To check your retention of the information you're learning, try recalling it at later times with minimal prompting. Try carrying around flashcards and glance at one or two from time to time or ask a friend who's also studying for the test to quiz you.

To enhance your retention, look for ways to put the information into practice so that you can apply it rather than simply recalling it. If you're using the information in practical ways, it will be much easier to remember. Similarly, it helps to solidify a concept in your mind if you're not only reading it to yourself but also explaining it to someone else. Ask a friend to let you teach them about a concept you're a little shaky on (or speak aloud to an imaginary audience if necessary). As you try to summarize, define, give examples, and answer your friend's questions, you'll understand the concepts better and they will stay with you longer. Finally, step back for a big picture view and ask yourself how each piece of information fits with the whole subject. When you link the different concepts together and see them working together as a whole, it's easier to remember the individual components.

Finally, practice showing your work on any multi-step problems, even if you're just studying. Writing out each step you take to solve a problem will help solidify the process in your mind, and you'll be more likely to remember it during the test.

Modality

Modality simply refers to the means or method by which you study. Choosing a study modality that fits your own individual learning style is crucial. No two people learn best in exactly the same way, so it's important to know your strengths and use them to your advantage.

For example, if you learn best by visualization, focus on visualizing a concept in your mind and draw an image or a diagram. Try color-coding your notes, illustrating them, or creating symbols that will trigger your mind to recall a learned concept. If you learn best by hearing or discussing information, find a study partner who learns the same way or read aloud to yourself. Think about how to put the information in your own words. Imagine that you are giving a lecture on the topic and record yourself so you can listen to it later.

For any learning style, flashcards can be helpful. Organize the information so you can take advantage of spare moments to review. Underline key words or phrases. Use different colors for different categories. Mnemonic devices (such as creating a short list in which every item starts with the same letter) can also help with retention. Find what works best for you and use it to store the information in your mind most effectively and easily.

3

Copyright © Mometrix Media. You have been licensed one copy of this document for personal use only. Any other reproduction or redistribution is strictly prohibited. All rights reserved.

Secret Key #3 – Practice the Right Way

Your success on test day depends not only on how many hours you put into preparing, but also on whether you prepared the right way. It's good to check along the way to see if your studying is paying off. One of the most effective ways to do this is by taking practice tests to evaluate your progress. Practice tests are useful because they show exactly where you need to improve. Every time you take a practice test, pay special attention to these three groups of questions:

- The questions you got wrong
- The questions you had to guess on, even if you guessed right
- The questions you found difficult or slow to work through

This will show you exactly what your weak areas are, and where you need to devote more study time. Ask yourself why each of these questions gave you trouble. Was it because you didn't understand the material? Was it because you didn't remember the vocabulary? Do you need more repetitions on this type of question to build speed and confidence? Dig into those questions and figure out how you can strengthen your weak areas as you go back to review the material.

 Additionally, many practice tests have a section explaining the answer choices. It can be tempting to read the explanation and think that you now have a good understanding of the concept. However, an explanation likely only covers part of the question's broader context. Even if the explanation makes perfect sense, **go back and investigate** every concept related to the question until you're positive you have a thorough understanding.

As you go along, keep in mind that the practice test is just that: practice. Memorizing these questions and answers will not be very helpful on the actual test because it is unlikely to have any of the same exact questions. If you only know the right answers to the sample questions, you won't be prepared for the real thing. **Study the concepts** until you understand them fully, and then you'll be able to answer any question that shows up on the test.

It's important to wait on the practice tests until you're ready. If you take a test on your first day of study, you may be overwhelmed by the amount of material covered and how much you need to learn. Work up to it gradually.

On test day, you'll need to be prepared for answering questions, managing your time, and using the test-taking strategies you've learned. It's a lot to balance, like a mental marathon that will have a big impact on your future. Like training for a marathon, you'll need to start slowly and work your way up. When test day arrives, you'll be ready.

Start with the strategies you've read in the first two Secret Keys—plan your course and study in the way that works best for you. If you have time, consider using multiple study resources to get different approaches to the same concepts. It can be helpful to see difficult concepts from more than one angle. Then find a good source for practice tests. Many times, the test website will suggest potential study resources or provide sample tests.

Copyright © Mometrix Media. You have been licensed one copy of this document for personal use only. Any other reproduction or redistribution is strictly prohibited. All rights reserved.

Practice Test Strategy

If you're able to find at least three practice tests, we recommend this strategy:

UNTIMED AND OPEN-BOOK PRACTICE

Take the first test with no time constraints and with your notes and study guide handy. Take your time and focus on applying the strategies you've learned.

TIMED AND OPEN-BOOK PRACTICE

Take the second practice test open-book as well, but set a timer and practice pacing yourself to finish in time.

TIMED AND CLOSED-BOOK PRACTICE

Take any other practice tests as if it were test day. Set a timer and put away your study materials. Sit at a table or desk in a quiet room, imagine yourself at the testing center, and answer questions as quickly and accurately as possible.

Keep repeating timed and closed-book tests on a regular basis until you run out of practice tests or it's time for the actual test. Your mind will be ready for the schedule and stress of test day, and you'll be able to focus on recalling the material you've learned.

Copyright © Mometrix Media. You have been licensed one copy of this document for personal use only. Any other reproduction or redistribution is strictly prohibited. All rights reserved.

Secret Key #4 – Pace Yourself

Once you're fully prepared for the material on the test, your biggest challenge on test day will be managing your time. Just knowing that the clock is ticking can make you panic even if you have plenty of time left. Work on pacing yourself so you can build confidence against the time constraints of the exam. Pacing is a difficult skill to master, especially in a high-pressure environment, so **practice is vital**.

Set time expectations for your pace based on how much time is available. For example, if a section has 60 questions and the time limit is 30 minutes, you know you have to average 30 seconds or less per question in order to answer them all. Although 30 seconds is the hard limit, set 25 seconds per question as your goal, so you reserve extra time to spend on harder questions. When you budget extra time for the harder questions, you no longer have any reason to stress when those questions take longer to answer.

Don't let this time expectation distract you from working through the test at a calm, steady pace, but keep it in mind so you don't spend too much time on any one question. Recognize that taking extra time on one question you don't understand may keep you from answering two that you do understand later in the test. If your time limit for a question is up and you're still not sure of the answer, mark it and move on, and come back to it later if the time and the test format allow. If the testing format doesn't allow you to return to earlier questions, just make an educated guess; then put it out of your mind and move on.

On the easier questions, be careful not to rush. It may seem wise to hurry through them so you have more time for the challenging ones, but it's not worth missing one if you know the concept and just didn't take the time to read the question fully. Work efficiently but make sure you understand the question and have looked at all of the answer choices, since more than one may seem right at first.

Even if you're paying attention to the time, you may find yourself a little behind at some point. You should speed up to get back on track, but do so wisely. Don't panic; just take a few seconds less on each question until you're caught up. Don't guess without thinking, but do look through the answer choices and eliminate any you know are wrong. If you can get down to two choices, it is often worthwhile to guess from those. Once you've chosen an answer, move on and don't dwell on any that you skipped or had to hurry through. If a question was taking too long, chances are it was one of the harder ones, so you weren't as likely to get it right anyway.

On the other hand, if you find yourself getting ahead of schedule, it may be beneficial to slow down a little. The more quickly you work, the more likely you are to make a careless mistake that will affect your score. You've budgeted time for each question, so don't be afraid to spend that time. Practice an efficient but careful pace to get the most out of the time you have.

6

Copyright © Mometrix Media. You have been licensed one copy of this document for personal use only. Any other reproduction or redistribution is strictly prohibited. All rights reserved.

Secret Key #5 – Have a Plan for Guessing

When you're taking the test, you may find yourself stuck on a question. Some of the answer choices seem better than others, but you don't see the one answer choice that is obviously correct. What do you do?

The scenario described above is very common, yet most test takers have not effectively prepared for it. Developing and practicing a plan for guessing may be one of the single most effective uses of your time as you get ready for the exam.

In developing your plan for guessing, there are three questions to address:

- When should you start the guessing process?
- How should you narrow down the choices?
- Which answer should you choose?

When to Start the Guessing Process

Unless your plan for guessing is to select C every time (which, despite its merits, is not what we recommend), you need to leave yourself enough time to apply your answer elimination strategies. Since you have a limited amount of time for each question, that means that if you're going to give yourself the best shot at guessing correctly, you have to decide quickly whether or not you will guess.

Of course, the best-case scenario is that you don't have to guess at all, so first, see if you can answer the question based on your knowledge of the subject and basic reasoning skills. Focus on the key words in the question and try to jog your memory of related topics. Give yourself a chance to bring the knowledge to mind, but once you realize that you don't have (or you can't access) the knowledge you need to answer the question, it's time to start the guessing process.

It's almost always better to start the guessing process too early than too late. It only takes a few seconds to remember something and answer the question from knowledge. Carefully eliminating wrong answer choices takes longer. Plus, going through the process of eliminating answer choices can actually help jog your memory.

Summary: Start the guessing process as soon as you decide that you can't answer the question based on your knowledge.

Copyright © Mometrix Media. You have been licensed one copy of this document for personal use only. Any other reproduction or redistribution is strictly prohibited. All rights reserved.

How to Narrow Down the Choices

The next chapter in this book (**Test-Taking Strategies**) includes a wide range of strategies for how to approach questions and how to look for answer choices to eliminate. You will definitely want to read those carefully, practice them, and figure out which ones work best for you. Here though, we're going to address a mindset rather than a particular strategy.

Your odds of guessing an answer correctly depend on how many options you are choosing from.

Number of options left	5	4	3	2	1
Odds of guessing correctly	20%	25%	33%	50%	100%

You can see from this chart just how valuable it is to be able to eliminate incorrect answers and make an educated guess, but there are two things that many test takers do that cause them to miss out on the benefits of guessing:

- Accidentally eliminating the correct answer
- Selecting an answer based on an impression

We'll look at the first one here, and the second one in the next section.

To avoid accidentally eliminating the correct answer, we recommend a thought exercise called **the $5 challenge**. In this challenge, you only eliminate an answer choice from contention if you are willing to bet $5 on it being wrong. Why $5? Five dollars is a small but not insignificant amount of money. It's an amount you could afford to lose but wouldn't want to throw away. And while losing

$5 once might not hurt too much, doing it twenty times will set you back $100. In the same way, each small decision you make—eliminating a choice here, guessing on a question there—won't by itself impact your score very much, but when you put them all together, they can make a big difference. By holding each answer choice elimination decision to a higher standard, you can reduce the risk of accidentally eliminating the correct answer.

The $5 challenge can also be applied in a positive sense: If you are willing to bet $5 that an answer choice *is* correct, go ahead and mark it as correct.

Summary: Only eliminate an answer choice if you are willing to bet $5 that it is wrong.

Copyright © Mometrix Media. You have been licensed one copy of this document for personal use only. Any other reproduction or redistribution is strictly prohibited. All rights reserved.

Which Answer to Choose

You're taking the test. You've run into a hard question and decided you'll have to guess. You've eliminated all the answer choices you're willing to bet $5 on. Now you have to pick an answer. Why do we even need to talk about this? Why can't you just pick whichever one you feel like when the time comes?

The answer to these questions is that if you don't come into the test with a plan, you'll rely on your impression to select an answer choice, and if you do that, you risk falling into a trap. The test writers know that everyone who takes their test will be guessing on some of the questions, so they intentionally write wrong answer choices to seem plausible. You still have to pick an answer though, and if the wrong answer choices are designed to look right, how can you ever be sure that you're not falling for their trap? The best solution we've found to this dilemma is to take the decision out of your hands entirely. Here is the process we recommend:

Once you've eliminated any choices that you are confident (willing to bet $5) are wrong, select the first remaining choice as your answer.

Whether you choose to select the first remaining choice, the second, or the last, the important thing is that you use some preselected standard. Using this approach guarantees that you will not be enticed into selecting an answer choice that looks right, because you are not basing your decision on how the answer choices look.

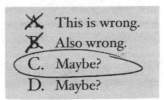

This is not meant to make you question your knowledge. Instead, it is to help you recognize the difference between your knowledge and your impressions. There's a huge difference between thinking an answer is right because of what you know, and thinking an answer is right because it looks or sounds like it should be right.

Summary: To ensure that your selection is appropriately random, make a predetermined selection from among all answer choices you have not eliminated.

9

Copyright © Mometrix Media. You have been licensed one copy of this document for personal use only. Any other reproduction or redistribution is strictly prohibited. All rights reserved.

Test-Taking Strategies

This section contains a list of test-taking strategies that you may find helpful as you work through the test. By taking what you know and applying logical thought, you can maximize your chances of answering any question correctly!

It is very important to realize that every question is different and every person is different: no single strategy will work on every question, and no single strategy will work for every person. That's why we've included all of them here, so you can try them out and determine which ones work best for different types of questions and which ones work best for you.

Question Strategies

⊘ READ CAREFULLY – No shit

Read the question and the answer choices carefully. Don't miss the question because you misread the terms. You have plenty of time to read each question thoroughly and make sure you understand what is being asked. Yet a happy medium must be attained, so don't waste too much time. You must read carefully and efficiently.

⊘ CONTEXTUAL CLUES

Look for contextual clues. If the question includes a word you are not familiar with, look at the immediate context for some indication of what the word might mean. Contextual clues can often give you all the information you need to decipher the meaning of an unfamiliar word. Even if you can't determine the meaning, you may be able to narrow down the possibilities enough to make a solid guess at the answer to the question.

⊘ PREFIXES

If you're having trouble with a word in the question or answer choices, try dissecting it. Take advantage of every clue that the word might include. Prefixes and suffixes can be a huge help. Usually, they allow you to determine a basic meaning. *Pre-* means before, *post-* means after, *pro-* is positive, *de-* is negative. From prefixes and suffixes, you can get an idea of the general meaning of the word and try to put it into context.

⊘ HEDGE WORDS

Watch out for critical hedge words, such as *likely, may, can, sometimes, often, almost, mostly, usually, generally, rarely*, and *sometimes*. Question writers insert these hedge phrases to cover every possibility. Often an answer choice will be wrong simply because it leaves no room for exception. Be on guard for answer choices that have definitive words such as *exactly* and *always*.

⊘ SWITCHBACK WORDS

Stay alert for *switchbacks*. These are the words and phrases frequently used to alert you to shifts in thought. The most common switchback words are *but, although*, and *however*. Others include *nevertheless, on the other hand, even though, while, in spite of, despite*, and *regardless of*. Switchback words are important to catch because they can change the direction of the question or an answer choice.

10

Copyright © Mometrix Media. You have been licensed one copy of this document for personal use only. Any other reproduction or redistribution is strictly prohibited. All rights reserved.

⊘ Face Value

When in doubt, use common sense. Accept the situation in the problem at face value. Don't read too much into it. These problems will not require you to make wild assumptions. If you have to go beyond creativity and warp time or space in order to have an answer choice fit the question, then you should move on and consider the other answer choices. These are normal problems rooted in reality. The applicable relationship or explanation may not be readily apparent, but it is there for you to figure out. Use your common sense to interpret anything that isn't clear.

Answer Choice Strategies

⊘ Answer Selection

The most thorough way to pick an answer choice is to identify and eliminate wrong answers until only one is left, then confirm it is the correct answer. Sometimes an answer choice may immediately seem right, but be careful. The test writers will usually put more than one reasonable answer choice on each question, so take a second to read all of them and make sure that the other choices are not equally obvious. As long as you have time left, it is better to read every answer choice than to pick the first one that looks right without checking the others.

⊘ Answer Choice Families

An answer choice family consists of two (in rare cases, three) answer choices that are very similar in construction and cannot all be true at the same time. If you see two answer choices that are direct opposites or parallels, one of them is usually the correct answer. For instance, if one answer choice says that quantity x increases and another either says that quantity x decreases (opposite) or says that quantity y increases (parallel), then those answer choices would fall into the same family. An answer choice that doesn't match the construction of the answer choice family is more likely to be incorrect. Most questions will not have answer choice families, but when they do appear, you should be prepared to recognize them.

⊘ Eliminate Answers

Eliminate answer choices as soon as you realize they are wrong, but make sure you consider all possibilities. If you are eliminating answer choices and realize that the last one you are left with is also wrong, don't panic. Start over and consider each choice again. There may be something you missed the first time that you will realize on the second pass.

⊘ Avoid Fact Traps

Don't be distracted by an answer choice that is factually true but doesn't answer the question. You are looking for the choice that answers the question. Stay focused on what the question is asking for so you don't accidentally pick an answer that is true but incorrect. Always go back to the question and make sure the answer choice you've selected actually answers the question and is not merely a true statement.

⊘ Extreme Statements

In general, you should avoid answers that put forth extreme actions as standard practice or proclaim controversial ideas as established fact. An answer choice that states the "process should be used in certain situations, if..." is much more likely to be correct than one that states the "process should be discontinued completely." The first is a calm rational statement and doesn't even make a definitive, uncompromising stance, using a hedge word *if* to provide wiggle room, whereas the second choice is far more extreme.

11

Copyright © Mometrix Media. You have been licensed one copy of this document for personal use only. Any other reproduction or redistribution is strictly prohibited. All rights reserved.

⏱ BENCHMARK

As you read through the answer choices and you come across one that seems to answer the question well, mentally select that answer choice. This is not your final answer, but it's the one that will help you evaluate the other answer choices. The one that you selected is your benchmark or standard for judging each of the other answer choices. Every other answer choice must be compared to your benchmark. That choice is correct until proven otherwise by another answer choice beating it. If you find a better answer, then that one becomes your new benchmark. Once you've decided that no other choice answers the question as well as your benchmark, you have your final answer.

⏱ PREDICT THE ANSWER

Before you even start looking at the answer choices, it is often best to try to predict the answer. When you come up with the answer on your own, it is easier to avoid distractions and traps because you will know exactly what to look for. The right answer choice is unlikely to be word-for-word what you came up with, but it should be a close match. Even if you are confident that you have the right answer, you should still take the time to read each option before moving on.

General Strategies

⏱ TOUGH QUESTIONS

If you are stumped on a problem or it appears too hard or too difficult, don't waste time. Move on! Remember though, if you can quickly check for obviously incorrect answer choices, your chances of guessing correctly are greatly improved. Before you completely give up, at least try to knock out a couple of possible answers. Eliminate what you can and then guess at the remaining answer choices before moving on.

⏱ CHECK YOUR WORK

Since you will probably not know every term listed and the answer to every question, it is important that you get credit for the ones that you do know. Don't miss any questions through careless mistakes. If at all possible, try to take a second to look back over your answer selection and make sure you've selected the correct answer choice and haven't made a costly careless mistake (such as marking an answer choice that you didn't mean to mark). This quick double check should more than pay for itself in caught mistakes for the time it costs.

⏱ PACE YOURSELF

It's easy to be overwhelmed when you're looking at a page full of questions; your mind is confused and full of random thoughts, and the clock is ticking down faster than you would like. Calm down and maintain the pace that you have set for yourself. Especially as you get down to the last few minutes of the test, don't let the small numbers on the clock make you panic. As long as you are on track by monitoring your pace, you are guaranteed to have time for each question.

⏱ DON'T RUSH

It is very easy to make errors when you are in a hurry. Maintaining a fast pace in answering questions is pointless if it makes you miss questions that you would have gotten right otherwise. Test writers like to include distracting information and wrong answers that seem right. Taking a little extra time to avoid careless mistakes can make all the difference in your test score. Find a pace that allows you to be confident in the answers that you select.

12

Copyright © Mometrix Media. You have been licensed one copy of this document for personal use only. Any other reproduction or redistribution is strictly prohibited. All rights reserved.

⊘ Keep Moving

Panicking will not help you pass the test, so do your best to stay calm and keep moving. Taking deep breaths and going through the answer elimination steps you practiced can help to break through a stress barrier and keep your pace.

Final Notes

The combination of a solid foundation of content knowledge and the confidence that comes from practicing your plan for applying that knowledge is the key to maximizing your performance on test day. As your foundation of content knowledge is built up and strengthened, you'll find that the strategies included in this chapter become more and more effective in helping you quickly sift through the distractions and traps of the test to isolate the correct answer.

Now that you're preparing to move forward into the test content chapters of this book, be sure to keep your goal in mind. As you read, think about how you will be able to apply this information on the test. If you've already seen sample questions for the test and you have an idea of the question format and style, try to come up with questions of your own that you can answer based on what you're reading. This will give you valuable practice applying your knowledge in the same ways you can expect to on test day.

Good luck and good studying!

Copyright © Mometrix Media. You have been licensed one copy of this document for personal use only. Any other reproduction or redistribution is strictly prohibited. All rights reserved.

Copyright © Mometrix Media. You have been licensed one copy of this document for personal use only. Any other reproduction or redistribution is strictly prohibited. All rights reserved.

Social Science Foundations

COLLECTING INFORMATION AND ORGANIZING AND REPORTING RESULTS

The first step of compiling data for useful implementation requires narrowing down on a **topic**. The student should first read background information to identify areas that are interesting or need further study and that the student does not have a strong opinion about. The research question should be identified, and the student should refer to general sources that can point to more specific information. When he or she begins to take notes, his or her information must be **organized** with a clear system to identify the source. Any information from outside sources must be acknowledged with **footnotes** or a **bibliography**. To gain more specific information about his or her topic, the student can then research bibliographies from general sources to narrow down on information pertinent to the topic at hand. He or she should draft a thesis statement that summarizes the main point of the research. This should lead to a working **outline** that incorporates all the ideas needed to support the main point in a logical order. A rough draft should incorporate the results of the research in the outlined order, with all citations clearly inserted. The paper should then be edited for clarity, style, flow, and content.

FORMULATING RESEARCH QUESTIONS OR HYPOTHESES

Formulating research questions or hypotheses is the process of finding questions to answer that have not yet been asked. The first step in the process is reading **background information**. Knowing about a general topic and reading about how other people have addressed it helps identify areas that are well understood. Areas that are not as well understood may either be lightly addressed in the available literature or distinctly identified as a topic that is not well understood and deserves further study. Research questions or hypotheses may address such an unknown aspect, or they may focus on drawing parallels between similar, well-researched topics that have not been connected before. Students usually need practice in developing research questions that are of the appropriate scope so that they will find enough information to answer the question, yet not so much that they become overwhelmed. Hypotheses tend to be more specific than research questions.

IDENTIFYING MAIN IDEAS IN A DOCUMENT

Main ideas in a paragraph are often found in the **topic sentence**, which is usually the first or second sentence in the paragraph. Every following sentence in the paragraph should relate to that initial information. Sometimes, the first or second sentence doesn't obviously set up the main idea. When that happens, each sentence in the paragraph should be read carefully to find the **common theme** between them all. This common theme is the main idea of the paragraph. Main ideas in an entire document can be found by analyzing the structure of the document. Frequently, the document begins with an introductory paragraph or abstract that will summarize the main ideas. Each paragraph often discusses one of the main ideas and contributes to the overall goal of the document. Some documents are divided up into chapters or sections, each of which discusses a main idea. The way that main ideas are described in a document (either in sentences, paragraphs, or chapters) depends on the length of the document.

USING ELECTRONIC RESOURCES AND PERIODICALS FOR REFERENCE

Electronic resources are often the quickest, most convenient way to get background information on a topic. One of the particular strengths of **electronic resources** is that they can also provide primary-source multimedia video, audio, or other visual information on a topic that would not be accessible in print. Information available on the internet is not often carefully screened for accuracy

15

Copyright © Mometrix Media. You have been licensed one copy of this document for personal use only. Any other reproduction or redistribution is strictly prohibited. All rights reserved.

or for bias, so choosing the **source** of electronic information is often very important. Electronic encyclopedias can provide excellent overview information, but publicly edited resources like Wikipedia are open to error, rapid change, incompleteness, or bias. Students should be made aware of the different types and reliabilities of electronic resources, and they should be taught how to distinguish between them. Electronic resources can often be too detailed and overwhelm students with irrelevant information. **Periodicals** provide current information on social science events, but they too must be screened for bias. Some amount of identifiable bias can actually be an important source of information, because it indicates prevailing culture and standards. Periodicals generally have tighter editorial standards than electronic resources, so completeness and overt errors are not usually as problematic. Periodicals can also provide primary-source information with interviews and photographs.

USING ENCYCLOPEDIAS, BIBLIOGRAPHIES, OR ALMANACS FOR SOCIAL SCIENCE RESEARCH

Encyclopedias are ideal for getting background information on a topic. They provide an overview of the topic and link it to other concepts that can provide additional keywords, information, or subjects. They can help students narrow their topic by showing the subtopics within the overall topic and by relating it to other topics. **Encyclopedias** may sometimes prove to be more useful than the internet because they provide a clearly organized, concise overview of material. **Bibliographies** are bound collections of references to periodicals and books, organized by topic. Students can begin researching more efficiently after they identify a topic, look it up in a bibliography, and look up the references listed there. This provides a branching network of information a student can follow. A pitfall of bibliographies is that when in textbooks or other journal articles, the references in them are chosen to support the author's point of view and so may be limited in scope. **Almanacs** are volumes of facts published annually. They provide numerical information on just about every topic, and are organized by subject or geographic region. They are often helpful for supporting arguments made using other resources and do not provide any interpretation of their own.

PRIMARY AND SECONDARY RESOURCES

Primary resources provide information about an event from the perspective of people who were present at the event. They might be letters, autobiographies, interviews, speeches, artworks, or anything created by people with first-hand experience. **Primary resources** are valuable because they provide not only facts about the event but also information about the surrounding circumstances; for example, a letter might provide commentary about how a political speech was received. The internet is a source of primary information, but care must be taken to evaluate the perspective of the website providing that information. Websites hosted by individuals or special-interest organizations are more likely to be biased than those hosted by public organizations, governments, educational institutions, or news associations. **Secondary resources** provide information about an event but were not written at the time the event occurred. They draw information from primary sources. Because secondary sources were written later, they have the added advantage of historical perspective, multiple points of view, or resultant outcomes. Newsmagazines that write about an event even a week after it occurred count as secondary sources. Secondary sources tend to analyze events more effectively or thoroughly than primary sources.

> **Review Video: What are Primary and Secondary Resources?**
> Visit mometrix.com/academy and enter code: 383328

ORGANIZING INFORMATION CHRONOLOGICALLY AND ANALYZING THE SEQUENCE OF EVENTS

To organize information chronologically, each piece of information must be associated with a time or a date. Events are ordered according to the time or date at which they happened. In social

Copyright © Mometrix Media. You have been licensed one copy of this document for personal use only. Any other reproduction or redistribution is strictly prohibited. All rights reserved.

sciences, chronological organization is the most straightforward way to arrange information, because it relies on a uniform, fixed scale—the passage of time. Information can also be organized based on any of the "who, what, when, where, why?" principles.

Analyzing the sequence of chronological events involves not only examining the event itself but the preceding and following events. This can put the event in question into perspective, showing how a certain thing might have happened based on preceding history. One large disadvantage of chronological organization is that it may not highlight important events clearly relative to less important events. Determining the relative importance of events depends more strongly on interpreting their relationships to neighboring events.

RECOGNIZING CAUSE-AND-EFFECT RELATIONSHIPS AND COMPARING SIMILARITIES AND DIFFERENCES

Cause-and-effect relationships are simply linkages between an event that happened (the **effect**) because of some other event (the **cause**). Effects are always chronologically ordered after causes. Effects can be found by asking why something happened or looking for information following words like *so, consequently, since, because, therefore, this led to, as a result,* and *thus.* Causes can also be found by asking what happened. **Comparing similarities and differences** involves mentally setting two concepts next to each other and then listing the ways they are the same and the ways they are different. The level of comparison varies by student level; for example, younger students may compare the physical characteristics of two animals while older students compare the themes of a book. Similarity/difference comparisons can be made by listing written descriptions in a point-by-point approach, or they can be done in several graphic ways. Venn diagrams are commonly used to organize information, showing non-overlapping clouds filled with information about the different characteristics of A and B, and the overlapping area shows ways in which A and B are the same. Idea maps using arrows and bubbles can also be developed to show these differences.

DISTINGUISHING BETWEEN FACT AND OPINION

Students easily recognize that **facts** are true statements that everyone agrees on, such as an object's name or a statement about a historical event. Students also recognize that **opinions** vary about matters of taste, such as preferences in food or music, that rely on people's interpretation of facts. Simple examples are easy to spot. **Fact-based passages** include certainty-grounded words like *is, did,* or *saw.* On the other hand, **passages containing opinions** often include words that indicate possibility rather than certainty, such as *would, should,* or *believe.* First-person verbs also indicate opinions, showing that one person is talking about his or her experience. Less clear are examples found in higher-level texts. For example, primary-source accounts of a Civil War battle might include facts ("*x* battle was fought today") and also opinions ("Union soldiers are not as brave as Confederate soldiers") that are not clearly written as such ("I believe Union soldiers..."). At the same time that students learn to interpret sources critically (Was the battle account written by a Southerner?), they should practice sifting fact from these types of opinion. Other examples where fact and opinion blend together are self-authored internet websites.

Review Video: Fact or Opinion
Visit mometrix.com/academy and enter code: 870899

DETERMINING THE ADEQUACY, RELEVANCE, AND CONSISTENCY OF INFORMATION

Before information is sought, a list of **guiding questions** should be developed to help determine whether information found is adequate, relevant, and consistent. These questions should be based on the **research goals**, which should be laid out in an outline or concept map. For example, a student writing a report on Navajo social structure might begin with questions concerning the

Copyright © Mometrix Media. You have been licensed one copy of this document for personal use only. Any other reproduction or redistribution is strictly prohibited. All rights reserved.

general lifestyle and location of Navajos and follow with questions about how Navajo society was organized. While researching his questions, he or she will come up with pieces of information. This information can be compared to his or her research questions to determine whether it is **relevant** to his or her report. Information from several sources should be compared to determine whether the information is **consistent**. Information that is **adequate** helps answer specific questions that are part of the research goals. Inadequate information for this particular student might be a statement such as "Navajos had a strong societal structure," because the student is probably seeking more specific information.

DRAWING CONCLUSIONS AND MAKING GENERALIZATIONS ABOUT A TOPIC

Students reading about a topic will encounter different facts and opinions that contribute to their overall impression of the material. The student can critically examine the material by thinking about what facts have been included, how they have been presented, what they show, what they relate to outside the written material, and what the author's conclusion is. Students may agree or disagree with the author's conclusion, based on the student's interpretation of the facts the author presented. When working on a research project, a student's research questions will help him or her gather details that will enable him or her to **draw a conclusion** about the research material.

Generalizations are blanket statements that apply to a wide number of examples. They are similar to conclusions but do not have to summarize the information as completely as conclusions. Generalizations in reading material may be flagged by words such as *all*, *most*, *none*, *many*, *several*, *sometimes*, *often*, *never*, *overall*, or *in general*. Generalizations are often followed by supporting information consisting of a list of facts. Generalizations can refer to facts or the author's opinions, and they provide a valuable summary of the text overall.

EVALUATING AND INTERPRETING MAPS

The **map legend** is an area that provides interpretation information such as the key, the scale, and how to interpret the map. The **key** is the area that defines symbols, abbreviations, and color schemes used on the map. Any feature identified on the map should be defined in the key. The **scale** is a feature of the map legend that tells how distance on the map relates to distance on the ground. It can either be presented mathematically in a ratio or visually with a line segment. For example, it could say that one inch on the map equals one foot on the ground, or it could show a line segment and tell how much distance on the map the line symbolizes. **Latitude** and **longitude** are often shown on maps to relate their area to the world. Latitude shows how far a location is north or south from Earth's equator, and longitude shows how far a location is east or west from Earth's prime meridian. Latitude runs from 90°N (North Pole) to 0° (equator) to 90°S (South Pole), and longitude runs 180°E (International Date Line) to 0° (prime meridian) to 180°W (International Date Line).

> **Review Video: 5 Elements of any Map**
> Visit mometrix.com/academy and enter code: 437727

POPULAR MAP PROJECTIONS

- **Globe**: Earth's features are shown on a sphere. No distortion of distances, directions, or areas occurs.
- **Mercator**: Earth's features are projected onto a cylinder wrapped around a globe. This generates a rectangular map that is not distorted at the equator but is greatly distorted near the poles. Lines of latitude and longitude form a square grid.
- **Robinson**: Earth's features are projected onto an oval-looking map. Areas near the poles are truer to size than in the Mercator. Some distortion affects every point.

Copyright © Mometrix Media. You have been licensed one copy of this document for personal use only. Any other reproduction or redistribution is strictly prohibited. All rights reserved.

- **Orthographic**: Earth's features are shown on a circle, which is tangent to the globe at any point chosen by the mapmaker. This generates a circular, 3D-appearing map similar to how Earth is seen from space.
- **Conic maps**: This family of maps is drawn by projecting the globe's features onto a cone set onto the globe. Some distortion affects most points.
- **Polar maps**: The land around the poles has been projected onto a circle. This provides much less distortion of Antarctica and the land around the North Pole than other map types.

CARTOGRAPHIC DISTORTION AND ITS INFLUENCE ON MAP PROJECTIONS

Cartographic distortion is the distortion caused by projecting a three-dimensional structure, in this case, Earth's surface, onto the two-dimensional surface of a map. Numerous map projections have been developed to minimize distortion, but the only way to eliminate distortion completely is to render Earth in three dimensions. Most map projections have minimal distortion in some location, usually the center, and the distortion becomes greater close to the edges of the map. Some map projections try to compromise and distribute the distortion more evenly across the map. Different categories of maps preserve, or do not distort, different features. Maps that preserve directions accurately are **azimuthal**, and maps that preserve shapes properly are **conformal**. Area-preserving maps are called **equal-area maps**, and maps that preserve distance are called **distance-preserving**. Maps that preserve the shortest routes are **gnomonic projections**.

> **Review Video: Map Projections**
> Visit mometrix.com/academy and enter code: 327303

COMPARING MAPS OF THE SAME PLACE FROM DIFFERENT TIME PERIODS

Maps of the same place from different time periods can often be initially aligned by **geographic features**. Political and land-use boundaries are most likely to change between time periods, whereas locations of waterways and geologic features such as mountains are relatively constant. Once geographic features have been used to align maps, they can be compared side-by-side to examine the changing locations of human settlement, smaller waterways, etc. This kind of map interpretation, at the smallest scale, provides information about how small groups of humans **interact with their environment**. For example, such analysis might show that major cities began around ports and then moved inland as modes of transportation, like railroads and cars, became more common. Lands that were initially used for agriculture might become incorporated into a nearby city as the population grows. This kind of map analysis can also show the evolution of the **socio-economics** of an area, providing information about the relative importance of economic activities (manufacturing, agriculture, or trade) and even the commuting behavior of workers.

NATURAL, POLITICAL, AND CULTURAL FEATURES ON MAPS

Map legends will provide information about the types of natural, political, or cultural features on a map. Some maps show only one of these three features. **Natural features** such as waterways, wetlands, beaches, deserts, mountains, highlands, and plains can be compared between regions by type, number, distribution, or any other physical characteristic. **Political features** such as state and county divisions or roads and railroads can be compared numerically, but examining their geographic distribution may be more informative. This provides information on settlement density and population. In addition, road and railroad density may show regions of intense urbanization, agricultural regions, or industrial centers. **Cultural features** may include roads and railroads, but might also include historic areas, museums, archaeological digs, early settlements, and even campgrounds. Comparing and contrasting the number, distribution, and types of these features may provide information on the history of an area, the duration of settlement of an area, or the current use of the area (for example, many museums are found in current-day cultural centers).

Copyright © Mometrix Media. You have been licensed one copy of this document for personal use only. Any other reproduction or redistribution is strictly prohibited. All rights reserved.

COMPARING MAPS WITH DATASETS OR TEXTS

Maps can provide a great deal of information about an area by showing specific locations where certain types of settlement, land use, or population growth occurred. **Datasets** and **texts** can provide more specific information about events that might only otherwise be hypothesized from maps. This specific information may provide dates of significant events (for example, the date of a fire that gutted a downtown region, forcing suburban development) or important numerical data (e.g., population growth by year). Written datasets and texts enable map interpretation to become concrete and allow observed trends to be linked with specific causes ("Real estate prices rose in 2004, causing middle-class citizens to move northwest of the city"). Without specific information from additional sources, inferences drawn from maps cannot be put in **context** and interpreted in more than a vague way.

EVALUATING AND INTERPRETING OTHER GRAPHIC FORMATS

The type of information being conveyed guides the choice of **format**. Textual information and numeric information must be displayed with different techniques. Text-only information may be most easily summarized in a diagram or a timeline. If the text includes numeric information, it may be converted into a chart that shows the size of groups, connects ideas in a table or graphic, or shows information in a hybridized format. Numeric information is often most helpfully presented in tables or graphs. When information will be referred to and looked up again and again, tables are often most helpful for the reader. When the trends in the numeric information are more important than the numbers themselves, graphs are often the best choice. Information that is linked to the land and has a spatial component is best conveyed using maps.

INTERPRETING CHARTS AND TABLES

Charts used in social science are a visual representation of data. They combine graphic and textual elements to convey information in a concise format. Often, **charts** divide the space up in blocks, which are filled with text and/or pictures to convey a point. Charts are often organized in tabular form, where blocks below a heading all have information in common. Charts also divide information into conceptual, non-numeric groups (for example, "favorite color"), which are then plotted against a numerical axis (e.g., "number of students"). Charts should be labeled in such a way that a reader can locate a point on the chart and then consult the surrounding axes or table headings to understand how it compares to other points. **Tables** are a type of chart that divides textual information into rows and columns. Each row and column represent a characteristic of the information. For example, a table might be used to convey demographic information. The first column would provide "year," and the second would provide "population." Reading across the rows, one could see that in the year 1966, the population of Middletown was 53,847. Tracking the columns would show how frequently the population was counted.

INTERPRET GRAPHS AND DIAGRAMS

Graphs are similar to charts, except that they graphically show numeric information on both axes. For example, a **graph** might show population through the years, with years on the x axis and population on the y axis. One advantage of graphs is that the population during the time in between censuses can be estimated by locating that point on the graph. Each axis should be labeled to allow the information to be interpreted correctly, and the graph should have an informative title.

Diagrams are usually drawings that show the progression of events. The drawings can be fairly schematic, as in a flow chart, or they can be quite detailed, as in a depiction of scenes from a battle. Diagrams usually have arrows connecting the events or boxes shown. Each event or box should be

Copyright © Mometrix Media. You have been licensed one copy of this document for personal use only. Any other reproduction or redistribution is strictly prohibited. All rights reserved.

labeled to show what it represents. Diagrams are interpreted by following the progression along the arrows through all events.

Review Video: Understanding Charts and Tables
Visit mometrix.com/academy and enter code: 882112

USING TIMELINES IN SOCIAL SCIENCE

Timelines are used to show the relationships between people, places, and events. They are ordered chronologically and usually are shown left-to-right or top-to-bottom. Each event on the **timeline** is associated with a date, which determines its location on the timeline. On electronic resources, timelines often contain hyperlinks associated with each event. Clicking on the event's hyperlink will open a page with more information about the event. **Cause-and-effect relationships** can be observed on timelines, which often show a key event and then resulting events following in close succession. These can be helpful for showing the order of events in time or the relationships between similar events. They help make the passage of time a concrete concept and show that large periods pass between some events, while other events cluster very closely.

USING POLITICAL CARTOONS IN SOCIAL SCIENCE STUDIES

Political cartoons are drawings that memorably convey an opinion. These opinions may be supportive or critical and may summarize a series of events or pose a fictional situation that summarizes an attitude. **Political cartoons** are, therefore, secondary sources of information that provide social and cultural context about events. Political cartoons may have captions that help describe the action or put it in context. They may also have dialogue, labels, or other recognizable cultural symbols. For example, Uncle Sam frequently appears in political cartoons to represent the United States government. Political cartoons frequently employ caricatures to call attention to a situation or a person. The nature of the caricature helps show the cartoonist's attitude toward the issue being portrayed. Every element of the cartoon is included to support the artist's point and should be considered in the cartoon's interpretation. When interpreting political cartoons, students should examine what issue is being discussed, what elements the artist chose to support his or her point, and what the message is. Considering who might agree or disagree with the cartoon is also helpful in determining the message of the cartoon.

ANALYZING ARTIFACTS

Artifacts, or everyday objects used by previous cultures, are useful for understanding life in those cultures. Students should first discover, or be provided with, a **description** of the item. This description should depict what time period the **artifact** was used in and what culture used it. From that description and/or from examination of the artifact, students should be able to discuss what the artifact is, what it is made of, its potential uses, and the people who likely used it. They should then be able to draw **conclusions** from all these pieces of evidence about life in that culture. For example, analysis of coins from an early American archaeological site might show that settlers brought coins with them, or that some classes of residents were wealthy, or that trade occurred with many different nations. The interpretation will vary depending on the circumstances surrounding the artifact. Students should consider these circumstances when drawing conclusions.

Copyright © Mometrix Media. You have been licensed one copy of this document for personal use only. Any other reproduction or redistribution is strictly prohibited. All rights reserved.

Disciplinary Literacy in Social Science

OVERVIEW OF CLASSROOM MANAGEMENT

- **Organization**—the state or manner of being organized
- **Discipline**—training expected to produce a specific character or pattern of behavior, especially training that produces moral or mental improvement
- **Procedures**—a set of established forms or methods for conducting the affairs of an organized body
- **Learner responsibility**—the student must have responsibility for their actions or non-actions
- **Interventions**—interference so as to modify a process or situation

INSTRUCTIONAL APPROACHES TO CLASSROOM MANAGEMENT AND STUDENT MOTIVATION

- Model-based classroom management
- Concise and efficient instructions
- Developmentally and age-appropriate instruction
- Large (whole) group instruction
- Small group instruction

Be able to create and maintain an atmosphere that encourages questions, conjectures, problem-solving, and experimentation.

RETEACHING, ENRICHMENT, AND EXTENSIONS

- **Reteaching**—The act of teaching over again
- **Enrichment**—above and beyond the given
- **Extensions**—small add-ons that help in teaching

CURRICULUM COMPONENTS

- **Scope and sequence**—effective instruction focusing on the essential skills and concepts commonly found on standardized tests.
- **Curricular materials**—equipment and materials needed to teach a subject.
- **Learner objectives**—types and levels of objectives of what will be taught.

PRIOR KNOWLEDGE

Prior knowledge is a combination of one's existing attitudes, experiences, and knowledge. Attitudes can range from beliefs about ourselves as learners or being aware of our own strengths and weaknesses. It can also be our level of motivation and responsibility for our own learning. The experiences from our daily activities, especially ones with our friends and families, give us a background from which we derive most of our understanding. Individual events in our lives provide us experiences we can draw from, both bad and good, and influence how we deal with future situations. This knowledge is drawn from a wide variety of things, from knowledge of specific content areas and the concepts within, to the goals that we have for ourselves academically.

USING COMPUTERS TO BETTER MANAGE THE CLASSROOM

Computers have revolutionized virtually every area of society, and teaching is no exception. Various forms of digitalization can significantly increase the efficiency of a teacher's ability to manage the classroom. Teachers can use the computer to do traditional paperwork and help free them from a

Copyright © Mometrix Media. You have been licensed one copy of this document for personal use only. Any other reproduction or redistribution is strictly prohibited. All rights reserved.

number of tasks that are classified as noninstructional. A computer will not make a classroom a success by itself, and a teacher must know, like a business manager, what programs will do and how they are used. Teachers can use computers to:

- Keep student progress records, tests, and cumulative and average scores.
- Prepare individualized notes and observations for each student.
- Keep thorough records of attendance.
- Keep an inventory of supplies that include what quantities are available and where they are located.
- Generate tests and worksheets, as well as often grade them instantly. Students may also be able to take the test on the computer.
- Produce posters and calendars and generally provide more options for time organization.
- Appreciably increase communication between the teacher, parents, and their children.

TEACHER PLANNING AND PREPARATION

Despite the status of the teacher's knowledge on instructional matters, he or she selects certain curricular content, makes decisions about groupings, and allocates specific time periods for activities. These are the crux of teacher preparation and planning. Teachers must turn curricular goals and related content into a plan that works; the planning may be informal, or it may be formal and explicit. This includes textbook and material selection, content strategies, learning assessments for particular pupils, scheduling lessons, and detailing instruction for particular days. A skillful teacher plans his or her school day before they ever enter into the classroom. Teachers have perceptions of the students' needs in different subject areas, but very little is accomplished if the teacher is hindered in their plans.

QUESTIONING STRATEGY IN RECIPROCAL TEACHING

One of the surest signs of proficiency in a subject is the ability to teach the concepts that have been learned to others. Reciprocal teaching provides students with the opportunity to absorb the information that has been read or taught and begin summarizing, questioning, clarifying, and ultimately predicting the content that they read, as though they might have to teach it to someone else. Students first identify the kind of information significant enough for the substance of a question when those questions are first generated as they read through a text. They then ask this information in the form of a question and test themselves to find out if they might answer their own questions. The generation of questions is a flexible strategy insofar as students can be taught and encouraged to ask questions on a number of different levels. When students know before reading that they need to think of questions about the text, they then read while aware of the important ideas in that text. This helps increase comprehension, process the meaning, and make inferences and connections to prior information before forming a question.

ORAL QUESTIONING IN CLASS

One easy way for teachers to conduct a formative assessment in class is to briefly quiz students on the material covered. Whether it is to be done for a grade or not, it is generally useful to give a brief overview of the previous day's lesson at the beginning of class. Oftentimes, this can be best accomplished by allowing students to articulate the material and to critique one another's understanding. Some probing questions from the teacher can ensure that the recent material is understood in the context of the material that has already been learned. It is not always necessary to formally grade students on their participation or performance in an informal question-and-answer session; the main thing is to develop an idea of the students' progress.

Copyright © Mometrix Media. You have been licensed one copy of this document for personal use only. Any other reproduction or redistribution is strictly prohibited. All rights reserved.

TRADITIONAL AND STANDARDIZED FORMS OF ASSESSMENTS, WHEN TO USE, AND USING STUDENTS' WORK TO GUIDE INSTRUCTION

- Identify what students are doing correctly.
- Identify the concepts that your class is developing.
- Point out your students' misconceptions and errors.
- Identify appropriate measures of scoring aptitude.
- Figure out appropriate methods of remediation and acceleration.
- Know the appropriate uses of rubrics.

HURDLES STUDENTS FACE STUDYING AT HOME

The personal difficulties students have and priorities that compete with classwork have drastically changed as the world has become digitally saturated. The presence and ubiquitous nature of social media influences culture and mindsets in ways that society still does not fully comprehend. Students may have difficulties with homework because parents come home tired after a hectic day and are unable to properly monitor the students' assignments, or the parents are less familiar with the more modernized methods of teaching and assignments and become frustrated or apathetic—choosing to simply remain in ignorance rather than confront the unfamiliar territory. Oftentimes, the parents do not actually realize that their child is having a problem until they see that their child's grades are suffering. Students may also be involved in various extracurricular activities that vie for their time or suffer specific personal difficulties such as an unstable home life, a lack of adult role models, or drug problems.

STRATEGIES TO HAVE STUDENTS COMPLETE HOMEWORK ASSIGNMENTS

Teachers should make known their expectations early in the school year before the first piece of homework is ever assigned. Ensuring that the students clearly understand the rules of the classroom, the types of assignments they are likely to encounter, the methods and means for turning the assignments in, and how those assignments will be graded, can prevent much of students' confusions and frustrations. A written explanation of expectations helps to increase the chances of students successfully completing homework. In elementary school, as well as to a certain extent in junior high and high school, homework can teach students the fundamentals of working independently, as well as encourage self-discipline through time management and meeting deadlines.

Students should know:

- Homework is important and has meaning.
- Doing assignments or not doing them has consequences such as lower grades if the assignments are not done.
- Students need to be held to a high standard. Research has shown that students make better gains academically when teachers set high expectations and tell the students of their expectations. Students also should know how much and when homework will be assigned.

CREATING ASSIGNMENTS WITH PURPOSE HELPS IN COMPLETING HOMEWORK AND STUDY SKILLS

Assignments that are given to students to complete outside of class should be given with a purpose rather than to provide busywork. If a student believes that the homework given is meaningful or beneficial to them, they will be more likely to consider it as something worth doing. While students may appreciate understanding an assignment's purpose, the purpose might not become clear until students are midway through the assignment or have completed it. The teacher should not just tell

Copyright © Mometrix Media. You have been licensed one copy of this document for personal use only. Any other reproduction or redistribution is strictly prohibited. All rights reserved.

a student to read something or answer questions without knowing why they are doing it. Students should be shown the bigger picture of how their assignments fit in the realm of what they are studying, even though the student may not entirely appreciate the project's significance until it is finished or partially finished.

The following are some of the main purposes of homework:

- To review and practice what the students have learned for implementation in the future
- To prepare for exams
- To improve overall study skills by learning to use resources such as the library, reference material, encyclopedias, or the internet
- To explore subjects more deeply than time allows while in class

HELPING STUDENTS BETTER UNDERSTAND AND STUDY WITH FOCUSING ASSIGNMENTS

Assignments that are focused are less difficult for students to complete and understand. Assignments that try to reinforce an overabundant number of ideas are not likely to help a student learn. This is especially the case for students who have not yet developed abstract thinking to the point where they can successfully integrate many of the concepts. Assignments need not be a large, overwhelming dissertation about what it is the teacher expects. The assignment should stick to one issue or concept, and it should ask for maybe four or five examples. A teacher can easily determine if the students are comprehending what is being taught and if not, help can be given in studying for the objective. Focus and the appropriate background information are also important in class discussions of assigned readings because some children can become overwhelmed if asked to read too much at once.

HELPING STUDENTS THINK THROUGH WHILE STUDYING WITH CHALLENGING ASSIGNMENTS

Homework can give a student the ability to apply concepts that are beyond the controlled environment of a classroom. It can also help students collect and connect information from a variety of sources, subjects, and places. The best assignments challenge students to expand or break away from how they normally think. Such an assignment might combine two unassociated ideas. Assignments can range from listing what one finds in a desk drawer to writing paragraphs about family members. In those assignments, students can break the punctuation or capitalization rules in order to better learn the rules. Integrating topics also helps the thinking process, such as putting together an art, writing, and science class.

HELPING STUDENTS STUDY AND COMPLETE THEIR WORK BY VARYING ASSIGNMENTS

If all assignments are alike, students are very likely to get bored. Mixing approaches and styles is one of the fastest ways to elicit change. All students will not be interested in a given assignment, but mixing it up creates better chances that some of the homework will be enjoyed by the students. Short-term assignments can help students practice and review material already covered in class. Long-term projects allow students to vary the pace of their work, get into subjects of interest to them, and to manage time and deadlines. Variety may also help keep teachers engaged and excited about the schoolyear and convince them to try experimenting with their approaches and styles.

ENHANCING STUDYING BY TYING ASSIGNMENTS TO THE PRESENT

Students may often feel that they cannot relate to assignments about events from long ago. It is hard to teach most types of history unless they are related somehow to the present, so assignments should draw comparisons between what is happening today and events years or centuries ago. For instance, students might approach an assignment on a Civil War battle by contrasting it with more modern battles. They might see the battle through the eyes of a television war correspondent who

Copyright © Mometrix Media. You have been licensed one copy of this document for personal use only. Any other reproduction or redistribution is strictly prohibited. All rights reserved.

interviews the principal leaders and ask what they might do differently if they were to "do over" the battle. Students learn the specifics of such battles through these interviews and can appreciate the significance of the events that took place. This is a way of piquing interest in studying.

HELPING STUDENTS STUDY A SUBJECT BY MATCHING SKILLS, INTERESTS, AND NEEDS

The chances are greater that a student will complete his or her homework assignments if they:

- Are not too hard or too easy.
- Match children's preferred learning styles.
- Let students work on material that they really like. Assignments cannot be customized for every student. But teachers can give assignments to a heterogeneous class that varies in content, format and style. This will better the chance that all students will have some elements of the assignments that are of interest.

Teachers can give the students choices. The student may be expected to master all the same material, but it can be done in different ways. This helps the student feel they control parts of their learning, which encourages studying and helps them to enjoy an assignment that they otherwise might not.

TEST-TAKING TIPS BENEFITING INTERMEDIATE STUDENTS

When it is time to take a test, the student should:

- Think positively about doing the best that he or she can do.
- Take some deep breaths and relax. Breathe slowly. Clear the mind of worries and anxious thoughts.
- Push his or her feet down on the floor to the count of five. Push them harder and hold. Relax and then repeat.
- Visualize by closing his or her eyes and picturing his or herself in a happy and peaceful place.
- Bring all materials needed for the test.
- Listen carefully to the directions and ask if they are not understood.
- Reread the directions carefully
- Look over the entire test to see what must be done before beginning.
- Determine how much time there is to spend on each question, allowing more time for essay questions.
- Skip difficult questions and go back later to answer those skipped.

IMPORTANCE OF CAREFULLY READING ENTIRE TEST ITEMS AND ALL POSSIBLE ANSWERS FOR ELEMENTARY STUDENTS

Students should carefully consider each possible option or alternative before selecting an answer on an assignment or exam. It is common for a student to stop reading after determining that one of the answer choices is an acceptable answer rather than ensuring that they have made the best choice. Students should be encouraged to very carefully go over each question and pay particular attention to key terms. This information may be translated by the student into different forms, such as changing the question into their own words or substituting common words. They can use their knowledge to anticipate what an answer might be and to select an answer that appears similar to the one they predicted. These skills may be practiced in regular classroom activities.

Copyright © Mometrix Media. You have been licensed one copy of this document for personal use only. Any other reproduction or redistribution is strictly prohibited. All rights reserved.

IMPORTANCE OF CHECKING WORK WHEN TAKING TESTS IN ELEMENTARY CLASSES

It is worthwhile to instill into students the idea of checking their work after completion. Confirming that they have correctly answered each question to the best of their ability is an excellent use of any extra time a student may have after finishing an assignment or test. When they check their work, they need to ensure that the answers are correctly marked on the answer sheet and that the answers match the number of questions on the answer sheet. Students should have time to check and reconsider their work if time has been efficiently managed, and they should be encouraged to change answers when they think a better answer is appropriate. Students need reinforcement that their work should be checked daily. Teachers can do this by refusing to accept work until it is confirmed the work has been checked.

HELPING ACHIEVE POSITIVE LEARNING OUTCOMES FROM HIGH TEACHER EXPECTATIONS

Most, if not all, teachers have high hopes for their students. However, some teachers may be better than others at consciously communicating those expectations. Others might unconsciously expect less of students who show little interest in learning or who have significant barriers to hurdle. But by holding all students to high standards, most teachers believe they can help students achieve their full potential. Studies do show that students tend to internalize beliefs teachers have about their ability. When students are not expected to make a lot of progress, they may tend to take on a defeatist outlook. Some students may think their teachers believe they are not capable of handling demanding assignments. Teachers must see themselves as responsible for finding ways to raise performance despite whatever circumstances the students face.

HOME, CULTURAL, AND PARENTAL INVOLVEMENT

Many of the differences in academic achievement in children can be explained by the quantity and quality of reading materials in the home, the number of pages read for homework, the number of days absent from school, the number of hours in which TV is watched and social media is consumed, and the presence of two parents in the home. There are other environmental factors that impact academic acheivemcnt. For instance, the activities in which children engage outside of school, such as reading storybooks, visiting libraries, or playing word games. Another factor is the potential difference between the home and school cultures. Culture is used in this sense as a broad term to include the behavior and attitudes of parents. If there is a wide gap between the home culture and school culture, children may perceive tasks like reading as unrewarding or devaluing their identity.

EFFECT OF PEER INFLUENCE ON LEARNING

Peer influence on children's behavior, as well as on learning, is well recognized in psychological literature. Peer influence can operate both positively and negatively. Teachers will try normally to exploit the positive influence on peers and promote many of the learning experiences the children may have by organizing them into small groups in which they can become involved in learning. The negative aspects of peer influence are obvious when parents of children expect them to show interest in school work and spend time on homework, but many of the children's peers do not have the same goals for themselves. There may be times where it might become necessary to have a child discontinue his or her association with those peers who are negative influences.

LITERACY PROBLEMS WITHIN THE SCHOOL SYSTEM

There are various statistics that indicate that the overall literacy rates of students within the US school system are well below desired values. According to the Literacy Project in 2019, almost 65% of fourth graders did not read at a proficient level, and roughly 90% of children who were below average readers at the end of first grade remained that way by the end of fourth grade. There also

27

Copyright © Mometrix Media. You have been licensed one copy of this document for personal use only. Any other reproduction or redistribution is strictly prohibited. All rights reserved.

appears to be at least some correlation between literacy and income, as over 80% of the fourth graders who were reading below the proficient level were from low-income families. While many solutions have been proffered, no major solution has been discovered to significantly reduce or eliminate this issue. To further complicate matters, recent studies have also shown that over 85% of juvenile offenders have difficulty reading. Debates over policy and methodology continue as no one-size-fits-all strategy has been determined to be effective at reducing overall illiteracy rates within the school system.

ENSURING LITERACY FOR STUDENTS OF LOWER SOCIOECONOMIC CLASSES

There are disagreements among scholars as to the nature of the correlation between a child's socioeconomic level and comprehension level in school. Some see a direct correlation, while others say the correlation is more in degrees. Most data shows that children who are from low-income families are significantly more likely to fall behind in reading. This typically compounds as those with poor literacy skills through school tend to maintain them into adulthood often resulting in lower paying jobs, which then continues the cycle of poverty. There are many debated reasons as to why certain children may not be excelling in school, but in order to progress effectively, one needs to have a good foundation, and that foundation is being able to read and to communicate.

IMPROVING SCHOOL LITERACY LEVELS

If a school performs poorly on assessments, they are sometimes required to adjust their entire curriculum. When such changes take place, there are many aims that are incorporated, much more than just a single program or a single type of instruction. These aims may include helping students' lifelong skills, improving the quality of teaching, and making sure all teachers recognize the role that language plays in learning. Another possible aim might be to include a set time for students to read, such as a literacy hour. The focus might include having staff mark all children's books for spelling and grammar as well as content, that all departments provide a glossary of subject-specific words for pupils, and that all departments would use a writing frame to provide writing structure for children in each subject.

IMPACT OF FAMILY BACKGROUND ON EDUCATION

The exact nature of the impact parental education and socioeconomic status has on student achievement is unknown, although it does have an impact. Studies have found that parental education and family socioeconomic status alone are not necessarily predictors of how students will achieve academically. Studies have found that parental education accounts for about a quarter of the variance in student test scores, while socioeconomic status accounts for slightly more than a quarter. Other research indicates that dysfunctional home environments, low expectations from parents, parenting that is ineffective, differences in language, and high mobility levels may account for the low achievement levels among those students that come from lower socioeconomic levels. Other impacts that family culture has on a student's performance might include cultural dispositions that end up isolating a student from his or her peer group. One of the most reliable ways of addressing family or socioeconomic background is by increasing the student's awareness of their future, whether that be in education or a particular career path. Having the student start thinking about his or her future will help to set and achieve short-term goals that will naturally lead to their long-term goals.

NEGATIVE PEER INFLUENCES OF LEARNING

Students, teenagers specifically, look to each other to learn, and this sometimes brings about problems. Teenagers are growing and learning, and through this development, the students look to each other to acquire what their peers deem to be acceptable. In many instances, this may lead to inaccurate understandings. Teenagers purposely acquire knowledge sometimes that is

Copyright © Mometrix Media. You have been licensed one copy of this document for personal use only. Any other reproduction or redistribution is strictly prohibited. All rights reserved.

unmistakably wrong and continue to use it in everyday situations. Some students are so influenced by their culture that, even though they are capable of speaking properly, they will not do so for fear they will not fit in with their peers. These students—who readily acknowledge that they have been taught formal language—choose to continue using slang because their culture has shaped them to do so.

INCORPORATING THE HISPANIC CULTURE IN READING LESSONS FOR ELEMENTARY STUDENTS

One of the greatest ways to expand cultural intelligence and remove barriers of ignorance is to simply expose children to various cultures and highlight what makes them unique. The Hispanic population is the fastest growing ethnic population in the United States. In order to better incorporate Hispanic culture into lesson plans, teachers will likely need to intentionally implement new strategies to properly engage and inform students. Assigning students the task of researching and presenting famous Hispanic Americans in history, presenting videos with Hispanic speakers and Spanish vocabulary, or reading about major historical events in the formation of Hispanic nations are all excellent ways to celebrate and better understand Hispanic culture. It is imperative to make sure that classrooms have ample amounts of resources for children to properly explore and engage with various cultures and their traditions. Showing how culture influences society, from foods eaten to the names of cities, children are better able to comprehend and understand one another and the larger world around them.

IEP

Special education teachers help to develop an Individualized Education Program (IEP) for each special education student. The IEP sets personalized goals for each student and is tailored to the student's individual needs and ability. When appropriate, the program includes a transition plan outlining specific steps to prepare students with disabilities for middle school or high school, or, in the case of older students, a job or post-secondary study. Teachers review the IEP with the student's parents, school administrators, and the student's general education teacher. Teachers work closely with parents to inform them of their child's progress and suggest techniques to promote learning at home.

OBSERVATIONS ASSESSING PREDICTION SKILLS

Teachers observing students will at some point hear the language of prediction. Students might say, "I think..." or "I wonder if..." By observing, the teachers can view certain reading behaviors that students show. When observing students making predictions about fiction text, the teacher should look out for these reading behaviors:

- Do students look at the text cover and make predictions that are based on the title or illustration?
- Do students stop prediction-making while they are reading?
- When reading the text, do students make predictions based on clues from the illustration or text?

These behaviors should be observed for nonfiction text reading:

- Do students use headings or subheadings in order to make predictions?
- Do students use charts, graphs, illustrations, or maps to make predictions?
- Do students predict what is likely to be learned based on clues from the illustration or text?

Copyright © Mometrix Media. You have been licensed one copy of this document for personal use only. Any other reproduction or redistribution is strictly prohibited. All rights reserved.

EFFECTIVELY USING PARAPROFESSIONAL SKILLS AND TIME

Especially with special education, teachers do not have enough time to meet all of the needs of every individual student in each classroom, and paraprofessionals are often sent into classrooms to help students with special needs. Regardless of the use, the roles and routines in which the paraprofessional is used need to be carefully and clearly laid out. Say the paraprofessional is in the classroom for reading a half-hour each day. It is important to consider the routines that could be put into place for that time period. One might discuss the benefits of the paraprofessional helping with readers who struggle. Also, one might plot the progress of students that are being helped by the paraprofessional. Ensuring that the paraprofessional is helpful to both the teacher and students and is not being pushed beyond the limitations of their expertise effectively manages the paraprofessional's skills and time.

ESTABLISHING A SUCCESSFUL LEARNING CENTER

Effective classrooms have a combination of direct instruction, cooperative learning, independent practice, and learning center activities. Learning centers help play an important part in classroom management and should be established one at a time. Possible centers include a writing center, an alphabet center, a science center, a writing center, or various other centers, but these can always be changed to meet the students' needs. Clear rules and routines for using each center should be understood, and a chart should be posted at each center that indicates how many children should be in the center or what materials and equipment may be used. The center will likely need to be closely supervised at first, as teachers begin determining when children are able to work both independently or cooperatively.

CURRICULUM STANDARDS

Standards focus on developing coherency across grade levels, teaching for understanding, and relevancy of subject matter, helping courses to build upon each other in age-appropriate ways. This farsighted statement sets an excellent vision for what students should be learning. The standards are broken into ten areas within two broader categories. Process Standards, the first category, defines how students should "do" the content and how they should be able to use their knowledge. The second category, the Content Standards, deals with the content that students should learn.

CONTROVERSY OVER TEACHER EXPECTATIONS ON LEARNING OUTCOMES

The original Pygmalion study gave teachers false information about the learning potential of certain students in grades 1-6 in a San Francisco elementary school. Teachers were told that one of their students had been tested and found to be on the edge of a period of rapid intellectual growth, but in actuality, the student had actually been selected at random and the tests were measuring how the expectations of the teacher towards a student can impact their success. At the end of the experimental period, some of the targeted students exhibited superior scores on IQ tests compared to those of similar abilities. The results led researchers to claim that inflated expectations of teachers for target students actually caused accelerated intellectual growth. A number of studies have since taken place, and some found technical defects serious enough to cast doubt on the original findings. Whether one accepts or doubts the Pygmalion study, educators and the public are very interested in the power of expectations affecting the outcomes of students.

POSITIVE EFFECT ON STUDENT OUTCOMES WITH HIGHER TEACHER EXPECTATIONS SUPPLEMENTED WITH OTHER MEASURES

High expectations may not be the magic trick needed to close achievement gaps, but raising expectations can make a difference when the effort is accompanied by a relevant and rigorous curriculum, adequate materials,current textbooks, effective teaching strategies, good classroom

Copyright © Mometrix Media. You have been licensed one copy of this document for personal use only. Any other reproduction or redistribution is strictly prohibited. All rights reserved.

management, tutoring programs, uncrowded classrooms, and involved parents. It is likely the case that in life, as well as in teaching, there is a need for balance. Teachers should believe and expect that students can learn given time and hard work, and students must be convinced that the reward of an education is worth the effort. When students and teachers mutually understand and believe that success is obtainable and that it can only be obtained through consistent and intentional work, both students and teachers are significantly more likely to achieve their goals.

Copyright © Mometrix Media. You have been licensed one copy of this document for personal use only. Any other reproduction or redistribution is strictly prohibited. All rights reserved.

History

American History Pre-Columbian to 1789

WELL-KNOWN NATIVE AMERICANS

The following are five well-known Native Americans and their roles in early US history:

1. **Squanto**, an Algonquian, helped early English settlers survive the hard winter by teaching them the native methods of planting corn, squash, and pumpkins.
2. **Pocahontas**, also Algonquian, became famous as a liaison with John Smith's Jamestown colony in 1607.
3. **Sacagawea**, a Shoshone, served a vital role in the Lewis and Clark expedition when the two explorers hired her as their guide in 1805.
4. **Crazy Horse** and **Sitting Bull** led Sioux and Cheyenne troops in the Battle of the Little Bighorn in 1876, soundly defeating George Armstrong Custer.
5. **Chief Joseph**, a leader of the Nez Perce who supported peaceful interaction with white settlers, attempted to relocate his tribe to Canada rather than move them to a reservation.

MAJOR REGIONAL NATIVE AMERICAN GROUPS

The major regional Native American groups and the major traits of each are as follows:

- The **Algonquians** in the eastern part of the United States lived in wigwams. The northern tribes subsisted on hunting and gathering, while those who were farther south grew crops such as corn.
- The **Iroquois**, also an east coast tribe, spoke a different language from the Algonquians and lived in rectangular longhouses.
- The **Plains tribes** lived between the Mississippi River and the Rocky Mountains. These nomadic tribes lived in teepees and followed the buffalo herds. Plains tribes included the Sioux, Cheyenne, Comanche, and Blackfoot.
- **Pueblo tribes** included the Zuni, Hopi, and Acoma. They lived in the Southwest deserts in homes made of stone or adobe. They domesticated animals and cultivated corn and beans.
- On the Pacific coast, tribes such as the **Tlingit**, **Chinook**, and **Salish** lived on fish, deer, native berries, and roots. Their rectangular homes housed large family groups, and they used totem poles.
- In the far north, the **Aleuts** and **Inuit** lived in skin tents or igloos. Talented fishermen, they built kayaks and umiaks and also hunted caribou, seals, whales, and walrus.

> **Review Video: Major Regional Native American Groups**
> Visit mometrix.com/academy and enter code: 550136

AGE OF EXPLORATION

The Age of Exploration is also called the **Age of Discovery**. It is generally considered to have begun in the early 15th century and continued into the 17th century. Major developments of the **Age of Exploration** included technological advances in navigation, mapmaking, and shipbuilding. These advances led to expanded European exploration of the rest of the world. Explorers set out from several European countries, including Portugal, Spain, France, and England, seeking new routes to

Copyright © Mometrix Media. You have been licensed one copy of this document for personal use only. Any other reproduction or redistribution is strictly prohibited. All rights reserved.

Asia. These efforts led to the discovery of new lands, as well as colonization in India, Asia, Africa, and North America.

Review Video: Age of Exploration
Visit mometrix.com/academy and enter code: 612972

IMPACT OF TECHNOLOGICAL ADVANCES IN NAVIGATION AND SEAFARING EXPLORATION

For long ocean journeys, it was important for sailors to be able to find their way home even when their vessels sailed far out to sea. A variety of navigational tools enabled them to launch ambitious journeys over long distances. The **compass** and **astrolabe** were particularly important advancements. Chinese navigators used the magnetic compass in approximately 200 BC, and knowledge of the astrolabe came to Europe from Arab navigators and traders who had refined designs developed by the ancient Greeks. The Portuguese developed a ship called a **caravel** in the 1400s that incorporated navigational advancements with the ability to make long sea journeys. Equipped with this advanced vessel, the Portuguese achieved a major goal of the Age of Exploration by discovering a **sea route** from Europe to Asia in 1498.

SIGNIFICANCE OF CHRISTOPHER COLUMBUS'S VOYAGE

In 1492, Columbus, a Genoan explorer, obtained financial backing from King Ferdinand and Queen Isabella of Spain to seek a sea route to Asia. He sought a trade route with the Asian Indies to the west. With three ships, the *Niña*, the *Pinta*, and the *Santa Maria*, he eventually landed in the **West Indies**. While Columbus failed in his effort to discover a western route to Asia, he is credited with the discovery of the **Americas**.

Review Video: Christopher Columbus
Visit mometrix.com/academy and enter code: 496598

FRENCH, SPANISH, DUTCH, AND BRITISH GOALS IN COLONIZATION OF THE AMERICAS

France, Spain, the Netherlands, and England each had specific goals in the colonization of the Americas:

- Initial **French colonies** were focused on expanding the fur trade. Later, French colonization led to the growth of plantations in Louisiana, which brought numerous African slaves to the New World.
- **Spanish colonists** came to look for wealth and to convert the natives to Christianity. For some, the desire for gold led to mining in the New World, while others established large ranches.
- The **Dutch** were also involved in the fur trade and imported slaves as the need for laborers increased.
- **British colonists** arrived with various goals. Some were simply looking for additional income, while others were fleeing Britain to escape religious persecution.

Review Video: Colonization of the Americas
Visit mometrix.com/academy and enter code: 438412

NEW ENGLAND COLONIES

The New England colonies were New Hampshire, Connecticut, Rhode Island and Massachusetts. These colonies were founded largely to escape **religious persecution** in England. The beliefs of the **Puritans**, who migrated to America in the 1600s, significantly influenced the development of these colonies. Situated in the northeast coastal areas of America, the New England colonies featured

Copyright © Mometrix Media. You have been licensed one copy of this document for personal use only. Any other reproduction or redistribution is strictly prohibited. All rights reserved.

numerous harbors as well as dense forests. The soil, however, was rocky and had a very short growing season, so was not well suited for agriculture. The economy of New England during the colonial period centered around fishing, shipbuilding and trade along with some small farms and lumber mills. Although some groups congregated in small farms, life centered mainly in towns and cities where **merchants** largely controlled the trade economy. Coastal cities such as Boston grew and thrived.

> **Review Video: The Massachusetts Bay Colony**
> Visit mometrix.com/academy and enter code: 407058

MIDDLE OR MIDDLE ATLANTIC COLONIES

The Middle or Middle Atlantic Colonies were New York, New Jersey, Pennsylvania, and Delaware. Unlike the New England colonies, where most colonists were from England and Scotland, the Middle Colonies founders were from various countries, including the Netherlands and Sweden. Various factors led these colonists to America. More fertile than New England, the Middle Colonies became major producers of **crops**, including rye, oats, potatoes, wheat, and barley. Some particularly wealthy inhabitants owned large farms and/or businesses. Farmers, in general, were able to produce enough to have a surplus to sell. Tenant farmers also rented land from larger landowners.

SOUTHERN COLONIES

The Southern Colonies were Maryland, Virginia, North Carolina, South Carolina, and Georgia. Of the Southern Colonies, Virginia was the first permanent English colony and Georgia the last. The warm climate and rich soil of the south encouraged **agriculture**, and the growing season was long. As a result, economy in the south was based largely on labor-intensive **plantations**. Crops included tobacco, rice, and indigo, all of which became valuable cash crops. Most land in the south was controlled by wealthy plantation owners and farmers. Labor on the farms came in the form of indentured servants and African slaves. The first of these **African slaves** arrived in Virginia in 1619.

> **Review Video: Southern Colonies: An Overview**
> Visit mometrix.com/academy and enter code: 703830
>
> **Review Video: The English Colony of Virginia**
> Visit mometrix.com/academy and enter code: 537399

SIGNIFICANCE OF THE FRENCH AND INDIAN WARS

The **British defeat of the Spanish Armada** in 1588 led to the decline of Spanish power in Europe. This, in turn, led the British and French into battle several times between 1689 and 1748. These wars were:

- King William's War, or the Nine Years War, 1689-1697. This war was fought largely in Flanders.
- The War of Spanish Succession, or Queen Anne's War, 1702-1713
- War of Austrian Succession, or King George's War, 1740-1748

The fourth and final war, the **French and Indian War** (1754-1763), was fought largely in the North American territory and resulted in the end of France's reign as a colonial power in North America. Although the French held many advantages, including more cooperative colonists and numerous Indian allies, the strong leadership of **William Pitt** eventually led the British to victory. Costs

34

Copyright © Mometrix Media. You have been licensed one copy of this document for personal use only. Any other reproduction or redistribution is strictly prohibited. All rights reserved.

incurred during the wars eventually led to discontent in the colonies and helped spark the **American Revolution**.

> **Review Video: French and Indian War**
> Visit mometrix.com/academy and enter code: 502183

NAVIGATION ACTS

The Navigation Acts, enacted in 1651, were an attempt by Britain to dominate international trade. Aimed largely at the Dutch, the acts banned foreign ships from transporting goods to the British colonies and from transporting goods to Britain from elsewhere in Europe. While the restrictions on trade angered some colonists, these acts were helpful to other American colonists who, as members of the British Empire, were legally able to provide ships for Britain's growing trade interests and use the ships for their own trading ventures. By the time the French and Indian War had ended, one-third of British merchant ships were built in the American colonies. Many colonists amassed fortunes in the shipbuilding trade.

BRITAIN'S TAXATION OF THE AMERICAN COLONIES AFTER THE FRENCH AND INDIAN WAR

The French and Indian War created circumstances for which the British desperately needed more revenue. These needs included:

- Paying off the war debt
- Defending the expanding empire
- Governing Britain's 33 far-flung colonies, including the American colonies

To meet these needs, the British passed additional laws, increasing revenues from the colonies. Because they had spent so much money to defend the American colonies, the British felt it was appropriate to collect considerably higher **taxes** from them. The colonists felt this was unfair, and many were led to protest the increasing taxes. Eventually, protest led to violence.

TRIANGULAR TRADE

Triangular trade began in the colonies with ships setting off for **Africa**, carrying rum. In Africa, the rum was traded for gold or slaves. Ships then went from Africa to the **West Indies**, trading slaves for sugar, molasses, or money. To complete the triangle, the ships returned to the **colonies** with sugar or molasses to make more rum, as well as stores of gold and silver. This trade triangle violated the Molasses Act of 1733, which required the colonists to pay high duties to Britain on molasses acquired from French, Dutch, and Spanish colonies. The colonists ignored these duties, and the British government adopted a policy of salutary neglect by not enforcing them.

EFFECTS OF NEW LAWS ON BRITISH-COLONIAL RELATIONS

While earlier revenue-generating acts such as the Navigation Acts brought money to the colonists, the new laws after 1763 required colonists to pay money back to **Britain**. The British felt this was fair since the colonists were British subjects and since they had incurred debt protecting the Colonies. The colonists felt it was not only unfair but illegal.

The development of **local government** in America had given the colonists a different view of the structure and role of government. This made it difficult for the British to understand the colonists' protests against what the British felt was a fair and reasonable solution to the mother country's financial problems.

Copyright © Mometrix Media. You have been licensed one copy of this document for personal use only. Any other reproduction or redistribution is strictly prohibited. All rights reserved.

FACTORS THAT LED TO INCREASING DISCONTENT IN THE AMERICAN COLONIES

More and more colonists were born on American soil, decreasing any sense of kinship with the far-away British rulers. Their new environment had led to new ideas of government and a strong view of the colonies as a separate entity from Britain. Colonists were allowed to **self-govern** in domestic issues, but **Britain** controlled international issues. In fact, the American colonies were largely left to form their own local government bodies, giving them more freedom than any other colonial territory. This gave the colonists a sense of **independence**, which led them to resent control from Britain. Threats during the French and Indian War led the colonists to call for unification in order to protect themselves.

COLONIAL GOVERNMENT AND BRITISH GOVERNMENT DIFFERENCES THAT LED TO "NO TAXATION WITHOUT REPRESENTATION"

As new towns and other legislative districts developed in America, the colonists began to practice **representative government**. Colonial legislative bodies were made up of elected representatives chosen by male property owners in the districts. These individuals represented the interests of the districts from which they had been elected.

By contrast, in Britain, the **Parliament** represented the entire country. Parliament was not elected to represent individual districts. Instead, they represented specific classes. Because of this drastically different approach to government, the British did not understand the colonists' statement that they had no representation in the British Parliament.

ACTS OF BRITISH PARLIAMENT THAT OCCURRED AFTER THE FRENCH AND INDIAN WARS

After the French and Indian Wars, the British Parliament passed four major acts:

1. The **Sugar Act**, 1764—this act not only required taxes to be collected on molasses brought into the colonies but gave British officials the right to search the homes of anyone suspected of violating it.
2. The **Stamp Act**, 1765—this act taxed printed materials such as newspapers and legal documents. Protests led the Stamp Act to be repealed in 1766, but the repeal also included the Declaratory Act, which stated that Parliament had the right to govern the colonies.
3. The **Quartering Act**, 1765—this act required colonists to provide accommodations and supplies for British troops. In addition, colonists were prohibited from settling west of the Appalachians until given permission by Britain.
4. The **Townshend Acts**, 1767—these acts taxed paper, paint, lead, and tea that came into the colonies. Colonists led boycotts in protest, and in Massachusetts leaders like Samuel and John Adams began to organize resistance against British rule.

FACTORS THAT LED TO THE BOSTON MASSACRE

With the passage of the **Stamp Act**, nine colonies met in New York to demand its repeal. Elsewhere, protest arose in New York City, Philadelphia, Boston, and other cities. These protests sometimes escalated into violence, often targeting ruling British officials. The passage of the **Townshend Acts** in 1767 led to additional tension in the colonies. The British sent troops to New York City and Boston. On March 5, 1770, protesters began to taunt the British troops, throwing snowballs. The soldiers responded by firing into the crowd. This clash between protesters and soldiers led to five deaths and eight injuries, and was christened the **Boston Massacre**. Shortly thereafter, Britain repealed the majority of the Townshend Acts.

Copyright © Mometrix Media. You have been licensed one copy of this document for personal use only. Any other reproduction or redistribution is strictly prohibited. All rights reserved.

TEA ACT THAT LED TO THE BOSTON TEA PARTY

The majority of the **Townshend Acts** were repealed after the Boston Massacre in 1770, but Britain kept the tax on tea. In 1773, the **Tea Act** was passed. This allowed the East India Company to sell tea for much lower prices and also allowed them to bypass American distributors, selling directly to shopkeepers instead. Colonial tea merchants saw this as a direct assault on their business. In December of 1773, the **Sons of Liberty** boarded ships in Boston Harbor and dumped 342 chests of tea into the sea in protest of the new laws. This act of protest came to be known as the **Boston Tea Party**.

COERCIVE ACTS PASSED AFTER THE BOSTON TEA PARTY

The Coercive Acts passed by Britain in 1774 were meant to punish Massachusetts for defying British authority. The following were also known as the **Intolerable Acts**:

- Shut down ports in Boston until the city paid back the value of the tea destroyed during the Boston Tea Party
- Required that local government officials in Massachusetts be appointed by the governor rather than being elected by the people
- Allowed trials of British soldiers to be transferred to Britain rather than being held in Massachusetts
- Required locals to provide lodging for British soldiers any time there was a disturbance, even if lodging required them to stay in private homes

These acts led to the assembly of the First Continental Congress in Philadelphia on September 5, 1774. Fifty-five delegates met, representing 12 of the American colonies. They sought compromise with England over England's increasingly harsh efforts to control the colonies.

FIRST CONTINENTAL CONGRESS

The goal of the First Continental Congress was to achieve a peaceful agreement with Britain. Made up of delegates from 12 of the 13 colonies, the Congress affirmed loyalty to Britain and the power of Parliament to dictate foreign affairs in the colonies. However, they demanded that the **Intolerable Acts** be repealed, and instituted a trade embargo with Britain until this came to pass.

In response, George III of England declared that the American colonies must submit or face military action. The British sought to end assemblies that opposed their policies. These assemblies gathered weapons and began to form militias. On April 19, 1775, the British military was ordered to disperse a meeting of the Massachusetts Assembly. A battle ensued on Lexington Common as the armed colonists resisted. The resulting battles became the **Battle of Lexington and Concord**—the first battles of the **American Revolution**.

SIGNIFICANCE OF THE SECOND CONTINENTAL CONGRESS

The Second Continental Congress met in Philadelphia on May 10, 1775, a month after Lexington and Concord. Their discussions centered on the defense of the American colonies and how to conduct the growing war, as well as local government. The delegates also discussed declaring independence from Britain, with many members in favor of this drastic move. They established an army, and on June 15, named **George Washington** as its commander in chief. By 1776, it was obvious that there was no turning back from full-scale war with Britain. The colonial delegates of the Continental Congress signed the **Declaration of Independence** on July 4, 1776.

> **Review Video: The First and Second Continental Congress**
> Visit mometrix.com/academy and enter code: 835211

Copyright © Mometrix Media. You have been licensed one copy of this document for personal use only. Any other reproduction or redistribution is strictly prohibited. All rights reserved.

ORIGINS AND BASIC IDEAS OF THE DECLARATION OF INDEPENDENCE

Penned by Thomas Jefferson and signed on July 4, 1776, the **Declaration of Independence** stated that King George III had violated the rights of the colonists and was establishing a tyrannical reign over them. Many of Jefferson's ideas of natural rights and property rights were shaped by 17th-century philosopher **John Locke**. Jefferson asserted all people's rights to "life, liberty and the pursuit of happiness." Locke's comparable idea asserted "life, liberty, and private property." Both felt that the purpose of government was to protect the rights of the people, and that individual rights were more important than individuals' obligations to the state.

> **Review Video: Declaration of Independence**
> Visit mometrix.com/academy and enter code: 256838

BATTLES OF THE REVOLUTIONARY WAR

The following are five major battles of the Revolutionary War and their significance:

- The **Battle of Lexington and Concord** (April 1775) is considered the first engagement of the Revolutionary War.
- The **Battle of Bunker Hill** (June 1775) was one of the bloodiest of the entire war. Although American troops withdrew, about half of the British army was lost. The colonists proved they could stand against professional British soldiers. In August, Britain declared that the American colonies were officially in a state of rebellion.
- The first colonial victory occurred in Trenton, New Jersey, when Washington and his troops **crossed the Delaware River** on Christmas Day, 1776, for a December 26 surprise attack on British and Hessian troops.
- The **Battle of Saratoga** effectively ended a plan to separate the New England colonies from their Southern counterparts. The surrender of British general John Burgoyne led to France joining the war as allies of the Americans and is generally considered a turning point of the war.
- On October 19, 1781, General Cornwallis surrendered after a defeat in the **Battle of Yorktown**, ending the Revolutionary War.

> **Review Video: The Revolutionary War**
> Visit mometrix.com/academy and enter code: 935282

SIGNIFICANCE OF THE TREATY OF PARIS

The Treaty of Paris was signed on September 3, 1783, bringing an official end to the Revolutionary War. In this document, Britain officially recognized the United States of America as an **independent nation**. The treaty established the Mississippi River as the country's western border. The treaty also restored Florida to Spain, while France reclaimed African and Caribbean colonies seized by the British in 1763. On November 25, 1783, the last British troops departed from the newly born United States of America.

SIGNIFICANCE OF THE ARTICLES OF CONFEDERATION

A precursor to the Constitution, the **Articles of Confederation** represented the first attempt of the newly independent colonies to establish the basics of government. The Continental Congress approved the Articles on November 15, 1777. They went into effect on March 1, 1781, following ratification by the thirteen states. The articles prevented a central government from gaining too much power, instead giving power to a **congressional body** made up of **delegates** from all thirteen states. However, the individual states retained final authority.

38

Copyright © Mometrix Media. You have been licensed one copy of this document for personal use only. Any other reproduction or redistribution is strictly prohibited. All rights reserved.

Without a strong central **executive**, though, this weak alliance among the new states proved ineffective in settling disputes or enforcing laws. The idea of a weak central government needed to be revised. Recognition of these weaknesses eventually led to the drafting of a new document, the **Constitution**.

Review Video: **Articles of Confederation**
Visit mometrix.com/academy and enter code: 927401

INITIAL PROPOSITION AND DRAFT OF THE CONSTITUTION

Delegates from twelve of the thirteen states (Rhode Island was not represented) met in Philadelphia in May of 1787, initially intending to revise the Articles of Confederation. However, it quickly became apparent that a simple revision would not provide the workable governmental structure the newly formed country needed. After vowing to keep all the proceedings secret until the final document was completed, the delegates set out to draft what would eventually become the **Constitution of the United States of America**. By keeping the negotiations secret, the delegates were able to present a completed document to the country for ratification, rather than having every small detail hammered out by the general public.

GENERAL STRUCTURE OF GOVERNMENT PROPOSED BY THE DELEGATES

The delegates agreed that the new nation required a **strong central government** but that its overall power should be **limited**. The various branches of the government should have **balanced power**, so that no one group could control the others. Final power belonged to the **citizens** who voted officials into office based on who would provide the best representation.

SIGNIFICANCE OF THE VIRGINIA PLAN, THE NEW JERSEY PLAN, AND THE GREAT COMPROMISE

Disagreement immediately occurred between delegates from large states and those from smaller states. James Madison and Edmund Randolph (the governor of Virginia) felt that representation in Congress should be based on state population. This was the **Virginia Plan**. The **New Jersey Plan**, presented by William Paterson from New Jersey, proposed that each state should have equal representation. Finally, Roger Sherman from Connecticut formulated the **Connecticut Compromise**, also called the Great Compromise. The result was the familiar structure we have today. Each state has the equal representation of two Senators in the Senate, with the number of representatives in the House of Representatives based on population. This is called a **bicameral congress**. Both houses may draft bills, but financial matters must originate in the House of Representatives.

EFFECTS OF THE THREE-FIFTHS COMPROMISE AND THE NUMBER OF REPRESENTATIVES FOR EACH STATE

During debate on the US Constitution, a disagreement arose between the Northern and Southern states involving how **slaves** should be counted when determining a state's quota of representatives. In the South, large numbers of slaves were commonly used to run plantations. Delegates wanted slaves to be counted to determine the number of representatives but not counted to determine the amount of taxes the states would pay. The Northern states wanted exactly the opposite arrangement. The final decision was to count three-fifths of the slave population both for tax purposes and to determine representation. This was called the **Three-fifths Compromise**.

PROVISIONS OF THE COMMERCE COMPROMISE

The Commerce Compromise also resulted from a North/South disagreement. In the North, the economy was centered on **industry and trade**. The Southern economy was largely **agricultural**.

Copyright © Mometrix Media. You have been licensed one copy of this document for personal use only. Any other reproduction or redistribution is strictly prohibited. All rights reserved.

The Northern states wanted to give the new government the ability to regulate exports as well as trade between the states. The South opposed this plan. Another compromise was in order. In the end, Congress received regulatory power over all trade, including the ability to collect **tariffs** on exported goods. In the South, this raised another red flag regarding the slave trade, as they were concerned about the effect on their economy if tariffs were levied on slaves. The final agreement allowed importing slaves to continue for twenty years without government intervention. Import taxes on slaves were limited, and after the year 1808, Congress could decide whether to allow continued imports of slaves.

OBJECTIONS AGAINST THE CONSTITUTION

Once the Constitution was drafted, it was presented for approval by the states. Nine states needed to approve the document for it to become official. However, debate and discussion continued. Major **concerns** included:

- There was nobill of rights to protect individual freedoms.
- States felt too much power was being handed over to the central government.
- Voters wanted more control over their elected representatives.

Discussion about necessary changes to the Constitution was divided into two camps: Federalists and Anti-Federalists. **Federalists** wanted a strong central government. **Anti-Federalists** wanted to prevent a tyrannical government from developing if a central government held too much power.

MAJOR PLAYERS IN THE FEDERALIST AND ANTI-FEDERALIST CAMPS

Major Federalist leaders included Alexander Hamilton, John Jay, and James Madison. They wrote a series of letters, called the **Federalist Papers**, aimed at convincing the states to ratify the Constitution. These were published in New York papers. Anti-Federalists included Thomas Jefferson and Patrick Henry. They argued against the Constitution as it was originally drafted in a series of **Anti-Federalist Papers**.

The final compromise produced a strong central government controlled by checks and balances. A **Bill of Rights** was also added, becoming the first ten amendments to the Constitution. These amendments protected rights such as freedom of speech, freedom of religion, and other basic rights. Aside from various amendments added throughout the years, the United States Constitution has remained unchanged.

INDIVIDUALS WHO FORMED THE FIRST ADMINISTRATION OF THE NEW GOVERNMENT

The individuals who formed the first administration of the new government were:

- **George Washington**—elected as the first President of the United States in 1789
- **John Adams**—finished second in the election and became the first Vice President
- **Thomas Jefferson**—appointed by Washington as Secretary of State
- **Alexander Hamilton**—appointed Secretary of the Treasury

Copyright © Mometrix Media. You have been licensed one copy of this document for personal use only. Any other reproduction or redistribution is strictly prohibited. All rights reserved.

American History 1790 to 1898

ALIEN AND SEDITION ACTS

When **John Adams** became president, a war was raging between Britain and France. While Adams and the **Federalists** backed the British, Thomas Jefferson and the **Republican Party** supported the French. The United States nearly went to war with France during this time period, while France worked to spread its international standing and influence under the leadership of **Napoleon Bonaparte**. The **Alien and Sedition Acts** grew out of this conflict and made it illegal to speak in a hostile fashion against the existing government. They also allowed the president to deport anyone in the US who was not a citizen and who was suspected of treason or treasonous activity. When Jefferson became the third president in 1800, he repealed these four laws and pardoned anyone who had been convicted under them.

DEVELOPMENT OF POLITICAL PARTIES IN EARLY US GOVERNMENT

Many in the US were against political parties after seeing the way parties, or factions, functioned in Britain. The factions in Britain were more interested in personal profit than the overall good of the country, and they did not want this to happen in the US.

However, the differences of opinion between Thomas Jefferson and Alexander Hamilton led to the formation of **political parties**. Hamilton favored a stronger central government, while Jefferson felt that more power should remain with the states. Jefferson was in favor of strict Constitutional interpretation, while Hamilton believed in a more flexible approach. As others joined the two camps, Hamilton backers began to call themselves **Federalists**, while those supporting Jefferson became identified as **Democratic-Republicans**.

DEVELOPMENT OF THE WHIG, THE DEMOCRATIC, AND THE REPUBLICAN PARTIES

Thomas Jefferson was elected president in 1800 and again in 1804. The **Federalist Party** began to decline, and its major figure, Alexander Hamilton, died in a duel with Aaron Burr in 1804. By 1816, the Federalist Party had virtually disappeared.

New parties sprang up to take its place. After 1824, the **Democratic-Republican Party** suffered a split. The **Whigs** rose, backing John Quincy Adams and industrial growth. The new Democratic Party formed in opposition to the Whigs, and their candidate, Andrew Jackson, was elected as president in 1828.

By the 1850s, issues regarding slavery led to the formation of the **Republican Party**, which was anti-slavery, while the Democratic Party, with a larger interest in the South, favored slavery. This Republican/Democrat division formed the basis of today's **two-party system**.

SIGNIFICANCE OF MARBURY V. MADISON

The main duty of the Supreme Court today is **judicial review**. This power was largely established by **Marbury v. Madison**. When John Adams was voted out of office in 1800, he worked during his final days in office to appoint Federalist judges to Supreme Court positions, knowing Jefferson, his replacement, held opposing views. As late as March 3, the day before Jefferson was to take office, Adams made last-minute appointments referred to as "Midnight Judges." One of the late appointments was William Marbury. The next day, March 4, Jefferson ordered his Secretary of State, James Madison, not to deliver Marbury's commission. This decision was backed by Chief Justice Marshall, who determined that the **Judiciary Act of 1789**, which granted the power to deliver

41

Copyright © Mometrix Media. You have been licensed one copy of this document for personal use only. Any other reproduction or redistribution is strictly prohibited. All rights reserved.

commissions, was illegal in that it gave the Judicial Branch powers not granted in the Constitution. This case set precedent for the Supreme Court to nullify laws it found to be **unconstitutional**.

Review Video: Marbury v Madison
Visit mometrix.com/academy and enter code: 573964

McCULLOCH V. MARYLAND

Judicial review was further exercised by the Supreme Court in **McCulloch v. Maryland**. When Congress chartered a national bank, the **Second Bank of the United States**, Maryland voted to tax any bank business dealing with banks chartered outside the state, including the federally chartered bank. Andrew McCulloch, an employee of the Second Bank of the US in Baltimore, refused to pay this tax. The resulting lawsuit from the State of Maryland went to the Supreme Court for judgment.

John Marshall, Chief Justice of the Supreme Court, stated that Congress was within its rights to charter a national bank. In addition, the State of Maryland did not have the power to levy a tax on the federal bank or on the federal government in general. In cases where state and federal government collided, precedent was set for the **federal government** to prevail.

EFFECT OF THE TREATY OF PARIS ON NATIVE AMERICANS

After the Revolutionary War, the **Treaty of Paris**, which outlined the terms of surrender of the British to the Americans, granted large parcels of land to the US that were occupied by Native Americans. The new government attempted to claim the land, treating the natives as a conquered people. This approach proved unenforceable.

Next, the government tried purchasing the land from the Indians via a series of **treaties** as the country expanded westward. In practice, however, these treaties were not honored, and Native Americans were simply dislocated and forced to move farther and farther west, often with military action, as American expansion continued.

INDIAN REMOVAL ACT OF 1830 AND THE TREATY OF NEW ECHOTA

The Indian Removal Act of 1830 gave the new American government power to form treaties with Native Americans. In theory, America would claim land east of the Mississippi in exchange for land west of the Mississippi, to which the natives would relocate voluntarily. In practice, many tribal leaders were forced into signing the treaties, and relocation at times occurred by force.

The **Treaty of New Echota** in 1835 was supposedly a treaty between the US government and Cherokee tribes in Georgia. However, the treaty was not signed by tribal leaders but rather by a small portion of the represented people. The leaders protested and refused to leave, but President Martin Van Buren enforced the treaty by sending soldiers. During their forced relocation, more than 4,000 Cherokee Indians died on what became known as the **Trail of Tears**.

Review Video: Indian Removal Act
Visit mometrix.com/academy and enter code: 666738

DEVELOPMENT OF ECONOMIC TRENDS AS THE US CONTINUED TO GROW

In the Northeast, the economy mostly depended on **manufacturing, industry, and industrial development**. This led to a dichotomy between rich business owners and industrial leaders and the much poorer workers who supported their businesses. The South continued to depend on **agriculture**, especially on large-scale farms or plantations worked mostly by slaves and indentured servants. In the West, where new settlements had begun to develop, the land was largely wild.

Copyright © Mometrix Media. You have been licensed one copy of this document for personal use only. Any other reproduction or redistribution is strictly prohibited. All rights reserved.

Growing communities were essentially **agricultural**, raising crops and livestock. The differences between regions led each to support different interests both politically and economically.

POLITICAL MOTIVATIONS BEHIND FRANCE SELLING THE LOUISIANA PURCHASE

With tension still high between France and Britain, Napoleon was in need of money to support his continuing war efforts. To secure necessary funds, he decided to sell the **Louisiana Territory** to the US. President **Thomas Jefferson** wanted to buy New Orleans, feeling US trade was made vulnerable to both Spain and France at that port. Instead, Napoleon sold him the entire territory for the bargain price of $15 million. The Louisiana Territory was larger than all the rest of the United States put together, and it eventually became 15 additional states.

Federalists in Congress were opposed to the purchase. They feared that the Louisiana Purchase would extend slavery, and that further western growth would weaken the power of the northern states.

MAJOR IDEAS DRIVING AMERICAN FOREIGN POLICY

The three major ideas driving American foreign policy during its early years were:

- **Isolationism**—the early US government did not intend to establish colonies, though they did plan to grow larger within the bounds of North America.
- **No entangling alliances**—both George Washington and Thomas Jefferson were opposed to forming any permanent alliances with other countries or becoming involved in other countries' internal issues.
- **Nationalism**—a positive patriotic feeling about the United States blossomed quickly among its citizens, particularly after the War of 1812, when the US once again defeated Britain. The Industrial Revolution also sparked increased nationalism by allowing even the most far-flung areas of the US to communicate with each other via telegraph and the expanding railroad.

CAUSES AND RESULT OF THE WAR OF 1812

The War of 1812 grew out of the continuing tension between France and Great Britain. Napoleon continued striving to conquer Britain, while the US continued trade with both countries but favored France and the French colonies. Because of what Britain saw as an alliance between America and France, they determined to bring an end to trade between the two nations.

With the British preventing US trade with the French and the French preventing trade with the British, James Madison's presidency introduced acts to **regulate international trade**. If either Britain or France removed their restrictions, America would not trade with the other country. Napoleon acted first, and Madison prohibited trade with England. England saw this as the US formally siding with the French, and war ensued in 1812.

The **War of 1812** has been called the **Second American Revolution**. It established the superiority of the US naval forces and reestablished US independence from Britain and Europe.

The British had two major objections to America's continued trade with France. First, they saw the US as helping France's war effort by providing supplies and goods. Second, the United States had grown into a competitor, taking trade and money away from British ships and tradesmen. In its attempts to end American trade with France, the British put into effect the **Orders in Council**,

Copyright © Mometrix Media. You have been licensed one copy of this document for personal use only. Any other reproduction or redistribution is strictly prohibited. All rights reserved.

which made any and all French-owned ports off-limits to American ships. They also began to seize American ships and conscript their crews.

Review Video: Overview of the War of 1812
Visit mometrix.com/academy and enter code: 507716

Review Video: Opinions About the War of 1812
Visit mometrix.com/academy and enter code: 274558

MAJOR MILITARY EVENTS OF THE WAR OF 1812

Two major naval battles, at **Lake Erie** and **Lake Champlain**, kept the British from invading the US via Canada. American attempts to conquer Canadian lands were not successful.

In another memorable British attack, the British invaded Washington, DC and burned the White House on August 24, 1814. Legend has it that **Dolley Madison**, the First Lady, salvaged the portrait of George Washington from the fire. On Christmas Eve, 1814, the **Treaty of Ghent** officially ended the war. However, Andrew Jackson, unaware that the war was over, managed another victory at New Orleans on January 8, 1815. This victory improved American morale and led to a new wave of national pride and support known as the "**Era of Good Feelings**."

MONROE DOCTRINE

On December 2, 1823, President Monroe delivered a message to Congress in which he introduced the **Monroe Doctrine**. In this address, he stated that any attempts by European powers to establish new colonies on the North American continent would be considered interference in American politics. The US would stay out of European matters, and expected Europe to offer America the same courtesy. This approach to foreign policy stated in no uncertain terms that America would not tolerate any new European colonies in the New World, and that events occurring in Europe would no longer influence the policies and doctrines of the US.

LEWIS AND CLARK EXPEDITION

The purchase of the **Louisiana Territory** from France in 1803 more than doubled the size of the United States. President Thomas Jefferson wanted to have the area mapped and explored, since much of the territory was wilderness. He chose Meriwether Lewis and William Clark to head an expedition into the Louisiana Territory. After two years, Lewis and Clark returned, having traveled all the way to the Pacific Ocean. They brought maps, detailed journals, and a multitude of information about the wide expanse of land they had traversed. The **Lewis and Clark Expedition** opened up the west in the Louisiana Territory and beyond for further exploration and settlement.

Review Video: Lewis and Clark Expedition
Visit mometrix.com/academy and enter code: 570657

EFFECTS OF MANIFEST DESTINY ON AMERICAN POLITICS

In the 1800s, many believed America was destined by God to expand west, bringing as much of the North American continent as possible under the umbrella of the US government. With the Northwest Ordinance and the Louisiana Purchase, over half of the continent became American. However, the rapid and relentless expansion brought conflict with the Native Americans, Great Britain, Mexico, and Spain. One result of "**Manifest Destiny**" was the **Mexican-American War** from 1846 to 1848. By the end of the war, Texas, California, and a large portion of what is now the American Southwest joined the growing nation. Conflict also arose over the **Oregon Territory**,

Copyright © Mometrix Media. You have been licensed one copy of this document for personal use only. Any other reproduction or redistribution is strictly prohibited. All rights reserved.

shared by the US and Britain. In 1846, President James Polk resolved this problem by compromising with Britain, establishing a US boundary south of the 49th parallel.

> **Review Video: What is the Manifest Destiny?**
> Visit mometrix.com/academy and enter code: 957409

MEXICAN-AMERICAN WAR

Spain had held colonial interests in America since the 1540s—earlier even than Great Britain. In 1810, **Mexico** revolted against Spain, becoming a free nation in 1821. **Texas** followed suit, declaring its independence after an 1836 revolution. In 1844, the Democrats pressed President Tyler to annex Texas. Unlike his predecessor, Andrew Jackson, Tyler agreed to admit Texas into the Union, and in 1845, Texas became a state.

During Mexico's war for independence, the nation incurred $4.5 million in war debts to the US. Polk offered to forgive the debts in return for New Mexico and Upper California, but Mexico refused. In 1846, war was declared in response to a Mexican attack on American troops along the southern border of Texas. Additional conflict arose in Congress over the **Wilmot Proviso**, which stated that slavery was prohibited in any territory the US acquired from Mexico as a result of the **Mexican-American War**. The war ended in 1848.

> **Review Video: When was the Mexican-American War?**
> Visit mometrix.com/academy and enter code: 271216
>
> **Review Video: Sectional Crisis: The Wilmot Proviso**
> Visit mometrix.com/academy and enter code: 974842

GADSDEN PURCHASE AND THE 1853 POST-WAR TREATY WITH MEXICO

After the Mexican-American war, a **second treaty** in 1853 determined hundreds of miles of America's southwest borders. In 1854, the **Gadsden Purchase** was finalized, providing even more territory to aid in the building of the transcontinental railroad. This purchase added what would eventually become the southernmost regions of Arizona and New Mexico to the growing nation. The modern outline of the United States was by this time nearly complete.

INFLUENCE OF THE AMERICAN SYSTEM ON AMERICAN ECONOMICS

Spurred by the trade conflicts of the War of 1812 and supported by Henry Clay among others, the **American System** set up tariffs to help protect American interests from competition with overseas products. Reducing competition led to growth in employment and an overall increase in American industry. The higher tariffs also provided funds for the government to pay for various improvements. Congress passed high tariffs in 1816 and also chartered a federal bank. The **Second Bank of the United States** was given the job of regulating America's money supply.

JACKSONIAN DEMOCRACY VS. PRECEDING POLITICAL CLIMATE

Jacksonian Democracy is largely seen as a shift from politics favoring the wealthy to politics favoring the common man. The right to vote was given to all free white males, not just property owners, as had been the case previously. Jackson's approach favored the patronage system, laissez-faire economics, and relocation of the Indian tribes from the Southeast portion of the country. Jackson opposed the formation of a federal bank and allowed the Second Bank of the United States to collapse by vetoing a bill to renew the charter. Jackson also faced the challenge of the **Nullification Crisis** when South Carolina claimed that it could ignore or nullify any federal law it

Copyright © Mometrix Media. You have been licensed one copy of this document for personal use only. Any other reproduction or redistribution is strictly prohibited. All rights reserved.

considered unconstitutional. Jackson sent troops to the state to enforce the protested tariff laws, and a compromise engineered by Henry Clay in 1833 settled the matter for the time being.

MAJOR EVENTS AND DEVELOPMENTS THAT BROUGHT THE NORTH AND SOUTH INTO CONFLICT

The conflict between the North and South coalesced around the issue of **slavery**, but other elements contributed to the growing disagreement. Though most farmers in the South worked small farms with little or no slave labor, the huge plantations run by the South's rich depended on slaves or indentured servants to remain profitable. They had also become more dependent on **cotton**, with slave populations growing in concert with the rapid increase in cotton production. In the North, a more diverse agricultural economy and the growth of **industry** made slaves rarer. The **abolitionist movement** grew steadily, with Harriet Beecher Stowe's *Uncle Tom's Cabin* giving many an idea to rally around. A collection of anti-slavery organizations formed, with many actively working to free slaves in the South, often bringing them to the northern states or Canada.

ANTI-SLAVERY ORGANIZATIONS

Five anti-slavery organizations and their significance are:

- **American Colonization Society**—Protestant churches formed this group, aimed at returning black slaves to Africa. Former slaves subsequently formed Liberia, but the colony did not do well, as the region was not well-suited for agriculture.
- **American Anti-Slavery Society**—William Lloyd Garrison, a Quaker, was the major force behind this group and its newspaper, *The Liberator*.
- **Philadelphia Female Anti-Slavery Society**—this women-only group was formed by Margaretta Forten because women were not allowed to join the Anti-Slavery Society formed by her father.
- **Anti-Slavery Convention of American Women**—this group continued meeting even after pro-slavery factions burned down their original meeting place.
- **Female Vigilant Society**—this organization raised funds to help the Underground Railroad, as well as slave refugees.

ATTITUDES TOWARD EDUCATION IN THE EARLY 19TH CENTURY

Horace Mann, among others, felt that schools could help children become better citizens, keep them away from crime, prevent poverty, and help American society become more unified. His *Common School Journal* brought his ideas of the importance of education into the public consciousness and proposed his suggestions for an improved American education system. Increased literacy led to increased awareness of current events, Western expansion, and other major developments of the time period. Public interest and participation in the arts and literature also increased. By the end of the 19th century, all children had access to a **free public elementary education**.

DEVELOPMENTS IN TRANSPORTATION

As America expanded its borders, it also developed new technology to travel the rapidly growing country. Roads and railroads traversed the nation, with the **Transcontinental Railroad** eventually allowing travel from one coast to the other. Canals and steamboats simplified water travel and made shipping easier and less expensive. The **Erie Canal** (1825) connected the Great Lakes to the Hudson River. Other canals connected other major waterways, further facilitating transportation and the shipment of goods.

Copyright © Mometrix Media. You have been licensed one copy of this document for personal use only. Any other reproduction or redistribution is strictly prohibited. All rights reserved.

With growing numbers of settlers moving into the West, **wagon trails** developed, including the Oregon Trail, California Trail, and the Santa Fe Trail. The most common vehicles seen along these westbound trails were covered wagons, also known as **prairie schooners**.

INDUSTRIAL ACTIVITY BEFORE AND AFTER 1800

During the 18th century, goods were often manufactured in houses or small shops. With increased technology allowing for the use of machines, **factories** began to develop. In factories, a large volume of salable goods could be produced in a much shorter amount of time. Many Americans, including increasing numbers of **immigrants**, found jobs in these factories, which were in constant need of labor. Another major invention was the **cotton gin**, which significantly decreased the processing time of cotton and was a major factor in the rapid expansion of cotton production in the South.

DEVELOPMENT OF LABOR MOVEMENTS IN THE 1800S

In 1751, a group of bakers held a protest in which they stopped baking bread. This was technically the first American **labor strike**. In the 1830s and 1840s, labor movements began in earnest. Boston's masons, carpenters, and stoneworkers protested the length of the workday, fighting to reduce it to ten hours. In 1844, a group of women in the textile industry also fought to reduce their workday to ten hours, forming the **Lowell Female Labor Reform Association**. Many other protests occurred and organizations developed through this time period with the same goal in mind.

SECOND GREAT AWAKENING

Led by Protestant evangelical leaders, the **Second Great Awakening** occurred between 1800 and 1830. Several missionary groups grew out of the movement, including the **American Home Missionary Society**, which formed in 1826. The ideas behind the Second Great Awakening focused on personal responsibility, both as an individual and in response to injustice and suffering. The **American Bible Society** and the **American Tract Society** provided literature, while various traveling preachers spread the word. New denominations arose, including the Latter-day Saints and Seventh-day Adventists.

Another movement associated with the Second Great Awakening was the **temperance movement**, focused on ending the production and use of alcohol. One major organization behind the temperance movement was the **Society for the Promotion of Temperance**, formed in 1826 in Boston.

EARLY LEADERS IN THE WOMEN'S RIGHTS MOVEMENT

The women's rights movement began in the 1840s, with leaders including Elizabeth Cady Stanton, Sojourner Truth, Ernestine Rose, and Lucretia Mott. In 1869, Elizabeth Cady Stanton and Susan B. Anthony formed the **National Woman Suffrage Association**, fighting for women's right to vote.

In 1848, in Seneca Falls, the first women's rights convention was held, with about 300 attendees. The two-day **Seneca Falls Convention** discussed the rights of women to vote (suffrage) as well as equal treatment in careers, legal proceedings, etc. The convention produced a "Declaration of Sentiments," which outlined a plan for women to attain the rights they deserved. **Frederick**

Copyright © Mometrix Media. You have been licensed one copy of this document for personal use only. Any other reproduction or redistribution is strictly prohibited. All rights reserved.

Douglass supported the women's rights movement, as well as the abolition movement. In fact, women's rights and abolition movements often went hand-in-hand during this time period.

> **Review Video: What was the Women's Rights Movement in America?**
> Visit mometrix.com/academy and enter code: 987734

EFFECTS OF THE MISSOURI COMPROMISE ON THE TENSIONS BETWEEN THE NORTH AND SOUTH

By 1819, the United States had developed a tenuous balance between slave and free states, with exactly 22 senators in Congress from each faction. However, Missouri was ready to join the union. As a slave state, it would tip the balance in Congress. To prevent this imbalance, the **Missouri Compromise** brought the northern part of Massachusetts into the union as Maine, establishing it as a free state to balance the admission of Missouri as a slave state. In addition, the remaining portion of the Louisiana Purchase was to remain free north of **latitude 36°30′**. Since cotton did not grow well this far north, this limitation was acceptable to congressmen representing the slave states.

However, the proposed Missouri constitution presented a problem, as it outlawed immigration of free blacks into the state. Another compromise was in order, this time proposed by **Henry Clay**. According to this new compromise, Missouri would never pass a law that prevented anyone from entering the state. Through this and other work, Clay earned his title of the "**Great Compromiser**."

> **Review Video: What was the Missouri Compromise?**
> Visit mometrix.com/academy and enter code: 848091

POPULAR SOVEREIGNTY AND THE COMPROMISE OF 1850

In addition to the pro-slavery and anti-slavery factions, a third group rose, who felt that each individual state should decide whether to allow or permit slavery within its borders. The idea that a state could make its own choices was referred to as **popular sovereignty**.

When California applied to join the union in 1849, the balance of congressional power was again threatened. The **Compromise of 1850** introduced a group of laws meant to bring an end to the conflict:

- California's admittance as a free state
- The outlaw of the slave trade in Washington, DC
- An increase in efforts to capture escaped slaves
- The right of New Mexico and Utah territories to decide individually whether to allow slavery

In spite of these measures, debate raged each time a new state prepared to enter the union.

KANSAS-NEBRASKA ACT TRIGGER OF ADDITIONAL CONFLICT

With the creation of the Kansas and Nebraska territories in 1854, another debate began. Congress allowed popular sovereignty in these territories, but slavery opponents argued that the Missouri Compromise had already made slavery illegal in this region. In Kansas, two separate governments

Copyright © Mometrix Media. You have been licensed one copy of this document for personal use only. Any other reproduction or redistribution is strictly prohibited. All rights reserved.

arose, one pro-slavery and one anti-slavery. Conflict between the two factions rose to violence, leading Kansas to gain the nickname of "**Bleeding Kansas.**"

Review Video: Sectional Crisis: The Kansas-Nebraska Act
Visit mometrix.com/academy and enter code: 982119

DRED SCOTT DECISION

Abolitionist factions coalesced around the case of **Dred Scott**, using his case to test the country's laws regarding slavery. Scott, a slave, had been taken by his owner from Missouri, which was a slave state. He then traveled to Illinois, a free state, then on to the Minnesota Territory, also free based on the Missouri Compromise. After several years, he returned to Missouri, and his owner subsequently died. Abolitionists took Scott's case to court, stating that Scott was no longer a slave but free, since he had lived in free territory. The case went to the Supreme Court.

The Supreme Court stated that, because Scott, as a slave, was not a US citizen, his time in free states did not change his status. He also did not have the right to sue. In addition, the Court determined that the **Missouri Compromise** was unconstitutional, stating that Congress had overstepped its bounds by outlawing slavery in the territories.

Review Video: What was the Dred Scott Decision?
Visit mometrix.com/academy and enter code: 364838

INCIDENTS AT HARPER'S FERRY AND JOHN BROWN'S ROLE

John Brown, an abolitionist, had participated in several anti-slavery activities, including killing five pro-slavery men in retaliation, after the sacking of Lawrence, Kansas, an anti-slavery town. He and other abolitionists also banded together to pool their funds and build a runaway slave colony.

In 1859, Brown seized a federal arsenal in **Harper's Ferry**, located in what is now West Virginia. Brown intended to seize guns and ammunition and lead a slave rebellion. **Robert E. Lee** captured Brown and 21 followers, who were subsequently tried and hanged. While Northerners took the executions as an indication that the government supported slavery, Southerners were of the opinion that most of the North supported Brown and were, in general, anti-slavery.

PRESIDENTIAL CANDIDATES FOR THE 1860 ELECTION

The 1860 presidential candidates represented four different parties, each with a different opinion on slavery:

- **John Breckinridge**, representing the Southern Democrats, was pro-slavery but urged compromise to preserve the Union.
- **Abraham Lincoln**, of the Republican Party, was anti-slavery.
- **Stephen Douglas**, of the Northern Democrats, felt that the issue should be determined locally, on a state-by-state basis.
- **John Bell**, of the Constitutional Union Party, focused primarily on keeping the Union intact.

In the end, Abraham Lincoln won both the popular and electoral election. Southern states, who had sworn to secede from the Union if Lincoln was elected, did so, led by South Carolina. Shortly thereafter, the Civil War began when Confederate shots were fired on **Fort Sumter** in Charleston.

Copyright © Mometrix Media. You have been licensed one copy of this document for personal use only. Any other reproduction or redistribution is strictly prohibited. All rights reserved.

NORTH VS. SOUTH IN THE CIVIL WAR

The Northern states had significant advantages, including:

- **Larger population**—the North consisted of 24 states, while the South had 11.
- **Better transportation and finances**—with railroads primarily in the North, supply chains were much more dependable, as was overseas trade.
- **Raw materials**—the North held the majority of America's gold, as well as iron, copper, and other minerals vital to wartime.

The South's advantages included the following:

- **Better-trained military officers**—many of the Southern officers were West Point trained and had commanded in the Mexican and Indian wars.
- **Familiarity with weapons**—the climate and lifestyle of the South meant most of the people were experienced with both guns and horses. The industrial North had less extensive experience.
- **Defensive position**—the South felt that victory was guaranteed, since they were protecting their own lands, while the North would be invading.
- **Well-defined goals**—the South fought an ideological war to be allowed to govern themselves and preserve their way of life. The North originally fought to preserve the Union and later to free the slaves.

> **Review Video: The Civil War: A North vs South Overview**
> Visit mometrix.com/academy and enter code: 370788

BENEFIT OF THE EMANCIPATION PROCLAMATION ON THE UNION'S MILITARY STRATEGY

The Emancipation Proclamation, issued by President Lincoln on January 1, 1863, freed all slaves in **Confederate states** that were still in rebellion against the Union. While the original proclamation did not free any slaves in the states actually under Union control, it did set a precedent for the emancipation of slaves as the war progressed.

The **Emancipation Proclamation** worked in the Union's favor, as many freed slaves and other black troops joined the **Union Army**. Almost 200,000 blacks fought in the Union army, and over 10,000 served in the navy. By the end of the war, over 4 million slaves had been freed, and in 1865 slavery was abolished in the **13th amendment** to the Constitution.

> **Review Video: The Civil War: The Emancipation Proclamation**
> Visit mometrix.com/academy and enter code: 181778

MAJOR EVENTS OF THE CIVIL WAR

Six major events of the Civil War and their outcomes or significance are:

- The **First Battle of Bull Run** (July 21, 1861)—this was the first major land battle of the war. Observers, expecting to enjoy an entertaining skirmish, set up picnics nearby. Instead, they found themselves witness to a bloodbath. Union forces were defeated, and the battle set the course of the Civil War as long, bloody, and costly.
- The **Capture of Fort Henry** by Ulysses S. Grant—this battle in February of 1862 marked the Union's first major victory.

Copyright © Mometrix Media. You have been licensed one copy of this document for personal use only. Any other reproduction or redistribution is strictly prohibited. All rights reserved.

- The **Battle of Gettysburg** (July 1-3, 1863)—often seen as the turning point of the war, Gettysburg also saw the largest number of casualties of the war, with over 50,000 dead, wounded, or missing. Robert E. Lee was defeated, and the Confederate army, significantly crippled, withdrew.
- The **Overland Campaign** (May and June of 1864)—Grant, now in command of all the Union armies, led this high casualty campaign that eventually positioned the Union for victory.
- **Sherman's March to the Sea**—William Tecumseh Sherman, in May of 1864, conquered Atlanta. He then continued to Savannah, destroying vast amounts of property as he went.
- Following Lee's defeat at the Appomattox Courthouse, General Grant accepted **Lee's surrender** in the home of Wilmer McLean in Appomattox, Virginia on April 9, 1865.

CIRCUMSTANCES OF LINCOLN'S ASSASSINATION

The Civil War ended with the surrender of the South on April 9, 1865. Five days later, Lincoln and his wife, Mary, went to the play *Our American Cousin* at the Ford Theater. John Wilkes Booth, who did not know that the war was over, did his part in a plot to help the Confederacy by shooting Lincoln. He was carried from the theater to a nearby house, where he died the next morning. Booth was tracked down and killed by Union soldiers twelve days later.

> **Review Video: Overview of the Civil War**
> Visit mometrix.com/academy and enter code: 239557

GOALS OF RECONSTRUCTION AND THE FREEDMEN'S BUREAU

In the aftermath of the Civil War, the South was left in chaos. From 1865 to 1877, government on all levels worked to help restore order to the South, ensure civil rights to the freed slaves, and bring the Confederate states back into the Union. This became known as the **Reconstruction period**. In 1866, Congress passed the **Reconstruction Acts**, placing former Confederate states under military rule and stating the grounds for readmission into the Union.

The **Freedmen's Bureau** was formed to help freedmen both with basic necessities like food and clothing and also with employment and finding of family members who had been separated during the war. Many in the South felt the Freedmen's Bureau worked to set freed slaves against their former owners. The Bureau was intended to help former slaves become self-sufficient, and to keep them from falling prey to those who would take advantage of them. It eventually closed due to lack of funding and to violence from the **Ku Klux Klan**.

POLICIES OF THE RADICAL AND MODERATE REPUBLICANS

The **Radical Republicans** wished to treat the South quite harshly after the war. **Thaddeus Stevens**, the House Leader, suggested that the Confederate states be treated as if they were territories again, with ten years of military rule and territorial government before they would be readmitted. He also wanted to give all black men the right to vote. Former Confederate soldiers would be required to swear they had never supported the Confederacy (knows as the "Ironclad Oath") in order to be granted full rights as American citizens.

In contrast, the **moderate Republicans** wanted only black men who were literate or who had served as Union troops to be able to vote. All Confederate soldiers except troop leaders would also be able to vote. Before his death, **Lincoln** had favored a more moderate approach to Reconstruction, hoping this approach might bring some states back into the Union before the end of the war.

Copyright © Mometrix Media. You have been licensed one copy of this document for personal use only. Any other reproduction or redistribution is strictly prohibited. All rights reserved.

BLACK CODES AND THE CIVIL RIGHTS BILL

The Black Codes were proposed to control freed slaves. They would not be allowed to bear arms, assemble, serve on juries, or testify against whites. Schools would be segregated, and unemployed blacks could be arrested and forced to work. The **Civil Rights Act** countered these codes, providing much wider rights for the freed slaves.

Andrew Johnson, who became president after Lincoln's death, supported the Black Codes and vetoed the Civil Rights Act in 1865 and again in 1866. The second time, Congress overrode his veto, and it became law.

Two years later, Congress voted to **impeach** Johnson, the culmination of tensions between Congress and the president. He was tried and came within a single vote of being convicted, but ultimately was acquitted and finished his term in office.

PURPOSE OF THE THIRTEENTH, FOURTEENTH, AND FIFTEENTH AMENDMENTS

The Thirteenth, Fourteenth and Fifteenth Amendments were all passed shortly after the end of the Civil War:

- The **Thirteenth Amendment** was ratified by the states on December 6, 1865. This amendment prohibited slavery in the United States.
- The **Fourteenth Amendment** overturned the Dred Scott decision and was ratified July 9, 1868. American citizenship was redefined: a citizen was any person born or naturalized in the US, with all citizens guaranteed equal legal protection by all states. It also guaranteed citizens of any race the right to file a lawsuit or serve on a jury.
- The **Fifteenth Amendment** was ratified on February 3, 1870. It states that no citizen of the United States can be denied the right to vote based on race, color, or previous status as a slave.

> **Review Video: What is the 13th Amendment?**
> Visit mometrix.com/academy and enter code: 800185
>
> **Review Video: What is the 14th Amendment?**
> Visit mometrix.com/academy and enter code: 851325
>
> **Review Video: What is the 15th Amendment?**
> Visit mometrix.com/academy and enter code: 287199

PHASES OF RECONSTRUCTION

The three phases of Reconstruction are:

- **Presidential Reconstruction**—largely driven by President Andrew Johnson's policies, the presidential phase of Reconstruction was lenient on the South and allowed continued discrimination against and control over blacks.
- **Congressional Reconstruction**—Congress, controlled largely by Radical Republicans, took a different stance, providing a wider range of civil rights for blacks and greater control over Southern government. Congressional Reconstruction is marked by military control of the former Confederate States.
- **Redemption**—gradually, the Confederate states were readmitted into the Union. During this time, white Democrats took over the government of most of the South. In 1877, President Rutherford Hayes withdrew the last federal troops from the South.

Copyright © Mometrix Media. You have been licensed one copy of this document for personal use only. Any other reproduction or redistribution is strictly prohibited. All rights reserved.

CARPETBAGGERS AND SCALAWAGS

The chaos in the South attracted a number of people seeking to fill the power vacuums and take advantage of the economic disruption. **Scalawags** were southern whites who aligned with freedmen to take over local governments. Many in the South who could have filled political offices refused to take the necessary oath required to grant them the right to vote, leaving many opportunities for Scalawags and others. **Carpetbaggers** were Northerners who traveled to the South for various reasons. Some provided assistance, while others sought to make money or to acquire political power during this chaotic period.

TRANSCONTINENTAL RAILROAD

In 1869, the **Union Pacific Railroad** completed the first section of a planned **transcontinental railroad**. This section went from Omaha, Nebraska to Sacramento, California. Ninety percent of the workers were Chinese, working in very dangerous conditions for very low pay. With the rise of the railroad, products were much more easily transported across the country. While this was positive overall for industry throughout the country, it was often damaging to family farmers, who found themselves paying high shipping costs for smaller supply orders while larger companies received major discounts.

MEASURES TO LIMIT IMMIGRATION IN THE 19TH CENTURY

In 1870, the **Naturalization Act** put limits on US citizenship, allowing full citizenship only to whites and those of African descent. The **Chinese Exclusion Act of 1882** put limits on Chinese immigration. The **Immigration Act of 1882** taxed immigrants, charging 50 cents per person. These funds helped pay administrative costs for regulating immigration. **Ellis Island** opened in 1892 as a processing center for those arriving in New York. The year 1921 saw the **Emergency Quota Act** passed, also known as the **Johnson Quota Act**, which severely limited the number of immigrants allowed into the country.

AGRICULTURE IN THE 19TH CENTURY

TECHNOLOGICAL ADVANCES IN AGRICULTURAL CHANGES

During the mid-1800s, irrigation techniques improved significantly. Advances occurred in cultivation and breeding, as well as fertilizer use and crop rotation. In the Great Plains, also known as the Great American Desert, the dense soil was finally cultivated with steel plows. In 1892, gasoline-powered tractors arrived, and they were widely used by 1900. Other advancements in agriculture's toolset included barbed wire fences, combines, silos, deep-water wells, and the cream separator.

MAJOR ACTIONS THAT HELPED IMPROVE AGRICULTURE

Four major government actions that helped improve US agriculture in the 19th century are:

- The **Department of Agriculture** came into being in 1862, working for the interests of farmers and ranchers across the country.
- The **Morrill Land-Grant Acts** were a series of acts passed between 1862 and 1890, allowing land-grant colleges.
- In conjunction with land-grant colleges, the **Hatch Act of 1887** brought agriculture experiment stations into the picture, helping discover new farming techniques.
- In 1914, the **Smith-Lever Act** provided cooperative programs to help educate people about food, home economics, community development, and agriculture. Related agriculture extension programs helped farmers increase crop production to feed the rapidly growing nation.

Copyright © Mometrix Media. You have been licensed one copy of this document for personal use only. Any other reproduction or redistribution is strictly prohibited. All rights reserved.

INVENTORS FROM THE 1800S

Major inventors from the 1800s and their inventions include:

- Alexander Graham Bell—the telephone
- Orville and Wilbur Wright—the airplane
- Richard Gatling—the machine gun
- Walter Hunt, Elias Howe, and Isaac Singer—the sewing machine
- Nikola Tesla—alternating current motor
- George Eastman—the Kodak camera
- Thomas Edison—light bulbs, motion pictures, the phonograph
- Samuel Morse—the telegraph
- Charles Goodyear—vulcanized rubber
- Cyrus McCormick—the reaper
- George Westinghouse—the transformer, the air brake

This was an active period for invention, with about 700,000 patents registered between 1860 and 1900.

GILDED AGE

The time period from the end of the Civil War to the beginning of the First World War is often referred to as the **Gilded Age**, or the **Second Industrial Revolution**. The US was changing from an agricultural-based economy to an **industrial economy**, with rapid growth accompanying the shift. In addition, the country itself was expanding, spreading into the seemingly unlimited west.

This time period saw the beginning of banks, department stores, chain stores, and trusts—all familiar features of the modern-day landscape. Cities also grew rapidly, and large numbers of immigrants arrived in the country, swelling the urban ranks.

> **Review Video: The Gilded Age: An Overview**
> Visit mometrix.com/academy and enter code: 684770
>
> **Review Video: The Gilded Age: Chinese Immigration**
> Visit mometrix.com/academy and enter code: 624166

FACTORS LEADING TO THE DEVELOPMENT OF THE POPULIST PARTY

A major **recession** struck the United States during the 1890s, with crop prices falling dramatically. **Drought** compounded the problems, leaving many American farmers in crippling debt. The **Farmers' Alliance** formed in 1875, drawing the rural poor into a single political entity.

Recession also affected the more industrial parts of the country. The **Knights of Labor**, formed in 1869 by **Uriah Stephens**, was able to unite workers into a union to protect their rights. Dissatisfied by views espoused by industrialists, the Farmers Alliance and the Knights of Labor, joined to form the **Populist Party**, also known as the People's Party, in 1892. Some of the elements of the party's platform included:

- National currency
- Graduated income tax
- Government ownership of railroads as well as telegraph and telephone systems
- Secret ballots for voting

Copyright © Mometrix Media. You have been licensed one copy of this document for personal use only. Any other reproduction or redistribution is strictly prohibited. All rights reserved.

- Immigration restriction
- Single-term limits for president and vice-president

The Populist Party was in favor of decreasing elitism and making the voice of the common man more easily heard in the political process.

GROWTH OF THE LABOR MOVEMENT THROUGH THE LATE 19TH CENTURY

One of the first large, well-organized strikes occurred in 1892. Called the **Homestead Strike**, it occurred when the Amalgamated Association of Iron and Steel Workers struck against the Carnegie Steel Company. Gunfire ensued, and Carnegie was able to eliminate the plant's union. In 1894, workers in the American Railway Union, led by Eugene Debs, initiated the **Pullman Strike** after the Pullman Palace Car Co. cut their wages by 28 percent. President Grover Cleveland called in troops to break up the strike on the grounds that it interfered with mail delivery. Mary Harris "Mother" Jones organized the **Children's Crusade** to protest child labor. A protest march proceeded to the home of President Theodore Roosevelt in 1903. Jones also worked with the United Mine Workers of America and helped found the **Industrial Workers of the World**.

PANIC OF 1893

Far from a US-centric event, the **Panic of 1893** was an economic crisis that affected most of the globe. As a response, President Grover Cleveland repealed the **Sherman Silver Purchase Act**, afraid it had caused the downturn rather than boosting the economy as intended. The Panic led to bankruptcies, with banks and railroads going under and factory unemployment rising as high as 25 percent. In the end, the **Republican Party** regained power due to the economic crisis.

PROGRESSIVE ERA

From the 1890s to the end of the First World War, **Progressives** set forth an ideology that drove many levels of society and politics. The Progressives were in favor of workers' rights and safety and wanted measures taken against waste and corruption. They felt science could help improve society and that the government could—and should—provide answers to a variety of social problems. Progressives came from a wide variety of backgrounds but were united in their desire to improve society.

> **Review Video: The Progressive Era**
> Visit mometrix.com/academy and enter code: 722394

MUCKRAKERS AND THE PROGRESSIVE MOVEMENT

"Muckrakers" was a term used to identify aggressive investigative journalists who exposed scandals, corruption, and many other wrongs in late 19th-century society. Among these intrepid writers were:

- **Ida Tarbell**—she exposed John D. Rockefeller's Standard Oil Trust.
- **Jacob Riis**—a photographer, he brought the living conditions of the poor in New York to the public's attention.
- **Lincoln Steffens**—he worked to expose political corruption in municipal government.
- **Upton Sinclair**—his book *The Jungle* led to reforms in the meat-packing industry.

Through the work of these journalists, many new policies came into being, including workmen's compensation, child labor laws, and trust-busting.

Copyright © Mometrix Media. You have been licensed one copy of this document for personal use only. Any other reproduction or redistribution is strictly prohibited. All rights reserved.

GOVERNMENT DEALINGS WITH NATIVE AMERICANS THROUGH THE END OF THE 19TH CENTURY

America's westward expansion led to conflict and violent confrontations with Native Americans such as the **Battle of Little Bighorn**. In 1876, the American government ordered all Indians to relocate to reservations. Lack of compliance led to the **Dawes Act** in 1887, which ordered assimilation rather than separation: Native Americans were offered American citizenship and a piece of their tribal land if they would accept the lot chosen by the government and live on it separately from the tribe. This act remained in effect until 1934. Reformers also forced Indian children to attend **Indian Boarding Schools**, where they were not allowed to speak their native language and were immersed into a Euro-American culture and religion. Children were often abused in these schools and were indoctrinated to abandon their identity as Native Americans.

In 1890, the massacre at **Wounded Knee**, accompanied by Geronimo's surrender, led the Native Americans to work to preserve their culture rather than fight for their lands.

> **Review Video: Government Dealings with Native Americans Through the End of the 19th Century**
> Visit mometrix.com/academy and enter code: 635645

ROLE OF NATIVE AMERICANS IN WARTIME THROUGH THE BEGINNING OF THE 20TH CENTURY

The **Spanish-American War** (1898) saw a number of Native Americans serving with Teddy Roosevelt in the Rough Riders. Apache scouts accompanied General John J. Pershing to Mexico, hoping to find **Pancho Villa**. More than 17,000 Native Americans were drafted into service for **World War I**, though at the time, they were not considered legal citizens. In 1924, Indians were finally granted official citizenship by the **Indian Citizenship Act**.

After decades of relocation, forced assimilation, and genocide, the number of Native Americans in the US has greatly declined. Though many Native Americans have chosen—or have been forced—to assimilate, about 300 reservations exist today, with most of their inhabitants living in abject poverty.

> **Review Video: Role of Native Americans in Wartime Through the Beginning of the 20th Century**
> Visit mometrix.com/academy and enter code: 419128

EVENTS LEADING UP TO THE SPANISH-AMERICAN WAR

Spain had controlled **Cuba** since the 15th century. Over the centuries, the Spanish had quashed a variety of revolts. In 1886, slavery ended in Cuba, and another revolt was rising.

In the meantime, the US had expressed interest in Cuba, offering Spain $130 million for the island in 1853, during Franklin Pierce's presidency. In 1898, the Cuban revolt was underway. In spite of various factions supporting the Cubans, the US President, William McKinley, refused to recognize the rebellion, preferring negotiation over involvement in war. Then, the *Maine*, a US battleship in Havana Harbor, was blown up, killing 266 crew members. The US declared war two months later, and the war ended with a **Spanish surrender** in less than four months.

Copyright © Mometrix Media. You have been licensed one copy of this document for personal use only. Any other reproduction or redistribution is strictly prohibited. All rights reserved.

Illinois History

POLITICAL CHANGES IN ILLINOIS DUE TO AND FOLLOWING CIVIL WAR

Illinois historically voted with the **Democratic party** before the Civil War, during the times of Stephen Douglas. After the election of Lincoln, a moderate Republican, and the Civil War, a majority of the citizens of Illinois switched their allegiance to the party of the Union, the **Republican party**. Lincoln's assassination only strengthened their loyalty. In addition, the Civil War stimulated the formation of a number of new organizations. In wartime, the **Union League Club** had supported the Republican Party in disputes with the "copperheads," who were against unification and for the southern Confederacy. After the war, members of this and other groups used their influence to support Republican elections. The **Grand Army of the Republic**, composed of Union war veterans, was another such group. The war also made Illinois' economy more industrial, so the state then supported the promotion of railroads and the high tariffs favored by the Republican Party.

CONFLICTS WITHIN REPUBLICAN PARTY DURING ADMINISTRATION OF ANDREW JOHNSON

Abraham Lincoln made **Andrew Johnson** his running mate in 1864 to balance the ticket by appealing to pro-Union Southerners. Johnson succeeded to the presidency upon Lincoln's assassination, inheriting the tasks of Reconstruction. Johnson agreed to emancipation of slaves by the 13th Amendment and to some civil rights for Blacks. However, he also responded to advances of southern White supremacists wanting re-acceptance to the Union while also wanting to control Black citizens. Johnson's lenient attitude toward the South alienated his **Republican constituents**. Radical Republicans wanted a Federal Reconstruction program; moderates wanted state legal rights without federal funding. Illinois Senator **Trumbull** disagreed with those wanting to oust Johnson. However, Johnson's veto of Trumbull's bills for Black civil rights caused moderate and radical Republicans in Illinois and the North to unite in rejecting him. The House of Representatives voted to impeach him in 1868; the Senate came one vote short of approving it.

FORMATION OF THE LIBERAL REPUBLICAN PARTY

During the Reconstruction, **political corruption** was common in the Republican Party, damaging its reputation both in Illinois and throughout the country. The Illinois State Constitution was amended to eliminate a number of legal loopholes of which corrupt officials had taken advantage. Nonetheless, the state government continued to give valuable state contracts to political cronies and to appoint political "hacks" to civil service jobs. In some places, Democrats took the place of Republicans whose reputations were damaged by being involved in scandals. In local Illinois elections in 1869, members of **both parties** often joined to run "citizen tickets" to oppose the "ring tickets" furthered by the Republican system. Political corruption became an issue that divided the Republican Party nationwide. Many Republicans, disenchanted with Ulysses S. Grant's presidency and administration, became political reformers, starting a movement that formed the **Liberal Republican Party** in 1872, a challenge to the traditional American two-party system.

INFLUENCES AND ACTIONS OF LIBERAL REPUBLICAN PARTY IN ILLINOIS AND RESULTS OF THE 1872 PRESIDENTIAL ELECTION

Once the Liberal Republican Party had formed as a reaction of Republican political reformers against Republican political corruption, a number of Illinois Republicans campaigned for the Liberal Republican Party's candidacy for **President**. These included Illinois Senator Lyman Trumbull; Illinois Governor John Palmer; Supreme Court Justice David Davis; and Gustave Koerner, a German-American politician. However, at the Liberal Republican convention in Cincinnati, Ohio, party members could not agree to the strongest candidate. They settled on **Horace Greeley**, the newspaper editor from New York. Democrats, also unable to select anyone else, endorsed Greeley as their candidate as well. The Liberal Republican Party represented a new middle class of many

Copyright © Mometrix Media. You have been licensed one copy of this document for personal use only. Any other reproduction or redistribution is strictly prohibited. All rights reserved.

Republican and some northern Democratic professionals. They wanted competent governmental administration, but they did not seek support from Democrats, farmers, or others disenchanted with the two-party system. The North, including Illinois, voted to re-elect **Ulysses S. Grant** for another corruption-riddled term (1872-1876).

CHALLENGES TO CHICAGO POLITICS IN LATE 1800S

The devastation caused by the Great Fire of Chicago in 1871, the economic Panic of 1873 and the ensuing depression, a huge influx of immigrants, and the new development of violent incidents over labor disputes, all presented **political challenges** in Chicago, Illinois. The Populist Movement formed the People's Party as part of movements against corruption for political reform. Chicago voters responded to conditions in 1873 by electing a candidate from the **People's Party** to be their mayor, and People's Party members to run their city council. Recent German immigrants to Chicago also formed a **Socialist Party** at this time. The Socialists had many disputes with the People's Party city leadership during the depression of the 1870s. The Chicago administration's response to unemployment was to recommend that individuals should use their own initiative and self-help, while the Socialists wanted the city government to provide jobs and/or relief funds to unemployed citizens.

INFLUENCE OF FARMERS ON AMERICAN POLITICS AND ECONOMY IN LATE 1800S

Following the Civil War, the United States Federal government had taken the wartime inflationary "greenbacks" out of circulation and had returned to adhering to the gold standard. This **deflated** American currency's value. The deflation caused great pressure to debtors, especially farmers, by making it impossible for them to make payments. During the 1870s, many farmers formed **Granges and Farmers' Alliances** for the purposes of political lobbies and helping themselves. This was concurrent with the Populist Movement. The Farmers' Alliances contributed to the Populists until, by 1892, the Populists became a national political organization for the Farmers' Alliances. Its platform advocated national government subtreasuries/warehouses to help farmers with crop storage pending better prices; and coining silver for economic expansion. This appealed to southern and western Democrats, dividing the party and defeating conservative President Grover Cleveland. Nationally, the Populist Party garnered over a million votes, carrying three states in the 1872 election.

CHANGES MADE TO ILLINOIS STATE LAW BY ITS NEW CONSTITUTION OF 1870

Illinois law had been governed by the same state constitution since 1848 when, in 1869, a **state constitutional convention** was held to rewrite it. This was largely in response to widespread political corruption. This corruption was characterized by state legislation that was passed annually to favor local special interests and/or certain individuals. Political rings of insiders raided state treasury funds via contracts that they had created with the new Illinois State Industrial University at Champaign, and with the Illinois State Penitentiary, to give two examples. Illinois voters insisted that the state constitution be **rewritten** to address these dealings. The new state constitution prohibited most legislation favoring special interests, as well as the legislature's power to override the governor's vetoes. Consistent with the Fifteenth Amendment, the new Illinois State Constitution granted **suffrage** to black citizens of Illinois, although many people in Illinois still resisted civil rights and social equality for black people.

ILLINOIS STATE CONSTITUTION OF 1870, INTERESTS OF ILLINOIS FARMERS, AND MUNN V. ILLINOIS

Political graft had long existed in the city of Chicago, the state of Illinois, and within the Republican Party on a national level. Corrupt political deals giving benefits of money and power to politicians at the expense of the public seemed to increase exponentially during the late 1860s after the Civil

58

Copyright © Mometrix Media. You have been licensed one copy of this document for personal use only. Any other reproduction or redistribution is strictly prohibited. All rights reserved.

War. Voters in Illinois finally demanded that their **state constitution**, ratified in 1848, should be rewritten to rein in these damaging and unethical practices, and the state legislature responded by convening a state constitutional convention in 1869 to **amend** the existing document. The new constitution was ratified in 1870 and regulated businesses that held state franchises or licenses to further public interest. When a merchant violated and then challenged these new laws, it culminated in the U.S. Supreme Court's ruling in Munn v. Illinois (1877), which affirmed the regulation of businesses enacted in the Illinois State Constitution.

ECONOMIC DEVELOPMENTS IN ILLINOIS AS RESULT OF CIVIL WAR

During the Civil War, Illinois **agriculture** became very important to the Union armies. The corn and grains that Illinois farmers grew supplied troops with rations. Illinois **industry** also supplied the Union armies, as its factories manufactured soldiers' uniforms, wagons, weapons, and other needed items. Because Chicago was located at the center of Northwest America's network of railroads, which was rapidly expanding, it became a main distribution point for goods manufactured in the East to be transported to troops fighting in the West. After the war, the first **Transcontinental Railroad** was finished, running from Omaha to San Francisco, in 1869. Since Chicago already had a railroad connection with Omaha, Chicago also became the center of the Western railroad system. But the war's end also lowered crop prices and European demand for crops, so farmers who had borrowed money to raise production for booming wartime markets could not repay them.

EFFECTS OF GREAT CHICAGO FIRE OF 1871 UPON ECONOMIC AND BUSINESS DEVELOPMENT

Although the Great Fire destroyed almost 40 percent of Chicago, the city was rebuilt very quickly because of Chicago's strategic geographical position and capital contributions from eastern commerce. Instead of devastation, the opportunities for new construction created by the fire made Chicago a mecca for innovative architecture. **Frank Lloyd Wright** and **Louis Sullivan** became prominent architectural designers in Chicago, gaining nationwide and worldwide fame. Chicago was the site of America's first **skyscrapers**. These were enabled by cement caissons sunk in bedrock deep underground and supporting steel frames. As Chicago also became the nexus of America's Western rail system, Chicago merchants collected lumber, corn, grain, et cetera, from Western and Midwestern farms, and then distributed products manufactured from these crops, such as tools, clothes, and pre-fabricated housing units. Also because of the railroad system, **Sears Roebuck** and **Montgomery Ward** in Chicago both became prominent mail-order businesses when trains enabled widespread delivery of orders.

MAJOR MANUFACTURING INDUSTRIES IN CHICAGO IN MID/LATE 1800S

A number of manufacturing companies developed to support the agrarian commerce of the Western United States after the Civil War. Many of these companies began in Chicago or relocated there. The **McCormick Harvester Company** began in Virginia, but in 1848 it moved to Chicago to avail itself of the city's closeness to the West's Grain Belt. This company built an enormous factory on Chicago's West Side, which provided jobs for thousands of employees in the city. On the southwest side of Chicago, the Cudahy, Swift, and Armour companies all built huge slaughterhouses and meat processing and packing plants; collectively, these were known as **Packingtown**. Before the Civil War, St. Louis and New Orleans had become significant to commerce via the Mississippi River steamboats' transportation. With the growth of the railroads, which took the place of steamboats, Chicago superseded St. Louis as the major **commercial center** of the Mississippi Valley region.

Copyright © Mometrix Media. You have been licensed one copy of this document for personal use only. Any other reproduction or redistribution is strictly prohibited. All rights reserved.

ILLINOIS WOMEN'S INVOLVEMENT IN LABOR, SOCIAL REFORM, AND POLITICS PRIOR TO 1900

During the Gilded Age, many women in Illinois had to work, especially immigrants. In 1878, **The Knights of Labor**, a powerful labor union at the time, was notable as the only union accepting African-Americans and women, giving women an unusual chance to participate in a labor organization. The Chicago chapter also afforded immigrant women and families opportunities for social activities by organizing social groups hosting festivals, rallies, and picnics. Affluent middle-class women formed many women's clubs in the 1880s, such as the **Chicago Women's Club**, which worked to prevent juvenile offenders from becoming career criminals. Clubwomen pushed for and got seats on boards of schools and other state and private institutions for women and children. In 1891, the state legislature passed a bill letting women vote in elections of school officials. In 1894, **Lucy Flower** was the first woman elected by Illinois voters as Trustee of the University of Illinois.

ILLINOIS POLITICS AND ECONOMY IN LATE 1890S

Republicans swept the 1894 election, defeating Democrats and damaging the administration of conservative Democratic President **Grover Cleveland**. Cleveland's promotion of the gold standard, high tariffs, and laissez-faire economics lost him the support of southern and western Democrats, who preferred the Populist Party's promotion of government support for farmers and others in debt. Illinois politics reflected the growing divisiveness in the party. **Altgeld**, the first non-American-born Illinois Governor, pardoned activists in the Haymarket Riot and refused to deploy State troops against striking Pullman workers. Altgeld's labor/union-friendly policies were overridden by Cleveland's support of management with U.S. Army troops and a court injunction. Illinois' **William Jennings Bryan** spoke in support of coining silver, appealing to many: Chicago was among cities where unemployment approached 20 percent and many women and children went to work for half of men's wages. Bryan's "Cross of Gold" speech advocating free silver won him the nomination at the Chicago Democratic Convention.

POLITICAL REFORM IN CHICAGO AT END OF 19TH CENTURY

In the election of 1896, **William McKinley** and the Republican Party overwhelmingly defeated the Populist Party. Regardless, the emphasis of industrialists on efficiency, technology, and expertise provided a new criticism of the graft inherent in party politics. In 1896, the **Municipal Voters' League** was established by citizens of Chicago. This group investigated the city's aldermen for corruption and wrongdoing and was successful in ousting many of the guilty from office. Social movements begun during the Gilded Age had given rise to such developments as the formation of women's clubs for social reform; the election of German-American John Altgeld as the first non-native-born Governor of Illinois; and the success of Jane Addams' Hull House, the first settlement house in the country, to organize immigrants and other poor people to help themselves, and promote Americans' learning about other cultures from immigrants. These movements continued on to become part of the **Progressive Era**.

NATIVE AMERICAN TRIBES OF ILLINOIS

The largest portion of what is now the state of Illinois was once populated by the **Illini**, their original name; this tribe was referred to in English as the Illinois Tribe. In fact, the name Illinois itself is derived from the Algonquian Indian language. In the Miami-Illinois tribal language, **Illiniwek** was a word thought to mean "the people/the men." More Miami Indians lived in Indiana and in Oklahoma than in Illinois. However, the Miami and Illinois tribes each spoke a dialect of the Algonquian language. Much smaller parts of what is now the state of Illinois were once populated by the Chickasaw Tribe; the Dakota Sioux Tribe; the Ho-Chunk Tribe, also referred to as the Winnebago tribe; the Miami Tribe; and the Shawnee Tribe. All of these Native American tribes

Copyright © Mometrix Media. You have been licensed one copy of this document for personal use only. Any other reproduction or redistribution is strictly prohibited. All rights reserved.

were living in the territory which became Illinois before the Europeans came to America to settle and colonize its land.

AFTER ARRIVAL OF EUROPEANS

The Illinois, Chickasaw, Dakota Sioux, Winnebago (Ho-Chunk), Miami, and Shawnee tribes were all living in the territory that is now the state of Illinois before Europeans came to America to settle. After European settlers had arrived in the Illinois area, additional Native American tribes migrated from other areas of the American continent. These tribes included the Delaware Tribe, the Kickapoo Tribe, the Ottawa Tribe, the Potawatomi Tribe, the Sac Tribe, the Fox Tribe, and the Wyandot Tribe. Today, there are no Native American tribes living in the state of Illinois officially **recognized** by the United States Federal Government. These tribes have not become extinct; rather, the United States government forced them to move to reservations, mostly in Oklahoma, though some also settled elsewhere; for example, while other groups of the Delaware tribe moved to Oklahoma, the Citizen Delaware Indians stayed in Kansas and are also known as the Kansas Delaware.

PEORIA INDIAN TRIBE

Historically, the Illinois, or Illini, Indians, founded the great **"mound" civilizations** in the central region of the American continent 2,000 to 3,000 years in the past. A number of separate tribes first lived in the areas of the continent that border on the Great Lakes, and which drain into the Mississippi River. These tribes included the Peoria Tribe, the Kaskaskia Tribe, the Piankeshaw Tribe, and the Wea Tribe. In 1854, these tribes merged to form a single tribe. They were then called the **Confederated Peorias**. Peoria Indian tribes lived in Illinois, Michigan, Ohio, and Missouri. When the United States government relocated them, they were first consolidated in Missouri; then they were moved to Kansas; and ultimately, they were resettled in the northeastern region of Oklahoma. Miami, in Ottawa County of Oklahoma, is now the Peorias' tribal headquarters. The United States Federal government now recognizes the Peoria tribe in Oklahoma (1997).

THEORIES OF LINGUISTIC ORIGIN OF THE NAME ILLINOIS

In the 17th century, the Jesuit missionary **Father Jacques Marquette** explored the northern Mississippi Valley with Louis Jolliet and founded **Sault Ste. Marie**, the first European settlement in Michigan. He claimed that the word Illinois was a tribal word meaning "the men." However, later research by linguists suggests that this word may have been derived instead from the Illinois Indian word **irenweewa**, which in translation means "he speaks in the ordinary way." Scholars believe that the Ojibwa Indians living in the eastern region of the Great Lakes area took this Illinois Indian word and used it as a name for these people; in the Ojibwa tribal language, irenweewa was changed to ilinwe, which French explorers then used, spelling it as "Illinois." The word **Illiniwek**, sometimes translated as "the people," is thought to have developed from the Ojibwa word ilinwek, or the plural of ilinwe.

STRUCTURE OF ILLINOIS INDIAN TRIBES' SOCIETY

Before European exploration of the Americas began, the society of the Illinois Indian tribes was **egalitarian**. The tribes had chiefs; however, the chiefs were not regarded as rulers. They did influence the members of their tribes, and they were chosen based on their capacity to preserve the well-being of the Illinois society. However, they did not exert significant authority or power over the people. The Illinois used consensual agreement for tribal decisions. Power and resources were distributed relatively equally among members of the tribe. In the late 1600s, French authorities who had been colonizing the land and governing the Illinois Indians exerted the influence of European traditions, requiring chiefs to be responsible for tribal members' activities. They

Copyright © Mometrix Media. You have been licensed one copy of this document for personal use only. Any other reproduction or redistribution is strictly prohibited. All rights reserved.

reinforced this by awarding chiefs with medals. By the 1760s, the role of chief had become an office holding the primary political power and requiring the approval of the colonial officials.

HISTORY OF ILLINOIS INDIAN TRIBES IN CONTEXT OF EUROPEAN COLONIZATION

In the 1650s, **Iroquois** attacked the Illinois, forcing them west of the Mississippi River until the 1670s. In 1671, **France** claimed the Illinois country. Around 1680, the Iroquois again attacked the Illinois at Starved Rock, driving them out of the Illinois Valley for a time. By 1712, they had returned: their population was around 6,730, and they were living in villages at Starved Rock, Kaskaskia, Cahokia, and Pimetoui. The Illinois country was incorporated into the French colony of **Louisiana** in 1717. In 1756, when the French and Indian War began, the Illinois allied with the **French** against the English and other Indian tribes. To escape British rule, many moved west of the Mississippi. Illinois gained statehood in 1818 and Peoria tribes ceded their Illinois land to the USA. Indians had been moved to reservations by 1832. The Peoria Tribe (a part of the Illinois) was incorporated in Oklahoma in 1940.

ILLINOIS INDIAN TRIBES' DETERIORATION

In 1673, the Illinois tribes were powerful, over 10,000 strong, occupying much land. Then by 1832, 159 years later, only one village of 300 people was left in Illinois. European **colonization**, attacks by other **tribes**, and **disease** decimated their population. Their conversion to European customs caused their loss of native traditions. The Illinois' historical enemies were Pawnee, Osage, and Arikara to their west; Sioux to their northwest; and Quapaw to their south. The Iroquois, who had gotten guns from Europeans, raided them from the 1650s to 1700s. Then hostilities broke out with northern tribes Kickapoo, Sauk, Fox, Potawatomi, and Dakota Sioux, as well as southern tribes Quapaw, Shawnee, and Chickasaw. French, British, and American armies using Indian allies caused some of these wars. Europeans also exposed the Indians to foreign diseases, especially smallpox, for which they had no immunity. Epidemics in 1704, 1732, and 1756 caused massive depopulation of Illinois tribes.

ECONOMY OF ILLINOIS INDIAN TRIBES BEFORE AND AFTER EUROPEAN SETTLEMENT

As noted by the explorer and Jesuit missionary Father Jacques Marquette from his visit in 1669, the Illinois Indians grew corn, squash, beans, and watermelon. Hunting available in the area included bear, wild cattle, deer, turkey, ducks, cranes, pigeons, and buzzards. Before European settlement, the Illinois Indians were mostly **self-sufficient** in their economy. In addition to growing their own produce and hunting, they traded with Indian tribes of the Great Lakes commodities such as animal furs, hides, and human slaves acquired from tribes west and south of them. When French settlers began to colonize the region, the Illinois also traded these goods with them in return for firearms and other European commodities. Over time, more and more French missionaries and traders settled on the Illinois land and lived among the Illinois Indians. The Illinois Indians gradually became more economically **dependent** on French commerce, and thus they became less self-sufficient.

ILLINOIS INDIAN SETTLEMENTS IN 17TH CENTURY

Historians and anthropologists refer to the Illinois tribes as **semi-sedentary**; they were not nomadic, but did not always stay in one place. Their settlements were **seasonal**, based on available food sources. They established summer villages near rivers for water, living there in April and May to plant maize (corn), and returning from mid-July to mid-October to harvest it. Some villages held 350 longhouses roofed with mats. On the prairies, the Illinois established summer hunting camps for communal bison hunts, staying there in shorter-term, bark-roofed lodges during June and July. The Illinois built winter villages in the river bottoms, where animals could be hunted. They lived in these winter villages from mid-October through March. To facilitate better hunting, they kept

Copyright © Mometrix Media. You have been licensed one copy of this document for personal use only. Any other reproduction or redistribution is strictly prohibited. All rights reserved.

winter villages smaller with fewer people than summer villages, usually having 5-20 wigwams with mat roofs. They sometimes built larger winter villages when under the threat of being attacked.

SETTLEMENT OF ILLINOIS AFTER CIVIL WAR

Illinois had been the frontier of young America, but by the end of the Civil War, westward expansion changed this. Instead of frontier, Illinois became part of America's **heartland**. Settlers had moved into Iowa, Nebraska, and Kansas looking for new land to cultivate. Gold prospectors had used Panama as a route to get to California. As Illinois became central to the United States, Chicago developed into the West's main **staging area**. New York City and Illinois were connected by the Erie Canal, facilitating transportation and commerce. Chicago's position, where the Mississippi Valley and the Great Lakes met, made it the perfect location as a railway hub, and railroad construction expanded swiftly after the war. Even as Chicago flourished and became wealthy, towns such as Alton, Cairo, and Quincy, Illinois suffered economically when commercial traffic on the Mississippi River declined, while the Illinois Central Railroad serviced ports on the Gulf of Mexico.

ILLINOIS URBANIZATION IN "GILDED AGE" FOLLOWING CIVIL WAR

As crop prices fell following the Civil War, European demand for American crops fell, and American currency was deflated, **farmers** suffered economically. Young people looking for work moved from rural areas to **urban** ones, especially Chicago, where industry created more jobs. Westward expansion beyond the Mississippi River also prompted this movement. Employment opportunities afforded by Chicago's growing wealth attracted many immigrants from other countries. Even Chicago's Great Fire in 1871 was not such a great setback: New York provided funds to rebuild the city and more construction jobs were created, attracting more **immigrants**. Most immigrated from Southern and Eastern Europe and Ireland. Many had family or friends who had arrived earlier and they followed them to the same cities, facilitating the establishment of new communities. However, immigrants also were met with segregation in housing, jobs, and unions. Many found solutions by establishing themselves in economic sectors neglected by native White Americans.

ETHNIC COMPOSITION OF CHICAGO IN 1870S AND 1880S AND DISAGREEMENTS OVER ALCOHOL

Due to a massive influx of **immigration** in the 1870s-1880s, the majority of Chicago's population became new arrivals who outnumbered the native-born elite society who had settled before the Civil War. During this time period, **Frances Willard**, founder of the Women's Christian Temperance Union, and other reformers from the northern United States advocated for the regulation or even the prohibition of **liquor**. They blamed the abuse of alcohol for poverty, starvation, the disruption of families, and men committing violent acts against women. However, many of the new immigrants from Germany came from social traditions in their country wherein drinking beer and wine were commonplace and important, causing major disagreements with reformers who were against alcohol. German-American members of the Republican Party were angered by the party's inclinations to align with these anti-alcohol reformers, and as a result, many German-American Republicans in Chicago converted to the Democratic Party during this time.

CONTRIBUTIONS OF IMMIGRANTS IN ILLINOIS TO RADICAL MOVEMENTS IN CHICAGO

Before the Civil War, many Irish people had immigrated to Illinois for decades to work on the construction of the **Illinois and Michigan Canal**. After the war, they established community organizations, often associated with the Catholic Church; these groups gained significant power. Many also supported the cause of Ireland's independence from England. Irish-Americans contributed substantially to the establishment of labor unions. One of the biggest of these unions was the **Knights of Labor**. The Irish brought their strategy of the boycott from Ireland to America.

Copyright © Mometrix Media. You have been licensed one copy of this document for personal use only. Any other reproduction or redistribution is strictly prohibited. All rights reserved.

Powerful labor unions such as the Knights of Labor employed boycotting against management's financial, legal, and political power. Eastern European and German immigrants brought radical ideas and politics, forming the Socialist and Anarchist movements, highlighted by the **Great Strike of 1877** and the **Haymarket Riot of 1886**. As a result, many middle-class White native-born Americans associated immigrants with labor violence and radical ideas and actions.

ASSIMILATION OF IMMIGRANTS INTO CHICAGO POLITICAL AND SOCIAL LIFE IN 1880's

By the 1880s, Chicago's population contained more immigrants than native-born Americans due to large waves of **immigration**. Job seekers came mostly from Eastern Europe, Germany, and Ireland for employment opportunities created in Chicago by rebuilding efforts following the 1871 Great Fire and by Chicago's rapidly growing wealth as the new hub of the railroad systems and as an industrial center. In 1892, the first non-American-born Chicago governor, **John Peter Altgeld**, was elected. By this time, many other immigrants had achieved positions of political leadership in Chicago. However, immigrants also encountered discrimination and fewer opportunities, relying on their ethnic communities socially and in business. **Jane Addams** wanted to learn about other cultures. While many reformers wanted to teach immigrants "Yankee virtues" of self-control and thriftiness, Addams formed **Hull House**, the first settlement house in America, partly for assisting immigrants in self-help and organizing themselves, as well as uplifting the poor.

RELIGION IN CHICAGO AND ILLINOIS DURING GILDED AGE

The Northern United States had been largely **Protestant** since its beginnings. In the 1850s, many **Catholics** immigrated to America from Eastern and Southern Europe and Ireland. Native American-born Protestants often disagreed religiously and culturally with these Catholic immigrants. American Protestants developed such an aversion to both Catholicism and immigration that some of them reacted by founding the **Know-Nothings**, also called the American Party. In 1870 **Dwight L. Moody**, a Chicago minister, recruited **Ira Sankey**, a gospel singer, and they toured America and Europe promoting Moody's new fundamentalist, ecumenical Christianity, which opposed Calvinist doctrine such as original sin and preached about the love of God. Though he had critics, Moody became the most popular evangelist of the Gilded Age. In 1880, in lower Illinois, **Augustine Tolton** was ordained as America's first Black priest. His first all-Black parish in Quincy met such opposition from local Whites that he relocated to a parish in Chicago.

ROLE OF CHICAGO IN AMERICAN REALIST LITERARY MOVEMENT IN 1890s AND 1900s

Chicago played a major part in the development of the **American Realist** school of literature during the 1890s. **Hamlin Garland** was a newspaper reporter in Chicago who had grown up on a farm in rural Wisconsin. In addition to his journalism, Garland wrote novels that depicted the grim realities of life on a farm, which disabused many American readers of their idealized notions about farm life. **Theodore Dreiser** also worked in Chicago as a journalist and wrote short stories and novels. He compiled research notes on the city, informing his famous work *Sister Carrie* about the ascent and decline of a young woman in Chicago. Pulitzer Prize-winning author **Upton Sinclair** worked undercover for seven weeks in Chicago's meat-packing plants as research for his best-selling, muckraking novel *The Jungle*. Its 1906 exposure of conditions prompted the passage of the Pure Food and Drug Act and the Meat Inspection Act that year.

WORLD'S COLUMBIAN EXPOSITION OF 1893 IN CHICAGO

The World's Columbian Exposition was held in Chicago in 1893 to commemorate the 400th anniversary of Columbus' New World landing and celebrate American culture, business, and society. More than 27 million people came to Chicago to attend this fair. The fairgrounds included fourteen main buildings and spanned 633 acres. The consistently neo-classical style and similar construction materials of all of the buildings caused people to nickname them the **White City**. The

Copyright © Mometrix Media. You have been licensed one copy of this document for personal use only. Any other reproduction or redistribution is strictly prohibited. All rights reserved.

fair had a centrally located classical statue, a large reflecting pool, and a fountain. The many exhibits included agriculture, machinery, manufacturing, transportation, electricity, and the liberal arts; a Palace of Fine Arts building with over 8,000 works of art; and a women's building devoted to women's accomplishments. Other, smaller buildings also displayed goods from the American states, the American territories, and from more than twenty other nations as well.

PRESAGE OF LEISURE AND RECREATIONAL ACTIVITIES OF 20TH CENTURY AMERICAN LIFESTYLES

In 1893, Chicago was host to the World's Columbian Exposition, a giant fair to celebrate Columbus' landing in America 400 years before, and the cultural, social, industrial, and business accomplishments of America. This fair featured many exhibits of an educational and informational nature. In addition, it featured many sources of entertainment. On the midway of the fair, the first Ferris Wheel in the world was constructed. In addition, the exposition included a fun house, a swimming pool, and even a zoo. Official exhibitions from other countries were contributed to the exposition. Business entrepreneurs set up exhibits depicting life in less affluent villages of other nations. Just outside of the fair grounds, Buffalo Bill's Wild West Show had been established, and many attendees went to see it when they visited the fair. The exposition thus pioneered the mass amusements and cultural accomplishments and activities characteristic of **20th century American leisure and recreation**.

TURNER'S "THE SIGNIFICANCE OF THE FRONTIER IN AMERICAN HISTORY"

The World's Columbian Exposition was a huge 1893 fair in Chicago to celebrate cultural and social achievements as well as Columbus' American landing 400 years earlier. One way that it was related to historian **Frederick Jackson Turner's** paper, "The Significance of the Frontier in American History," was that Turner presented this piece in connection with the Exposition. Another way it was related was that Turner's argument both contradicted the social achievements highlighted in the Exposition by casting doubt on their future, and struck a chord among listeners. Turner argued that according to the 1890 census, there was no more frontier to conquer on the American continent. He found that the American frontier experience had forged the national character and democracy, asking what would happen in a future without this experience. He voiced a concern of many Americans about their modern society's future. Thus, while controversial, Turner's thesis was also influential.

LOUIS SULLIVAN

Louis Sullivan was an architect who was known for creating innovative building designs. **Sullivan** emerged in the later 1800s as the leader of the new **Chicago School of Architects**. When the "White City" buildings of the 1893 World's Columbian Exposition fair were constructed in Chicago, all using similar building materials and conforming to a neo-classical style, Sullivan protested that these buildings would set back architectural progress by fifty years. Rebuilding much of Chicago after the Great Fire of 1871 presented increased opportunities for architects. New designers invented a construction method enabling skyscrapers to be erected. Two landmarks in Chicago designed by Sullivan near the end of his career were the **Auditorium Theater** in 1889 and the **Chicago Stock Exchange Building** in 1893. He influenced generations of younger architects, including Frank Lloyd Wright, who after working for Sullivan started his own practice in Chicago and pioneered the Prairie School of Architecture.

JOHN DEWEY

John Dewey was a philosopher from Vermont who taught at the University of Michigan in the 1890s. At the end of the World's Columbian Exposition, which was held in Chicago in 1893, the Midway Plaisance which had hosted the fair remained, and the University of Chicago built a new campus on those grounds. **John D. Rockefeller**, founder of the Standard Oil Company and

Copyright © Mometrix Media. You have been licensed one copy of this document for personal use only. Any other reproduction or redistribution is strictly prohibited. All rights reserved.

millionaire, donated funds to recruit faculty members from the Northeast to teach at the new campus, including **John Dewey**. Dewey was a major proponent of the new **Pragmatist philosophy**. In Chicago he was inspired by Jane Addams' Hull House to develop a new instrumentalist philosophy for living. He believed our experiences are problem-solving instruments. He endorsed the **scientific method** and felt students should learn by experimenting and interacting with their environments. Dewey founded the University of Chicago's Laboratory School, which became a national center for educational reform.

EMPLOYMENT CONDITIONS IN ILLINOIS FOLLOWING PASSAGE OF CIVIL RIGHTS LAWS

The **Fourteenth Amendment** and the Reconstruction's **Civil Rights acts** allowed Black people to vote and serve as jurors. Illinois was required to change its state laws to conform to the federal legislation. During this time, Chicago schools became **integrated**, and state-funded colleges also admitted Black students. However, in the northern United States, less than 2 percent of the population was African-American. Because many northern Whites resisted integration or were unsure about it, social progress for Blacks in the North, including Illinois, was slow. Many White Illinois employees wanted to limit Black workers to unskilled labor to prevent competition. The Knights of Labor admitted Black members, but it was the exception among labor unions. In central and southern Illinois, many Blacks were recruited from the South to work in **coal mines**, often because White miners were on strike. The United Mine Workers organized integrated local unions, gaining over 20,000 Black members by 1900.

ACTIVISTS FOR RACIAL EQUALITY IN CHICAGO

In Illinois as in the rest of the North, many African-American people worked as unskilled laborers or servants during this time. They received lower pay than White workers for the same work. Housing in the North at this time was also strictly **segregated**, so Blacks were forced to live only in certain neighborhoods. As Chicago became a big city, it became a mecca for African-American political and intellectual activity. **Lucy Parsons**, a prominent African-American speaker, organized the **Chicago Working Women's Union** and began publishing her own newspaper, "Freedom," in 1891. Her husband, **Albert Parsons**, was White. Together the Parsons came to be among the most famous organizers and radical social critics in Chicago. **Ferdinand Barnett**, a graduate of City of Chicago Law School, became the first African-American Assistant State's Attorney in Illinois. Barnett was also founder and editor of the **Chicago Conservator**, a newspaper devoted to Black civil rights.

IDA B. WELLS

Ida B. Wells was the daughter of slaves in Mississippi. She managed to obtain an education and started teaching school while still in her teens. She challenged segregation of facilities while teaching in Memphis by suing a railroad company. She became a journalist focusing on **social injustices against African-Americans**, writing exposés of lynch mobs after three of her friends were lynched. These pieces garnered national fame. She confronted Frances Willard's Women's Christian Temperance Union for supporting Southern reformers' acceptance of lynching. Wells published a piece entitled Why the Colored American Is Not in the World's Columbian Exposition in 1894 to call attention to the exclusion by White fair organizers of Black people and exhibits. She became a touring lecturer to further her political activism and to escape threats against her in Memphis. She then married **Ferdinand Barnett**, Illinois' first Black Assistant State's Attorney and Chicago Conservator founder/editor, moving to Chicago.

WOMEN'S SUFFRAGE MOVEMENT

Women's suffrage got national attention from an 1848 Seneca Falls, New York convention, but thereafter it was eclipsed by the issue of abolition of slavery before, during, and after the Civil War.

Copyright © Mometrix Media. You have been licensed one copy of this document for personal use only. Any other reproduction or redistribution is strictly prohibited. All rights reserved.

When the **Fifteenth Amendment** gave Black men the vote, overlooking women, the movement became divided by disagreement whether women's suffrage should/should not be attached to this amendment. Reformers founded the **Illinois Woman Suffrage Association** in 1869, but women did not get the vote under the 1870 Illinois State Constitution. Reformers **Alta Hulett**, **Judge James**, and **Myra Colby Bradwell** got laws passed from 1860-1890 giving women rights to equal post-divorce child guardianship, to control their own earnings, control and maintain their own property, pursue any profession or occupation, and benefit from the estates of deceased husbands. Bradwell helped pass an 1873 law allowing qualified women to hold school offices; in 1874, ten women were elected to be county school superintendents.

WOMEN'S CHRISTIAN TEMPERANCE UNION

Frances Willard, of Chicago suburb Evanston, Illinois, founded the **Women's Christian Temperance Union** in 1874. This organization based its concept of "home protection," or defense of the family unit, upon the natural role of women as mothers. Willard and the WCTU united the women's rights movement with the philosophy that only women's morality could reform corrupt male political practices. Many pursued women's right to vote for this purpose. The WCTU's motto was "Agitate – Educate – Legislate." In 1877, Frances Willard was the first woman in history to speak before an official session of the Illinois General Assembly. In addition to working for women's suffrage and for temperance, the WCTU also advocated for social reform. For example, in 1889, the Chicago chapter of the organization ran a mission shelter accommodating 4,000 homeless women annually, a men's lodging house, an industrial school, two Sunday schools, a free medical dispensary, and a low-priced restaurant.

Copyright © Mometrix Media. You have been licensed one copy of this document for personal use only. Any other reproduction or redistribution is strictly prohibited. All rights reserved.

American History 1899 to Present

PROVISIONS OF THE SIXTEENTH, SEVENTEENTH, EIGHTEENTH, AND NINETEENTH AMENDMENTS

The early 20th century saw several amendments made to the US Constitution:

- The **Sixteenth Amendment** (1913) established a federal income tax.
- The **Seventeenth Amendment** (1913) allowed popular election of senators.
- The **Eighteenth Amendment** (1919) prohibited the sale, production, and transportation of alcohol. This amendment was later repealed by the Twenty-first Amendment.
- The **Nineteenth Amendment** (1920) gave women the right to vote.

These amendments largely grew out of the Progressive Era, as many citizens worked to improve American society.

ROLE OF THE FEDERAL TRADE COMMISSION IN ELIMINATING TRUSTS

Muckrakers such as Ida Tarbell and Lincoln Steffens brought to light the damaging trend of trusts—huge corporations working to monopolize areas of commerce so they could control prices and distribution. The **Sherman Antitrust Act** and the **Clayton Antitrust Act** set out guidelines for competition among corporations and set out to eliminate these trusts. The **Federal Trade Commission** was formed in 1914 in order to enforce antitrust measures and ensure that companies were operated fairly and did not create controlling monopolies.

IMPORTANCE OF THE PANAMA CANAL

Initial work began on the **Panama Canal** in 1881, though the idea had been discussed since the 1500s. The canal greatly reduces the length and time needed to sail from one ocean to the other by connecting the Atlantic to the Pacific through the Isthmus of Panama, which joins South America to North America. Before the canal was built, travelers had to sail around the entire perimeter of South America to reach the West Coast of the US. The French began the work after successfully completing the **Suez Canal**, which connected the Mediterranean Sea to the Red Sea. However, due to disease and high expense, the work moved slowly, and after eight years, the company went bankrupt, suspending work. The US purchased the holdings, and the first ship sailed through the canal in 1914. The Panama Canal was constructed as a lock-and-lake canal, with ships lifted on locks to travel from one lake to another over the rugged, mountainous terrain. In order to maintain control of the Canal Zone, the US assisted Panama in its battle for independence from **Columbia**.

INFLUENCE OF BIG STICK DIPLOMACY ON AMERICAN FOREIGN POLICY IN LATIN AMERICA

Theodore Roosevelt's famous quote, "Speak softly and carry a big stick," is supposedly of African origins, at least according to Roosevelt. He used this proverb to justify expanded involvement in foreign affairs during his tenure as President. The US military was deployed to protect American interests in **Latin America**. Roosevelt also worked to maintain an equal or greater influence in Latin America than those held by European interests. As a result, the US Navy grew larger, and the US generally became more involved in foreign affairs. Roosevelt felt that if any country was left vulnerable to control by Europe due to economic issues or political instability, the US had not only a right to intervene but was **obligated** to do so. This led to US involvement in Cuba, Nicaragua, Haiti, and the Dominican Republic over several decades leading into the First and Second World Wars.

TAFT'S DOLLAR DIPLOMACY VS. ROOSEVELT'S DIPLOMATIC THEORIES

During William Howard Taft's presidency, Taft instituted "**Dollar Diplomacy**." This approach was America's effort to influence Latin America and East Asia through economic rather than military

Copyright © Mometrix Media. You have been licensed one copy of this document for personal use only. Any other reproduction or redistribution is strictly prohibited. All rights reserved.

means. Taft saw past efforts in these areas to be political and warlike, while his efforts focused on peaceful economic goals. His justification of the policy was to protect the **Panama Canal**, which was vital to US trade interests.

In spite of Taft's assurance that Dollar Diplomacy was a peaceful approach, many interventions proved violent. During Latin American revolts, such as those in **Nicaragua**, the US sent troops to settle the revolutions. Afterward, bankers moved in to help support the new leaders through loans. Dollar Diplomacy continued until 1913, when Woodrow Wilson was elected president.

WILSON'S APPROACH TO INTERNATIONAL DIPLOMACY

Turning away from Taft's "Dollar Diplomacy," Wilson instituted a foreign policy he referred to as **"moral diplomacy."** This approach still influences American foreign policy today.

Wilson felt that **representative government and democracy** in all countries would lead to worldwide stability. Democratic governments, he felt, would be less likely to threaten American interests. He also saw the US and Great Britain as the great role models in this area, as well as champions of world peace and self-government. Free trade and international commerce would allow the US to speak out regarding world events.

Main elements of Wilson's policies included:

- Maintaining a strong military
- Promoting democracy throughout the world
- Expanding international trade to boost the American economy

MAJOR EVENTS OF WORLD WAR I

World War I occurred from 1914 to 1918 and was fought largely in Europe. Triggered by the assassination of Austrian Archduke Franz Ferdinand, the war rapidly escalated. At the beginning of the conflict, Woodrow Wilson declared the US neutral. Major events influencing US involvement included:

- **Sinking of the *Lusitania***—the British passenger liner RMS *Lusitania* was sunk by a German U-boat in 1915. Among the 1,000 civilian victims were over 100 American citizens. Outraged by this act, many Americans began to push for US involvement in the war, using the *Lusitania* as a rallying cry.
- **German U-boat aggression**—Wilson continued to keep the US out of the war, using as his 1916 reelection slogan, "He kept us out of war." While he continued to work toward an end of the war, German U-boats began to indiscriminately attack American and Canadian merchant ships carrying supplies to Germany's enemies in Europe.
- **Zimmerman Telegram** —the final event that brought the US into World War I was the interception of the Zimmerman Telegram (also known as the Zimmerman Note). In this telegram, Germany proposed forming an alliance with Mexico if the US entered the war.

EFFORTS IN THE US DURING WORLD WAR I SUPPORTING THE WAR EFFORT

American **railroads** came under government control in December 1917. The widespread system was consolidated into a single system, with each region assigned a director. This greatly increased the efficiency of the railroad system, allowing the railroads to supply both domestic and military needs. Control returned to private ownership in 1920. In 1918, **telegraph, telephone, and cable services** also came under Federal control, to be returned to private management the next year. The **American Red Cross** supported the war effort by knitting clothes for Army and Navy troops. They also helped supply hospital and refugee clothing and surgical dressings. Over 8 million people

Copyright © Mometrix Media. You have been licensed one copy of this document for personal use only. Any other reproduction or redistribution is strictly prohibited. All rights reserved.

participated in this effort. To generate wartime funds, the US government sold **Liberty Bonds**. In four issues, they sold nearly $25 billion—more than one-fifth of Americans purchased them. After the war, a fifth bond drive was held but sold "**Victory Liberty Bonds**."

Review Video: WWI Overview
Visit mometrix.com/academy and enter code: 659767

INFLUENCE OF WILSON'S FOURTEEN POINTS ON THE FINAL PEACE TREATIES THAT ENDED WORLD WAR I

President Woodrow Wilson proposed **Fourteen Points** as the basis for a peace settlement to end the war. Presented to the US Congress in January 1918, the Fourteen Points included:

- Five points outlining **general ideals**
- Eight points to resolve **immediate problems** of political and territorial nature
- One point proposing an **organization of nations** (the League of Nations) with the intent of maintaining world peace

In November of that same year, Germany agreed to an **armistice**, assuming the final treaty would be based on the Fourteen Points. However, during the peace conference in Paris 1919, there was much disagreement, leading to a final agreement that punished Germany and the other Central Powers much more than originally intended. Henry Cabot Lodge, who had become the Foreign Relations Committee chairman in 1918, wanted an unconditional surrender from Germany and was concerned about the article in the **Treaty of Versailles** that gave the League of Nations power to declare war without a vote from the US Congress. A **League of Nations** was included in the Treaty of Versailles at Wilson's insistence. The Senate rejected the Treaty of Versailles, and in the end, Wilson refused to concede to Lodge's demands. As a result, the US did not join the League of Nations.

MAJOR CHANGES AND EVENTS THAT TOOK PLACE IN AMERICA DURING THE 1920S

The post-war 1920s saw many Americans moving from the farm to the city, with growing prosperity in the US. The **Roaring Twenties**, or the **Jazz Age**, was driven largely by growth in the automobile and entertainment industries. Individuals like Charles Lindbergh, the first aviator to make a solo flight across the Atlantic Ocean, added to the American admiration of individual accomplishment. Telephone lines, distribution of electricity, highways, the radio, and other inventions brought great changes to everyday life.

Review Video: 1920's
Visit mometrix.com/academy and enter code: 124996

MAJOR CULTURAL MOVEMENTS OF THE 1920S INFLUENCED BY AFRICAN AMERICANS

The **Harlem Renaissance** saw a number of African-American artists settling in Harlem in New York. This community produced a number of well-known artists and writers, including Langston Hughes, Nella Larsen, Zora Neale Hurston, Claude McKay, Countee Cullen, and Jean Toomer. The growth of jazz, also largely driven by African Americans, defined the **Jazz Age**. Its unconventional, improvisational style matched the growing sense of optimism and exploration of the decade. Originating as an offshoot of the blues, jazz began in New Orleans. Some significant jazz musicians were Duke Ellington, Louis Armstrong, and Jelly Roll Morton. **Big Band** and **Swing Jazz** also developed in the 1920s. Well-known musicians of this movement included Bing Crosby, Frank Sinatra, Count Basie, Benny Goodman, Billie Holiday, Ella Fitzgerald, and The Dorsey Brothers.

Copyright © Mometrix Media. You have been licensed one copy of this document for personal use only. Any other reproduction or redistribution is strictly prohibited. All rights reserved.

PROVISIONS AND IMPORTANCE OF THE NATIONAL ORIGINS ACT OF 1924

The National Origins Act (Johnson-Reed Act) placed limitations on **immigration**. The number of immigrants allowed into the US was based on the population of each nationality of immigrants who were living in the country in 1890. Only two percent of each nationality's 1890 population numbers were allowed to immigrate. This led to great disparities between immigrants from various nations, and Asian immigration was not allowed at all. Some of the impetus behind the Johnson-Reed Act came as a result of paranoia following the **Russian Revolution**. Fear of communist influences in the US led to a general fear of immigrants.

ORIGINS OF THE RED SCARE

World War I created many jobs, but after the war ended, these jobs disappeared, leaving many unemployed. In the wake of these employment changes, the **International Workers of the World** and the **Socialist Party**, headed by Eugene Debs, became more and more visible. Workers initiated strikes in an attempt to regain the favorable working conditions that had been put into place before the war. Unfortunately, many of these strikes became violent, and the actions were blamed on "Reds," or Communists, for trying to spread their views into America. With the recent Bolshevik Revolution in Russia, many Americans feared a similar revolution might occur in the US. The **Red Scare** ensued, with many individuals jailed for supposedly holding communist, anarchist, or socialist beliefs.

GROWTH OF CIVIL RIGHTS FOR AFRICAN AMERICANS

Marcus Garvey founded the **Universal Negro Improvement Association and African Communities League (UNIA-ACL)**, which became a large and active organization focused on building black nationalism. In 1909, the **National Association for the Advancement of Colored People (NAACP)** came into being, working to defeat Jim Crow laws. The NAACP also helped prevent racial segregation from becoming federal law, fought against lynchings, helped black soldiers in WWI become officers, and helped defend the Scottsboro Boys, who were unjustly accused of rape.

KU KLUX KLAN

In 1866, Confederate Army veterans came together to fight against Reconstruction in the South, forming a group called the **Ku Klux Klan (KKK)**. With white supremacist beliefs, including anti-Semitism, nativism, anti-Catholicism, and overt racism, this organization relied heavily on violence to get its message across. In 1915, they grew again in power, using a film called *The Birth of a Nation*, by D.W. Griffith, to spread their ideas. In the 1920s, the reach of the KKK spread far into the north and midwest, and members controlled a number of state governments. Its membership and power began to decline during the Great Depression but experienced a resurgence later.

AMERICAN CIVIL LIBERTIES UNION

In 1866, Confederate Army veterans came together to fight against Reconstruction in the South, forming a group called the Ku Klux Klan (KKK). With white supremacist beliefs, including anti-Semitism, nativism, anti-Catholicism, and overt racism, this organization relied heavily on violence to get its message across. In 1915, they grew again in power, using a film called The Birth of a Nation, by D.W. Griffith, to spread their ideas. In the 1920s, the reach of the KKK spread far into the north and midwest, and members controlled a number of state governments. Its membership and power began to decline during the Great Depression but experienced a resurgence later.

Copyright © Mometrix Media. You have been licensed one copy of this document for personal use only. Any other reproduction or redistribution is strictly prohibited. All rights reserved.

GOALS OF THE ANTI-DEFAMATION LEAGUE

In 1913, the Anti-Defamation League was formed to prevent anti-Semitic behavior and practices. Its actions also worked to prevent all forms of racism and to prevent individuals from being discriminated against for any reason involving their race. They spoke against the Ku Klux Klan, as well as other racist or anti-Semitic organizations. This organization still works to fight discrimination against all minorities.

ROOSEVELT'S NEW DEAL

The **Great Depression**, which began in 1929 with the stock market crash, grew out of several factors that had developed over the previous years, including:

- Growing economic disparity between the rich and middle classes, with the rich amassing wealth much more quickly than the lower classes
- Disparity in economic distribution in industries
- Growing use of credit, leading to an inflated demand for some goods
- Government support of new industries rather than agriculture
- Risky stock market investments, leading to the stock market crash

Additional factors contributing to the Depression also included the **Labor Day Hurricane** in the Florida Keys (1935) and the **Great Hurricane of 1938** in New England, along with the **Dust Bowl** in the Great Plains, which destroyed crops and resulted in the displacement of as many as 2.5 million people.

> **Review Video: What Caused the Great Depression?**
> Visit mometrix.com/academy and enter code: 635912

Franklin D. Roosevelt was elected president in 1932 with his promise of a "**New Deal**" for Americans. His goals were to provide government work programs to provide jobs, wages, and relief to numerous workers throughout the beleaguered US. Congress gave Roosevelt almost free rein to produce relief legislation. The goals of this legislation were:

- **Relief**—creating jobs for the high numbers of unemployed
- **Recovery**—stimulating the economy through the National Recovery Administration
- **Reform**—passing legislation to prevent future, similar economic crashes

The Roosevelt Administration also passed legislation regarding ecological issues, including the Soil Conservation Service, aimed at preventing another Dust Bowl.

ROOSEVELT'S ALPHABET ORGANIZATIONS

So-called "alphabet organizations" set up during Roosevelt's administration included:

- **Civilian Conservation Corps** (CCC)—provided jobs in the forestry service
- **Agricultural Adjustment Administration** (AAA)—increased agricultural income by adjusting both production and prices
- **Tennessee Valley Authority** (TVA)—organized projects to build dams in the Tennessee River for flood control and production of electricity, resulting in increased productivity for industries in the area, and easier navigation of the Tennessee River

Copyright © Mometrix Media. You have been licensed one copy of this document for personal use only. Any other reproduction or redistribution is strictly prohibited. All rights reserved.

- **Public Works Administration** (PWA) and Civil Works Administration (CWA)—provided a multitude of jobs, initiating over 34,000 projects
- **Works Progress Administration** (WPA)—helped unemployed persons to secure employment on government work projects or elsewhere

ACTIONS TAKEN DURING THE ROOSEVELT ADMINISTRATION TO PREVENT FUTURE CRASHES

The Roosevelt administration passed several laws and established several institutions to initiate the "reform" portion of the New Deal, including:

- **Glass-Steagall Act**—separated investment from commercial banking
- **Securities Exchange Commission (SEC)**—helped regulate Wall Street investment practices, making them less dangerous to the overall economy
- **Wagner Act**—provided worker and union rights to improve relations between employees and employers
- **Social Security Act of 1935**—provided pensions as well as unemployment insurance

Other actions focused on insuring bank deposits and adjusting the value of American currency. Most of these regulatory agencies and government policies and programs still exist today.

MAJOR REGULATIONS REGARDING LABOR AFTER THE GREAT DEPRESSION

Three major regulations regarding labor that were passed after the Great Depression are:

- The **Wagner Act** (1935)—also known as the National Labor Relations Act, it established that unions were legal, protected members of unions, and required collective bargaining. This act was later amended by the Taft-Hartley Act of 1947 and the Landrum-Griffin Act of 1959, which further clarified certain elements.
- **Davis-Bacon Act** (1931)—provided fair compensation for contractors and subcontractors.
- **Walsh-Healey Act** (1936)—established a minimum wage, child labor laws, safety standards, and overtime pay.

ACCOMPLISHMENTS OF THE LYNDON B. JOHNSON PRESIDENCY

Kennedy's vice president, **Lyndon Johnson**, assumed the presidency after Kennedy's **assassination**. He supported civil rights bills, tax cuts, and other wide-reaching legislation that Kennedy had also supported. Johnson saw America as a "**Great Society**," and enacted legislation to fight disease and poverty, renew urban areas, and support education and environmental conservation. Medicare and Medicaid were instituted under his administration. He continued Kennedy's support of space exploration, and he is also known, although less positively, for his handling of the **Vietnam War**.

FACTORS THAT LED TO THE GROWTH OF THE CIVIL RIGHTS MOVEMENT

In the 1950s, post-war America was experiencing a rapid growth in prosperity. However, African-Americans found themselves left behind. Following the lead of **Mahatma Gandhi**, who led similar

Copyright © Mometrix Media. You have been licensed one copy of this document for personal use only. Any other reproduction or redistribution is strictly prohibited. All rights reserved.

class struggles in India, African-Americans began to demand equal rights. Major figures in this struggle included:

- **Rosa Parks**—often called the "mother of the Civil Rights Movement," her refusal to give up her seat on the bus to a white man served as a seed from which the movement grew.
- **Martin Luther King, Jr.**—the best-known leader of the movement, King drew on Gandhi's beliefs and encouraged non-violent opposition. He led a march on Washington in 1963, received the Nobel Peace Prize in 1964, and was assassinated in 1968.
- **Malcolm X**—espousing less peaceful means of change, Malcolm X became a Black Muslim and supported black nationalism.

IMPACT OF STOKELY CARMICHAEL, ADAM CLAYTON POWELL, AND JESSE JACKSON ON THE CIVIL RIGHTS MOVEMENT

- **Stokely Carmichael**—Carmichael originated the term "Black Power" and served as head of the Student Nonviolent Coordinating Committee. He believed in black pride and black culture and felt separate political and social institutions should be developed for blacks.
- **Adam Clayton Powell**—chairman of the Coordinating Committee for Employment, he led rent strikes and other actions, as well as a bus boycott, to increase the hiring of blacks.
- **Jesse Jackson**—Jackson was selected to head the Chicago Operation Breadbasket in 1966, and went on to organize boycotts and other actions. He also had an unsuccessful run for president.

EVENTS OF THE CIVIL RIGHTS MOVEMENT

Three major events of the Civil Rights Movement are:

- **Montgomery Bus Boycott**—in 1955, Rosa Parks refused to give her seat on the bus to a white man. As a result, she was tried and convicted of disorderly conduct and of violating local ordinances. A 381-day bus boycott ensued, protesting segregation on public buses.
- **Desegregation of Little Rock**—in 1957, after the Supreme Court decision on Brown v. Board of Education, which declared "separate but equal" unconstitutional, the Arkansas school board voted to desegregate their schools. Even though Arkansas was considered progressive, its governor brought in the Arkansas National Guard to prevent nine black students from entering Central High School in Little Rock. President Eisenhower responded by federalizing the National Guard and ordering them to stand down.
- **Birmingham Campaign**—protestors organized a variety of actions such as sit-ins and an organized march to launch a voting campaign. When the City of Birmingham declared the protests illegal, the protestors, including Martin Luther King, Jr., persisted and were arrested and jailed.

PIECES OF LEGISLATION PASSED AS A RESULT OF THE CIVIL RIGHTS MOVEMENT

Three major pieces of legislation passed as a result of the Civil Rights movement are:

- **Brown v. Board of Education** (1954)—the Supreme Court declared that "separate but equal" accommodations and services were unconstitutional.
- **Civil Rights Act of 1964**—this declared discrimination illegal in employment, education, or public accommodation.
- **Voting Rights Act of 1965**—this act ended various activities practiced, mostly in the South, to bar blacks from exercising their voting rights. These included poll taxes and literacy tests.

Copyright © Mometrix Media. You have been licensed one copy of this document for personal use only. Any other reproduction or redistribution is strictly prohibited. All rights reserved.

US PERSPECTIVE ON THE PROGRESSION OF THE VIETNAM WAR

After World War II, the US pledged, as part of its foreign policy, to come to the assistance of any country threatened by **communism**. When Vietnam was divided into a communist North and democratic South, much like Korea before it, the eventual attempts by the North to unify the country under Communist rule led to intervention by the US. On the home front, the **Vietnam War** became more and more unpopular politically, with Americans growing increasingly discontent with the inability of the US to achieve the goals it had set for the Asian country. When President **Richard Nixon** took office in 1969, his escalation of the war led to protests at Kent State in Ohio, during which several students were killed by National Guard troops. Protests continued, eventually resulting in the end of the compulsory draft in 1973. In that same year, the US departed Vietnam. In 1975, the South surrendered, and Vietnam became a unified country under communist rule.

EFFECTS OF US COLD WAR FOREIGN POLICY ACTS ON THE INTERNATIONAL RELATIONSHIPS

The following are US Cold War foreign policy acts and how they affected international relationships, especially between the US and the Soviet Union:

- **Marshall Plan**—this sent aid to war-torn Europe after WWII, largely focusing on preventing the spread of communism.
- **Containment Policy**—proposed by George F. Kennan, the containment policy focused on containing the spread of Soviet communism.
- **Truman Doctrine**—Harry S. Truman stated that the US would provide both economic and military support to any country threatened by Soviet takeover.
- **National Security Act**—passed in 1947, this act reorganized the government's military departments into the Department of Defense and created the Central Intelligence Agency and the National Security Council.

The combination of these acts led to the **Cold War**, with Soviet communists attempting to spread their influence and the US and other countries trying to contain or stop this spread.

NATO, WARSAW PACT, AND THE BERLIN WALL

NATO, the **North Atlantic Treaty Organization**, came into being in 1949. It essentially amounted to an agreement among the US and Western European countries that an attack on any one of these countries was to be considered an attack against the entire group. Under the influence of the Soviet Union, the Eastern European countries of the USSR, Bulgaria, East Germany, Poland, Romania, Albania, Hungary, and Czechoslovakia responded with the **Warsaw Pact**, which created a similar agreement among those nations. In 1961, a wall was built to separate communist East Berlin from democratic West Berlin. This was a literal representation of the "**Iron Curtain**" that separated the democratic and communist countries throughout the world.

EFFECT OF THE ARMS RACE ON POST WWII INTERNATIONAL RELATIONS

After World War II, major nations, particularly the US and USSR, rushed to develop highly advanced weapons systems such as the **atomic bomb** and later the **hydrogen bomb**. These countries seemed determined to outpace each other with the development of numerous, deadly weapons. These weapons were expensive and extremely dangerous, and it is possible that the war between US and Soviet interests remained "cold" due to the fear that one side or the other would use these powerful weapons.

END OF THE COLD WAR AND THE DISSOLUTION OF THE SOVIET UNION

In the late 1980s, **Mikhail Gorbachev** led the Soviet Union. He introduced a series of reform programs. **Ronald Reagan** famously urged Gorbachev to tear down the **Berlin Wall** as a gesture of

Copyright © Mometrix Media. You have been licensed one copy of this document for personal use only. Any other reproduction or redistribution is strictly prohibited. All rights reserved.

growing freedom in the Eastern Bloc, and in 1989 it was demolished, ending the separation of East and West Germany. The Soviet Union relinquished its power over the various republics in Eastern Europe, and they became independent nations with their own individual governments. In 1991, the **USSR** was dissolved and the Cold War also came to an end.

> **Review Video: How Did the Cold War End?**
> Visit mometrix.com/academy and enter code: 278032

TECHNOLOGICAL ADVANCES THAT OCCURRED THROUGHOUT THE 1900S

Numerous technological advances throughout the 1900s led to more effective treatment of diseases, more efficient communication and transportation, and new means of generating power. Advances in **medicine** increased the human lifespan in developed countries, and near-instantaneous **communication** opened up a myriad of possibilities. Some of these advances include:

- Discovery of penicillin (1928)
- Supersonic air travel (1947)
- Nuclear power plants (1951)
- Orbital satellite leading to manned space flight (Sputnik, 1957)
- First man on the moon (1969)

US POLICY TOWARD IMMIGRANTS AFTER WORLD WAR II

Prior to WWII, the US had been limiting **immigration** for several decades. After WWII, policy shifted slightly to accommodate political refugees from Europe and elsewhere. So many people were displaced by the war that in 1946, the UN formed the **International Refugee Organization** to deal with the problem. In 1948, the US Congress passed the **Displaced Persons Act**, which allowed over 400,000 European refugees to enter the US, most of them concentration camp survivors and refugees from Eastern Europe.

In 1952, the **United States Escapee Program (USEP)** increased the quotas, allowing refugees from communist Europe to enter the US, as did the **Refugee Relief Act**, passed in 1953. At the same time, however, the **Internal Security Act of 1950** allowed deportation of declared communists, and Asians were subjected to a quota based on race, rather than country of origin. Later changes included:

- **Migration and Refugee Assistance Act** (1962)—provided aid for refugees in need
- **Immigration and Nationality Act** (1965)—ended quotas based on nation of origin
- **Immigration Reform and Control Act** (1986)—prohibited the hiring of illegal immigrants but also granted amnesty to about three million illegals already in the country

POLICIES AND LEGISLATION ENACTED EXPANDING MINORITY RIGHTS

Several major acts have been passed, particularly since WWII, to protect the rights of minorities in America. These include:

- Civil Rights Act (1964)
- Voting Rights Act (1965)
- Age Discrimination Act (1967)
- Americans with Disabilities Act (1990)

Copyright © Mometrix Media. You have been licensed one copy of this document for personal use only. Any other reproduction or redistribution is strictly prohibited. All rights reserved.

Other important movements for civil rights included a prisoner's rights movement, movements for immigrant rights, and the women's rights movement. The National Organization for Women (NOW) was established in 1966 and worked to pass the Equal Rights Amendment. The amendment was passed, but not enough states ratified it for it to become part of the US Constitution.

INTERVENTIONIST AND ISOLATIONIST APPROACHES IN WORLD WAR II

When war broke out in Europe in 1939, President Roosevelt stated that the US would remain **neutral**. However, his overall approach was considered "**interventionist**," as he was willing to provide aid to the Allies without actually entering the conflict. Thus, the US supplied a wide variety of war materials to the Allied nations in the early years of the war.

Isolationists believed the US should not provide any aid to the Allies, including supplies. They felt Roosevelt, by assisting the Allies, was leading the US into a war for which it was not prepared. Led by Charles Lindbergh, the Isolationists believed that any involvement in the European conflict endangered the US by weakening its national defense.

SEQUENCE OF EVENTS THAT LED THE US TO DECLARE WAR AND ENTER WORLD WAR II

In 1937, Japan invaded China, prompting the US to eventually halt exports to Japan. Roosevelt also did not allow Japanese interests to withdraw money held in US banks. In 1941, **General Tojo** rose to power as the Japanese prime minister. Recognizing America's ability to bring a halt to Japan's expansion, he authorized the bombing of **Pearl Harbor** on December 7. The US responded by declaring war on Japan. Partially because of the **Tripartite Pact** among the Axis Powers, Germany and Italy then declared war on the US, later followed by Bulgaria, Hungary, and other Axis nations.

> **Review Video: World War II Overview**
> Visit mometrix.com/academy and enter code: 759402

OCCURRENCES OF WORLD WAR II THAT LED TO THE SURRENDER OF GERMANY

In 1941, **Hitler** violated the non-aggression pact he had signed with Stalin two years earlier by invading the USSR. **Stalin** then joined the **Allies**. Stalin, Roosevelt, and Winston Churchill planned to defeat Germany first, then Japan, bringing the war to an end.

In 1942-1943, the Allies drove **Axis** forces out of Africa. In addition, the Germans were soundly defeated at Stalingrad.

The **Italian Campaign** involved Allied operations in Italy between July 1943 and May 1945, including Italy's liberation. On June 6, 1944, known as **D-Day**, the Allies invaded France at Normandy. Soviet troops moved on the eastern front at the same time, driving German forces back. By April 25, 1945, Berlin was surrounded by Soviet troops. On May 7, Germany surrendered.

MAJOR EVENTS OF WORLD WAR II THAT LED TO THE SURRENDER OF JAPAN

War continued with **Japan** after Germany's surrender. Japanese forces had taken a large portion of Southeast Asia and the Western Pacific, all the way to the Aleutian Islands in Alaska. **General Doolittle** bombed several Japanese cities while American troops scored a victory at Midway. Additional fighting in the Battle of the Coral Sea further weakened Japan's position. As a final blow, the US dropped two **atomic bombs** on Japan, one on Hiroshima and the other on Nagasaki. This was the first time atomic bombs had been used in warfare, and the devastation was horrific and demoralizing. Japan surrendered on September 2, 1945, which became **V-J Day** in the US.

Copyright © Mometrix Media. You have been licensed one copy of this document for personal use only. Any other reproduction or redistribution is strictly prohibited. All rights reserved.

SIGNIFICANCE OF THE 442ND REGIMENTAL COMBAT TEAM, THE TUSKEGEE AIRMEN, AND THE NAVAJO CODE TALKERS DURING WORLD WAR II

The 442nd Regimental Combat Team consisted of Japanese-Americans fighting in Europe for the US. The most highly decorated unit per member in US history, they suffered a 93% casualty rate during the war. The **Tuskegee Airmen** were African American aviators, the first black Americans allowed to fly for the military. In spite of being ineligible to become official navy pilots, they flew over 15,000 missions and were highly decorated. The **Navajo Code Talkers** were native Navajo who used their traditional language to transmit information among Allied forces. Because Navajo is a language and not simply a code, the Axis powers were never able to translate it. The use of Navajo Code Talkers to transmit information was instrumental in the taking of Iwo Jima and other major victories of the war.

CIRCUMSTANCES AND OPPORTUNITIES FOR WOMEN DURING WORLD WAR II

Women served widely in the military during WWII, working in numerous positions, including the **Flight Nurses Corps**. Women also moved into the workforce while men were overseas, leading to over 19 million women in the US workforce by 1944. **Rosie the Riveter** stood as a symbol of these women and a means of recruiting others to take needed positions. Women, as well as their families left behind during wartime, also grew **Victory Gardens** to help provide food.

IMPORTANCE OF THE ATOMIC BOMB DURING WORLD WAR II

The atomic bomb, developed during WWII, was the most powerful bomb ever invented. A single bomb, carried by a single plane, held enough power to destroy an entire city. This devastating effect was demonstrated with the bombing of **Hiroshima** and **Nagasaki** in 1945 in what later became a controversial move, but ended the war. The bombings resulted in as many as 150,000 immediate deaths and many more as time passed after the bombings, mostly due to **radiation poisoning**.

Whatever the arguments against the use of "The Bomb," the post-WWII era saw many countries develop similar weapons to match the newly expanded military power of the US. The impact of those developments and use of nuclear weapons continues to haunt international relations today.

IMPORTANCE OF THE YALTA CONFERENCE AND THE POTSDAM CONFERENCE

In February 1945, Joseph Stalin, Franklin D. Roosevelt, and Winston Churchill met in Yalta to discuss the post-war treatment of the **Axis nations**, particularly Germany. Though Germany had not yet surrendered, its defeat was imminent. After Germany's official surrender, Joseph Stalin, Harry Truman (Roosevelt's successor), and Clement Attlee (replacing Churchill partway through the conference) met to formalize those plans. This meeting was called the **Potsdam Conference**. Basic provisions of these agreements included:

- Dividing Germany and Berlin into four zones of occupation
- Demilitarization of Germany
- Poland remaining under Soviet control
- Outlawing the Nazi Party
- Trials for Nazi leaders
- Relocation of numerous German citizens
- The USSR joining the United Nations, established in 1945
- Establishment of the United Nations Security Council, consisting of the US, the UK, the USSR, China, and France

Copyright © Mometrix Media. You have been licensed one copy of this document for personal use only. Any other reproduction or redistribution is strictly prohibited. All rights reserved.

AGREEMENTS MADE WITH POST-WAR JAPAN

General Douglas MacArthur led the American **military occupation of Japan** after the country surrendered. The goals of the US occupation included removing Japan's military and making the country a democracy. A 1947 constitution removed power from the emperor and gave it to the people, as well as granting voting rights to women. Japan was no longer allowed to declare war, and a group of 28 government officials were tried for war crimes. In 1951, the US finally signed a peace treaty with Japan. This treaty allowed Japan to rearm itself for purposes of self-defense but stripped the country of the empire it had built overseas.

US TREATMENT OF IMMIGRANTS DURING AND AFTER WORLD WAR II

In 1940, the US passed the **Alien Registration Act**, which required all aliens older than fourteen to be fingerprinted and registered. They were also required to report changes of address within five days.

Tension between whites and Japanese immigrants in **California**, which had been building since the beginning of the century, came to a head with the bombing of **Pearl Harbor** in 1941. Believing that even those Japanese living in the US were likely to be loyal to their native country, the president ordered numerous Japanese to be arrested on suspicion of subversive action and isolated in exclusion zones known as **War Relocation Camps**. Approximately 120,000 Japanese-Americans, two-thirds of them US citizens, were sent to these camps during the war.

GENERAL STATE OF THE US AFTER WORLD WAR II

Following WWII, the US became the strongest political power in the world, becoming a major player in world affairs and foreign policies. The US determined to stop the spread of **communism**, having named itself the "**arsenal of democracy**" during the war. In addition, America emerged with a greater sense of itself as a single, integrated nation, with many regional and economic differences diminished. The government worked for greater equality, and the growth of communications increased contact among different areas of the country. Both the aftermath of the Great Depression and the necessities of WWII had given the government greater **control** over various institutions as well as the economy. This also meant that the American government took on greater responsibility for the well-being of its citizens, both in the domestic arena, such as providing basic needs, and in protecting them from foreign threats. This increased role of providing basic necessities for all Americans has been criticized by some as "**the welfare state**."

ACCOMPLISHMENTS OF HARRY S. TRUMAN

Harry S. Truman took over the presidency from Franklin D. Roosevelt near the end of WWII. He made the final decision to drop atomic bombs on Japan and played a major role in the final decisions regarding the treatment of post-war Germany. On the domestic front, Truman initiated a 21-point plan known as the **Fair Deal**. This plan expanded Social Security, provided public housing, and made the Fair Employment Practice Committee permanent. Truman helped support Greece and Turkey (which were under threat from the USSR), supported South Korea against communist North Korea, and helped with recovery in Western Europe. He also participated in the formation of **NATO**, the North Atlantic Treaty Organization.

EVENTS AND IMPORTANCE OF THE KOREAN WAR

The Korean War began in 1950 and ended in 1953. For the first time in history, a world organization—the **United Nations**—played a military role in a war. North Korea sent communist troops into South Korea, seeking to bring the entire country under communist control. The UN sent out a call to member nations, asking them to support South Korea. Truman sent troops, as did many other UN member nations. The war ended three years later with a **truce** rather than a peace treaty,

Copyright © Mometrix Media. You have been licensed one copy of this document for personal use only. Any other reproduction or redistribution is strictly prohibited. All rights reserved.

and Korea remains divided at the **38th parallel north**, with communist rule remaining in the North and a democratic government ruling the South.

ACCOMPLISHMENTS OF DWIGHT D. EISENHOWER

Eisenhower carried out a middle-of-the-road foreign policy and brought the US several steps forward in equal rights. He worked to minimize tensions during the Cold War and negotiated a peace treaty with Russia after the death of Stalin. He enforced desegregation by sending troops to Little Rock Central High School in Arkansas, as well as ordering the desegregation of the military. Organizations formed during his administration included the Department of Health, Education, and Welfare, and the National Aeronautics and Space Administration (NASA).

PRESIDENCY OF JOHN F. KENNEDY

Although his term was cut short by his assassination, **JFK** instituted economic programs that led to a period of continuous expansion in the US unmatched since before WWII. He formed the Alliance for Progress and the Peace Corps, organizations intended to help developing nations. He also oversaw the passage of new civil rights legislation and drafted plans to attack poverty and its causes, along with support of the arts. Kennedy's presidency ended when he was assassinated by **Lee Harvey Oswald** in 1963.

EVENTS OF THE CUBAN MISSILE CRISIS

The Cuban Missile Crisis occurred in 1962, during John F. Kennedy's presidency. Russian Premier **Nikita Khrushchev** decided to place nuclear missiles in **Cuba** to protect the island from invasion by the US. An American U-2 plane flying over the island photographed the missile bases as they were being built. Tensions rose, with the US concerned about nuclear missiles so close to its shores, and the USSR concerned about American missiles that had been placed in **Turkey**. Eventually, the missile sites were removed, and a US naval blockade turned back Soviet ships carrying missiles to Cuba. During negotiations, the US agreed to remove their missiles from Turkey and agreed to sell surplus wheat to the USSR. A telephone hotline between Moscow and Washington was set up to allow instant communication between the two heads of state to prevent similar incidents in the future.

EVENTS OF THE RICHARD NIXON PRESIDENCY

Richard Nixon is best known for the **Watergate scandal** during his presidency, but other important events marked his tenure as president, including:

- End of the Vietnam War
- Improved diplomatic relations between the US and China, and the US and the USSR
- National Environmental Policy Act passed, providing for environmental protection
- Compulsory draft ended
- Supreme Court legalized abortion in Roe v. Wade
- Watergate

The Watergate scandal of 1972 ended Nixon's presidency. Rather than face impeachment and removal from office, he **resigned** in 1974.

EVENTS OF THE GERALD FORD PRESIDENCY

Gerald Ford was appointed to the vice presidency after Nixon's vice president **Spiro Agnew** resigned in 1973 under charges of tax evasion. With Nixon's resignation, Ford became president.

Copyright © Mometrix Media. You have been licensed one copy of this document for personal use only. Any other reproduction or redistribution is strictly prohibited. All rights reserved.

Ford's presidency saw negotiations with Russia to limit nuclear arms, as well as struggles to deal with inflation, economic downturn, and energy shortages. Ford's policies sought to reduce governmental control of various businesses and reduce the role of government overall. He also worked to prevent escalation of conflicts in the Middle East.

EVENTS OF THE JIMMY CARTER PRESIDENCY

Jimmy Carter was elected as president in 1976. Faced with a budget deficit, high unemployment, and continued inflation, Carter also dealt with numerous matters of international diplomacy, including:

- **Torrijos-Carter Treaties**—the US gave control of the Panama Canal to Panama.
- **Camp David Accords**—negotiations between Anwar el-Sadat, the president of Egypt, and Menachem Begin, the Israeli Prime Minister, led to a peace treaty between Egypt and Israel.
- **Strategic Arms Limitation Talks (SALT)**—these led to agreements and treaties between the US and the Soviet Union.
- **Iran Hostage Crisis**—after the Shah of Iran was deposed, an Islamic cleric, Ayatollah Khomeini, came to power. The shah came to the US for medical treatment, and Iran demanded his return so he could stand trial. In retaliation, a group of Iranian students stormed the US Embassy in Iran. Fifty-two American hostages were held for 444 days.

Jimmy Carter was awarded the **Nobel Peace Prize** in 2002.

EVENTS OF THE RONALD REAGAN PRESIDENCY

Ronald Reagan, at 69, became the oldest American president. The two terms of his administration included notable events such as:

- Reaganomics, also known as supply-side, trickle-down, or free-market economics, involving major tax cuts
- Economic Recovery Tax Act of 1981
- First female justice appointed to the Supreme Court—Sandra Day O'Connor
- Massive increase in the national debt—from $1 trillion to $3 trillion
- Reduction of nuclear weapons via negotiations with Mikhail Gorbachev
- Iran-Contra scandal—cover-up of US involvement in revolutions in El Salvador and Nicaragua
- Deregulation of savings and loan industry
- Loss of the space shuttle *Challenger*

EVENTS OF THE GEORGE H. W. BUSH PRESIDENCY

Reagan's presidency was followed by a term under his former vice president, **George H. W. Bush**. Bush's run for president included the famous "**thousand points of light**" speech, which was instrumental in increasing his standing in the election polls. During Bush's presidency, numerous international events took place, including:

- Fall of the Berlin wall and Germany's unification
- Panamanian dictator Manuel Noriega captured and tried on drug and racketeering charges
- Dissolution of the Soviet Union
- Gulf War, or Operation Desert Storm, triggered by Iraq's invasion of Kuwait
- Tiananmen Square Massacre in Beijing, China
- Ruby Ridge
- The arrival of the World Wide Web

Copyright © Mometrix Media. You have been licensed one copy of this document for personal use only. Any other reproduction or redistribution is strictly prohibited. All rights reserved.

EVENTS OF THE WILLIAM CLINTON PRESIDENCY

William Jefferson "Bill" Clinton was the second president in US history to be impeached, but he was not convicted, and maintained high approval ratings in spite of the impeachment. Major events during his presidency included:

- Family and Medical Leave Act
- "Don't Ask, Don't Tell," a compromise position regarding homosexuals serving in the military
- North American Free Trade Agreement, or NAFTA
- Defense of Marriage Act
- Oslo Accords
- Siege at Waco, Texas, involving the Branch Davidians led by David Koresh
- Bombing of the Murrah Federal Building in Oklahoma City, Oklahoma
- Troops sent to Haiti, Bosnia, and Somalia to assist with domestic problems in those areas

EVENTS OF THE GEORGE W. BUSH PRESIDENCY

George W. Bush, son of George H. W. Bush, became president after Clinton. Major events during his presidency included:

- September 11, 2001, al-Qaeda terrorists hijack commercial airliners and fly into the World Trade Center towers and the Pentagon, killing nearly 3,000 Americans
- US troops sent to Afghanistan to hunt down al-Qaeda leaders, including the head of the organization, Osama Bin Laden; beginning of the War on Terror
- US troops sent to Iraq, along with a multinational coalition, to depose Saddam Hussein and prevent his deployment of suspected weapons of mass destruction
- Subprime mortgage crisis and near collapse of the financial industry, leading to the Great Recession; first of multiple government bailouts of the financial industry

BARACK OBAMA

In 2008, Barack Obama, a senator from Illinois, became the first African American US president. His administration focused on improving the lot of a country suffering from a major recession. His major initiatives included:

- Economic bailout packages
- Improvements in women's rights
- Moves to broaden LGBT rights
- Health care reform legislation
- Reinforcement of the war in Afghanistan

DONALD TRUMP

In 2016, Donald Trump, previously a real estate developer and television personality, was elected 45th president after a tumultuous election in which he won the electoral college but lost the popular vote. Marked by tension between the administration and domestic media, Trump's initiatives included:

- Appointing three Supreme Court Justices: Neil Gorsuch, Brett Kavanaugh, and Amy Coney Barrett
- Passing a major tax reform bill

Copyright © Mometrix Media. You have been licensed one copy of this document for personal use only. Any other reproduction or redistribution is strictly prohibited. All rights reserved.

- Enacting travel and emigration restrictions on eight nations: Iran, Libya, Syria, Yemen, Somalia, Chad, North Korea, and Venezuela
- Recognizing Jerusalem, rather than Tel Aviv, as the capital of Israel
- Responding to the novel coronavirus (SARS-CoV-2) outbreak

Almost completely along party lines, Donald Trump was impeached by the House on charges of abuse of power and obstruction of Congress; he was acquitted by the Senate.

Copyright © Mometrix Media. You have been licensed one copy of this document for personal use only. Any other reproduction or redistribution is strictly prohibited. All rights reserved.

World History Pre-1400

DIFFERENT PERIODS OF PREHISTORY

Prehistory is the period of human history before writing was developed. The three major periods of prehistory are:

- **Lower Paleolithic**—Humans used crude tools.
- **Upper Paleolithic**—Humans began to develop a wider variety of tools. These tools were better made and more specialized. They also began to wear clothes, organize in groups with definite social structures, and practice art. Most lived in caves during this time period.
- **Neolithic**—Social structures became even more complex, including the growth of a sense of family and the ideas of religion and government. Humans learned to domesticate animals and produce crops, build houses, start fires with friction tools, and to knit, spin and weave.

ANTHROPOLOGY

Anthropology is the study of human culture. Anthropologists study groups of humans, how they relate to each other, and the similarities and differences between these different groups and cultures. Anthropological research takes two approaches: **cross-cultural research** and **comparative research**. Most anthropologists work by living among different cultures and participating in those cultures in order to learn about them.

There are four major **divisions** within anthropology:

- Biological anthropology
- Cultural anthropology
- Linguistic anthropology
- Archaeology

SCIENCE OF ARCHAEOLOGY

Archaeology is the study of past human cultures by evaluating what they leave behind. This can include bones, buildings, art, tools, pottery, graves, and even trash. Archaeologists maintain detailed notes and records of their findings and use special tools to evaluate what they find. Photographs, notes, maps, artifacts, and surveys of the area can all contribute to the evaluation of an archaeological site. By studying all these elements of numerous archeological sites, scientists have been able to theorize that humans or near-humans have existed for about 600,000 years. Before that, more primitive humans are believed to have appeared about one million years ago. These humans eventually developed into **Cro-Magnon man**, and then **Homo sapiens**, or modern man.

HUMAN DEVELOPMENT FROM THE LOWER PALEOLITHIC TO THE IRON AGE

Human development has been divided into several phases:

- **Lower Paleolithic or Early Stone Age**, beginning two to three million years ago—early humans used tools like needles, hatchets, awls, and cutting tools.
- **Middle Paleolithic or Middle Stone Age**, beginning approximately 300,000 BC—sophisticated stone tools were developed, along with hunting, gathering, and ritual practices.
- **Upper Paleolithic or Late Stone Age**, beginning approximately 40,000 BC—including the Mesolithic and Neolithic eras, textiles and pottery were developed. Humans of this era discovered the wheel, began to practice agriculture, made polished tools, and had some domesticated animals.

Copyright © Mometrix Media. You have been licensed one copy of this document for personal use only. Any other reproduction or redistribution is strictly prohibited. All rights reserved.

- **Bronze Age**, beginning approximately 3000 BC—metals are discovered and the first civilizations emerge as humans become more technologically advanced.
- **Iron Age**, beginning 1200 to 1000 BC—metal tools replace stone tools as humans develop knowledge of smelting.

REQUIREMENTS FOR CIVILIZATION AND STATE WHERE THE EARLIEST CIVILIZATIONS DEVELOPED

Civilizations are defined as having the following characteristics:

- Use of metal to make weapons and tools
- Written language
- A defined territorial state
- A calendar

The **earliest civilizations** developed in river valleys where reliable, fertile land was easily found, including:

- The Nile River Valley in Egypt
- Mesopotamia
- The Indus Valley
- Hwang Ho in China

The very earliest civilizations developed in the **Tigris-Euphrates valley** in Mesopotamia, which is now part of Iraq, and in Egypt's **Nile valley**. These civilizations arose between 5000 and 3000 BC. The area where these civilizations grew is known as the Fertile Crescent. Geography and the availability of water made large-scale human habitation possible.

IMPORTANCE OF RIVERS AND WATER TO THE GROWTH OF EARLY CIVILIZATIONS

The earliest civilizations are also referred to as **fluvial civilizations** because they were founded near rivers. Rivers and the water they provide were vital to these early groupings, offering:

- Water for drinking, cultivating crops, and caring for domesticated animals
- A gathering place for wild animals that could be hunted
- Rich soil deposits as a result of regular flooding

Irrigation techniques helped direct water where it was most needed, to sustain herds of domestic animals and to nourish crops of increasing size and quality.

FERTILE CRESCENT

James Breasted, an archaeologist from the University of Chicago, popularized the term "**Fertile Crescent**" to describe the area in Southwest Asia and the Mediterranean basin where the earliest civilizations arose. The region includes modern-day Iraq, Syria, Lebanon, Israel, Palestine, and Jordan. It is bordered on the south by the Syrian and Arabian Deserts, the west by the Mediterranean Sea, and to the north and east by the Taurus and Zagros Mountains, respectively. This area not only provided the raw materials for the development of increasingly advanced civilizations but also saw waves of migration and invasion, leading to the earliest wars and genocides as groups conquered and absorbed each other's cultures and inhabitants.

Copyright © Mometrix Media. You have been licensed one copy of this document for personal use only. Any other reproduction or redistribution is strictly prohibited. All rights reserved.

ACCOMPLISHMENTS OF THE EGYPTIAN, SUMERIAN, BABYLONIAN, AND ASSYRIAN CULTURES

The **Egyptians** were one of the most advanced ancient cultures, having developed construction methods to build the great pyramids, as well as a form of writing known as hieroglyphics. Their religion was highly developed and complex and included advanced techniques for the preservation of bodies after death. They also made paper by processing papyrus, a plant commonly found along the Nile, invented the decimal system, devised a solar calendar, and advanced overall knowledge of mathematics.

The **Sumerians** were the first to invent the wheel, and also brought irrigation systems into use. Their cuneiform writing was simpler than Egyptian hieroglyphs, and they developed the timekeeping system we still use today.

The **Babylonians** are best known for the Code of Hammurabi, an advanced law code.

The **Assyrians** developed horse-drawn chariots and an organized military.

ACCOMPLISHMENTS OF THE HEBREW, PERSIAN, MINOAN, AND MYCENAEAN CULTURES

The **Hebrew** or ancient Israelite culture developed the monotheistic religion that eventually developed into modern Judaism and Christianity.

The **Persians** were conquerors, but those they conquered were allowed to keep their own laws, customs, and religious traditions rather than being forced to accept those of their conquerors. They also developed an alphabet and practiced Zoroastrianism and Mithraism, religions that have influenced modern religious practice.

The **Minoans** used a syllabic writing system and built large, colorful palaces. These ornate buildings included sewage systems, running water, bathtubs, and even flushing toilets. Their script, known as Linear A, has yet to be deciphered.

The **Mycenaeans** practiced a religion that grew into the Greek pantheon, worshipping Zeus and other Olympian gods. They developed Linear B, a writing system used to write the earliest known form of Greek.

PHOENICIANS AND EARLY CULTURE IN INDIA AND ANCIENT CHINA

Skilled seafarers and navigators, the Phoenicians used the stars to navigate their ships at night. They developed a purple dye that was in great demand in the ancient world, and worked with glass and metals. They also devised a phonetic alphabet, using symbols to represent individual sounds rather than whole words or syllables.

The Indus Valley Civilization (IVC) was an urban civilization arose in the Indus Valley, located in between the modern countries of Iran, India, and Pakistan. These ancient humans developed the concept of zero in mathematics, practiced an early form of the Hindu religion, and developed the caste system which is still prevalent in India today. Archeologists are still uncovering information about this highly developed ancient civilization.

In ancient **China**, human civilization developed along the **Yangtze River**. These people produced silk, grew millet, and made pottery, including Longshan black pottery.

Copyright © Mometrix Media. You have been licensed one copy of this document for personal use only. Any other reproduction or redistribution is strictly prohibited. All rights reserved.

CIVILIZATIONS OF MESOPOTAMIA

The major civilizations of Mesopotamia, in what is now called the **Middle East**, were:

- Sumerians
- Amorites
- Hittites
- Assyrians
- Chaldeans
- Persians

These cultures controlled different areas of Mesopotamia during various time periods but were similar in that they were **autocratic**: a single ruler served as the head of the government and often was the main religious ruler as well. These rulers were often tyrannical, militaristic leaders who controlled all aspects of life, including law, trade, and religious activity. Portions of the legacies of these civilizations remain in cultures today. These include mythologies, religious systems, mathematical innovations, and even elements of various languages.

SUMERIANS

Sumer, located in the southern part of Mesopotamia, consisted of a dozen **city-states**. Each city-state had its own gods, and the leader of each city-state also served as the high priest. Cultural legacies of Sumer include:

- The invention of writing
- The invention of the wheel
- The first library—established in Assyria by Ashurbanipal
- The Hanging Gardens of Babylon—one of the Seven Wonders of the Ancient World
- First written laws—Ur-Nammu's Codes and the Codes of Hammurabi
- The *Epic of Gilgamesh*—the first recorded epic story

> **Review Video: How was Sumerian Culture Spread Throughout Mesopotamia?**
> Visit mometrix.com/academy and enter code: 939880

KUSHITES

Kush, or Cush, was located in Nubia, south of ancient Egypt, and the earliest existing records of this civilization were found in Egyptian texts. At one time, Kush was the largest empire on the Nile River, ruling not only Nubia but Upper and Lower Egypt as well.

In Neolithic times, Kushites lived in villages, with buildings made of mud bricks. They were settled rather than nomadic and practiced hunting and fishing, cultivated grain, and also herded cattle. **Kerma**, the capital, was a major center of trade.

Kush determined leadership through **matrilineal descent** of their kings, as did Egypt. Their heads of state, the Kandake or Kentake, were female. Their polytheistic religion included the primary Egyptian gods as well as regional gods, including a lion-headed god, which is commonly found in African cultures.

Kush was conquered by the **Aksumite Empire** in the 4th century AD.

Copyright © Mometrix Media. You have been licensed one copy of this document for personal use only. Any other reproduction or redistribution is strictly prohibited. All rights reserved.

MINOANS

The Minoans lived on the island of Crete, just off the coast of Greece. This civilization reigned from approximately 4000 to 1400 BC and is considered to be the first advanced civilization in Europe. The Minoans developed writing systems known to linguists as **Linear A** and **Linear B**. Linear A has not yet been translated; Linear B evolved into classical Greek script. "Minoans" is not the name they used for themselves but is instead a variation on the name of King Minos, a king in Greek mythology believed by some to have been a denizen of Crete. The Minoan civilization subsisted on trade, and their way of life was often disrupted by earthquakes and volcanoes. Much is still unknown about the Minoans, and archaeologists continue to study their architecture and archaeological remains. The Minoan culture eventually fell to Greek invaders and was supplanted by the **Mycenaean civilization**.

ANCIENT INDIA

The civilizations of ancient India gave rise to both **Hinduism** and **Buddhism**, major world religions that have influenced countries far from their place of origin. Practices such as yoga, increasingly popular in the West, can trace their roots to these earliest Indian civilizations, and the poses are still formally referred to by Sanskrit names. Literature from ancient India includes the *Mahabharata* containing the *Bhagavad Gita*, the *Ramayana*, *Arthashastra*, and the *Vedas*, a collection of sacred texts. Indo-European languages, including English, find their beginnings in these ancient cultures. Ancient Indo-Aryan languages such as Sanskrit are still used in some formal Hindu practices.

EARLIEST CIVILIZATIONS IN CHINA

Many historians believe **Chinese civilization** is the oldest uninterrupted civilization in the world. The **Neolithic age** in China goes back to 10,000 BC, with agriculture in China beginning as early as 5000 BC. Their system of writing dates to 1500 BC. The Yellow River served as the center for the earliest Chinese settlements. In Ningxia, in northwest China, there are carvings on cliffs that date back to the Paleolithic Period, indicating the extreme antiquity of Chinese culture. Literature from ancient China includes Confucius' *Analects*, the *Tao Te Ching*, and a variety of poetry.

ANCIENT CULTURES IN THE AMERICAS

Less is known of ancient American civilizations since less was left behind. Some of the more well-known cultures include:

- The **Norte Chico civilization** in Peru, an agricultural society of up to 30 individual communities, existed over 5,000 years ago. This culture is also known as the Caral-Supe civilization, and is the oldest known civilization in the Americas.
- The **Anasazi**, or Ancestral Pueblo People, lived in what is now the southwestern United States. Emerging about 1200 BC, the Anasazi built complex adobe dwellings and were the forerunners of later Pueblo Indian cultures.
- The **Maya** emerged in southern Mexico and northern Central America as early as 2600 BC. They developed a written language and a complex calendar.

MYCENAEANS

In contrast to the Minoans, whom they displaced, the **Mycenaeans** relied more on conquest than on trade. Mycenaean states included Sparta, Athens, and Corinth. The history of this civilization, including the **Trojan War**, was recorded by the Greek poet **Homer**. His work was largely considered mythical until archaeologists discovered evidence of the city of **Troy** in Hisarlik, Turkey. Archaeologists continue to add to the body of information about this ancient culture, translating documents written in Linear B, a script derived from the Minoan Linear A. It is theorized that the

88

Copyright © Mometrix Media. You have been licensed one copy of this document for personal use only. Any other reproduction or redistribution is strictly prohibited. All rights reserved.

Mycenaean civilization was eventually destroyed in either a Dorian invasion or an attack by Greek invaders from the north.

DORIAN INVASION

A Dorian invasion does not refer to an invasion by a particular group of people, but rather is a hypothetical theory to explain the end of the **Mycenaean civilization** and the growth of **classical Greece**. Ancient tradition refers to these events as "the return of the Heracleidae," or the sons (descendants) of Hercules. Archaeologists and historians still do not know exactly who conquered the Mycenaeans, but it is believed to have occurred around 1200 BC, contemporaneous with the destruction of the **Hittite civilization** in what is now modern Turkey. The Hittites speak of an attack by people of the Aegean Sea, or the "Sea People." Only Athens was left intact.

SPARTANS VS. ATHENIANS

Both powerful city-states, Sparta and Athens fought each other in the **Peloponnesian War** (431-404 BC). Despite their proximity, the Spartans and the Athenians nurtured contrasting cultures:

- The **Spartans**, located in Peloponnesus, were ruled by an oligarchic military state. They practiced farming, disallowed trade for Spartan citizens, and valued military arts and strict discipline. They emerged as the strongest military force in the area and maintained this status for many years. In one memorable encounter, a small group of Spartans held off a huge army of Persians at Thermopylae.
- The **Athenians** were centered in Attica, where the land was rocky and unsuitable for farming. Like the Spartans, they descended from invaders who spoke Greek. Their government was very different from Sparta's; it was in Athens that democracy was created by Cleisthenes of Athens in 508 BC. Athenians excelled in art, theater, architecture, and philosophy.

CONTRIBUTIONS OF ANCIENT GREECE THAT STILL EXIST TODAY

Ancient Greece made numerous major contributions to cultural development, including:

- **Theater**—Aristophanes and other Greek playwrights laid the groundwork for modern theatrical performance.
- **Alphabet**—the Greek alphabet, derived from the Phoenician alphabet, developed into the Roman alphabet, and then into our modern-day alphabet.
- **Geometry**—Pythagoras and Euclid pioneered much of the system of geometry still taught today. Archimedes made various mathematical discoveries, including calculating a very accurate value of pi.
- **Historical writing**—much of ancient history doubles as mythology or religious texts. Herodotus and Thucydides made use of research and interpretation to record historical events.
- **Philosophy**—Socrates, Plato, and Aristotle served as the fathers of Western philosophy. Their work is still required reading for philosophy students.

> **Review Video: Ancient Greece Timeline**
> Visit mometrix.com/academy and enter code: 800829

ALEXANDER THE GREAT

Born to Philip II of Macedon and tutored by Aristotle, **Alexander the Great** is considered one of the greatest conquerors in history. He conquered Egypt and the Achaemenid/Persian Empire, a powerful empire founded by Cyrus the Great that spanned three continents, and he traveled as far

Copyright © Mometrix Media. You have been licensed one copy of this document for personal use only. Any other reproduction or redistribution is strictly prohibited. All rights reserved.

as India and the Iberian Peninsula. Though Alexander died from malaria at age 32, his conquering efforts spread **Greek culture** into the east. This cultural diffusion left a greater mark on history than did his empire, which fell apart due to internal conflict not long after his death. Trade between the East and West increased, as did an exchange of ideas and beliefs that influenced both regions greatly. The **Hellenistic traditions** his conquest spread were prevalent in Byzantine culture until as late as the 15th century.

HITTITES

The Hittites were centered in what is now Turkey, but their empire extended into Palestine and Syria. They conquered the Babylonian civilization, but adopted their religion, laws, and literature. Overall, the Hittites tended to tolerate other religions, unlike many other contemporary cultures, and absorbed foreign gods into their own belief systems rather than forcing their religion onto peoples they conquered. The **Hittite Empire** reached its peak in 1600-1200 BC. After a war with Egypt, which weakened them severely, they were eventually conquered by the **Assyrians**.

PERSIAN WARS

The Persian Empire, ruled by **Cyrus the Great**, encompassed an area from the Black Sea to Afghanistan and beyond into Central Asia. After the death of Cyrus, **Darius I** became king in 522 BC. The empire reached its zenith during his reign, and Darius attempted to conquer Greece as well. From 499 to 449 BC, the Greeks and Persians fought in the **Persian Wars**. The **Peace of Callias** brought an end to the fighting, after the Greeks were able to repel the invasion.

Battles of the Persian Wars included:

- The **Battle of Marathon**—heavily outnumbered Greek forces managed to achieve victory.
- The **Battle of Thermopylae**—a small band of Spartans held off a throng of Persian troops for several days before Persia defeated the Greeks and captured an evacuated Athens.
- The **Battle of Salamis**—this was a naval battle that again saw outnumbered Greeks achieving victory.
- The **Battle of Plataea**—this was another Greek victory, but one in which they outnumbered the Persians. This ended the invasion of Greece.

MAURYA EMPIRE

The Maurya Empire was a large, powerful empire established in India. It was one of the largest ever to rule in the Indian subcontinent and existed from 322 to 185 BC, ruled by **Chandragupta Maurya** after the withdrawal from India of Alexander the Great. The Maurya Empire was highly developed, including a standardized economic system, waterways, and private corporations. Trade to the Greeks and others became common, with goods including silk, exotic foods, and spices. Religious development included the rise of Buddhism and Jainism. The laws of the Maurya Empire protected not only civil and social rights of the citizens, but they also protected animals, establishing protected zones for economically important creatures such as elephants, lions, and tigers. This period of time in Indian history was largely peaceful, perhaps due to the strong Buddhist beliefs of many of its leaders. The empire finally fell after a succession of weak leaders and was taken over by **Demetrius**, a Greco-Bactrian king who took advantage of this lapse in leadership to conquer southern Afghanistan and Pakistan around 180 BC, forming the **Indo-Greek Kingdom**.

Copyright © Mometrix Media. You have been licensed one copy of this document for personal use only. Any other reproduction or redistribution is strictly prohibited. All rights reserved.

DEVELOPMENT AND GROWTH OF THE CHINESE EMPIRES

In China, history was divided into a series of **dynasties**. The most famous of these, the **Han dynasty**, existed from 206 BC to AD 220. Accomplishments of the Chinese empires included:

- Building the Great Wall of China
- Numerous inventions, including paper, paper money, printing, and gunpowder
- High level of artistic development
- Silk production

The Chinese dynasties were comparable to Rome as far as their artistic and intellectual accomplishments, as well as the size and scope of their influence.

ROMAN EMPIRE AND REPUBLIC

Rome began humbly, in a single town that grew out of Etruscan settlements and traditions, founded, according to legend, by twin brothers Romulus and Remus, who were raised by wolves. Romulus killed Remus, and from his legacy grew Rome. A thousand years later, the **Roman Empire** covered a significant portion of the known world, from what is now Scotland, across Europe, and into the Middle East. **Hellenization**, or the spread of Greek culture throughout the world, served as an inspiration and a model for the spread of Roman culture. Rome brought in belief systems of conquered peoples as well as their technological and scientific accomplishments, melding the disparate parts into a Roman core. Rome began as a **republic** ruled by consuls, but after the assassination of **Julius Caesar**, it became an **empire** led by emperors. Rome's overall government was autocratic, but local officials came from the provinces where they lived. This limited administrative system was probably a major factor in the long life of the empire.

> **Review Video: Roman Republic Part One**
> Visit mometrix.com/academy and enter code: 360192
>
> **Review Video: Roman Republic Part Two**
> Visit mometrix.com/academy and enter code: 881514

DEVELOPMENT OF THE BYZANTINE EMPIRE FROM THE ROMAN EMPIRE

In the early 4th century, the Roman Empire split, with the eastern portion becoming the Eastern Empire, or the **Byzantine Empire**. In AD 330, **Constantine** founded the city of **Constantinople**, which became the center of the Byzantine Empire. Its major influences came from Mesopotamia and Persia, in contrast to the Western Empire, which maintained traditions more closely linked to Greece and Carthage. Byzantium's position gave it an advantage over invaders from the West and the East, as well as control over trade from both regions. It protected the Western empire from invasion from the Persians and the Ottomans, and practiced a more centralized rule than in the West. The Byzantines were famous for lavish art and architecture, as well as the Code of Justinian, which collected Roman law into a clear system. The Byzantine Empire finally fell to the **Ottomans** in 1453.

SIGNIFICANCE OF THE NICENE CREED

The **Byzantine Empire** was Christian-based but incorporated Greek language, philosophy, and literature and drew its law and government policies from Rome. However, there was as yet no unified doctrine of Christianity, as it was a relatively new religion that had spread rapidly and without a great deal of organization. In 325, the **First Council of Nicaea** addressed this issue. From this conference came the **Nicene Creed**, addressing the Trinity and other basic Christian beliefs. The **Council of Chalcedon** in 451 further defined the view of the Trinity.

Copyright © Mometrix Media. You have been licensed one copy of this document for personal use only. Any other reproduction or redistribution is strictly prohibited. All rights reserved.

FACTORS THAT LED TO THE FALL OF THE WESTERN ROMAN EMPIRE

Germanic tribes, including the Visigoths, Ostrogoths, Vandals, Saxons, and Franks, controlled most of Europe. The Roman Empire faced major opposition on that front. The increasing size of the empire also made it harder to manage, leading to dissatisfaction throughout the empire as Roman government became less efficient. Germanic tribes refused to adhere to the Nicene Creed, instead following **Arianism**, which led the Roman Catholic Church to declare them heretics. The **Franks** proved a powerful military force in their defeat of the Muslims in 732. In 768, **Charlemagne** became king of the Franks. These tribes waged several wars against Rome, including the invasion of Britannia by the Angles and Saxons. Far-flung Rome lost control over this area of its empire, and eventually, Rome itself was **invaded**.

ICONOCLASM AND THE CONFLICT BETWEEN THE ROMAN CATHOLIC AND EASTERN ORTHODOX CHURCHES

Emperor Leo III ordered the destruction of all icons throughout the Byzantine Empire. Images of Jesus were replaced with crosses, and images of Jesus, Mary, or other religious figures were considered blasphemy on the grounds of idolatry. **Pope Gregory II** called a synod to discuss the issue. The synod declared that the images were not heretical and that strong disciplinary measures would result for anyone who destroyed them. Leo's response was an attempt to kill Pope Gregory, but this plan ended in failure.

EFFECT OF THE VIKING INVASIONS ON THE CULTURE OF ENGLAND AND EUROPE

Vikings invaded Northern France in the 10th century, eventually becoming the **Normans**. Originating in Scandinavia, the **Vikings** were accomplished seafarers with advanced knowledge of trade routes. With overpopulation plaguing their native lands, they began to travel. From the 8th to the 11th centuries, they spread throughout Europe, conquering and colonizing. Vikings invaded and colonized England in several waves, including the **Anglo-Saxon invasions** that displaced Roman control. Their influence remained significant in England, affecting everything from the language of the country to place names and even the government and social structure. By 900, Vikings had settled in **Iceland**. They proceeded then to **Greenland** and eventually to **North America**, arriving in the New World even before the Spanish and British who claimed the lands several centuries later. They also traded with the Byzantine Empire until the 11th century, when their significant level of activity came to an end.

WEST VS. EAST 10TH-CENTURY EVENTS

In **Europe**, the years AD 500-1000 are largely known as the **Dark Ages**. In the 10th century, numerous Viking invasions disrupted societies that had been more settled under Roman rule. Vikings settled in Northern France, eventually becoming the Normans. By the 11th century, Europe would rise again into the **High Middle Ages** with the beginning of the **Crusades**.

In **China**, wars also raged. This led the Chinese to make use of gunpowder for the first time in warfare.

In the **Americas**, the **Mayan Empire** was winding down while the **Toltec** became more prominent. **Pueblo** Indian culture was also at its zenith.

In the **East**, the **Muslims** and the **Byzantine Empire** were experiencing a significant period of growth and development.

Copyright © Mometrix Media. You have been licensed one copy of this document for personal use only. Any other reproduction or redistribution is strictly prohibited. All rights reserved.

World History 1400 to 1914

FEUDALISM IN EUROPE IN THE MIDDLE AGES

A major element of the social and economic life of Europe, **feudalism** developed as a way to ensure European rulers would have the wherewithal to quickly raise an army when necessary. **Vassals** swore loyalty and promised to provide military service for lords, who in return offered a **fief**, or a parcel of land, for them to use to generate their livelihood. Vassals could work the land themselves, have it worked by **peasants** or **serfs**—workers who had few rights and were little more than slaves—or grant the fief to someone else. The king legally owned all the land, but in return, promised to protect the vassals from invasion and war. Vassals returned a certain percentage of their income to the lords, who in turn, passed a portion of their income on to the king. A similar practice was **manorialism**, in which the feudal system was applied to a self-contained manor. These manors were often owned by the lords who ran them but were usually included in the same system of loyalty and promises of protection that drove feudalism.

> **Review Video: The Middle Ages: Feudalism**
> Visit mometrix.com/academy and enter code: 165907

INFLUENCE OF THE ROMAN CATHOLIC CHURCH OVER MEDIEVAL SOCIETY

The Roman Catholic Church extended significant influence both politically and economically throughout medieval society. The church supplied **education**, as there were no established schools or universities. To a large extent, the church had filled a power void left by various invasions throughout the former Roman Empire, leading it to exercise a role that was far more **political** than religious. Kings were heavily influenced by the pope and other church officials, and churches controlled large amounts of land throughout Europe.

EFFECT OF BLACK DEATH ON MEDIEVAL POLITICS AND ECONOMIC CONDITIONS

The Black Death, believed to be **bubonic plague**, most likely came to Europe on fleas carried by rats on sailing vessels. The plague killed more than a third of the entire population of Europe and effectively ended **feudalism** as a political system. Many who had formerly served as peasants or serfs found different work, as a demand for skilled labor grew. Nation-states grew in power, and in the face of the pandemic, many began to turn away from faith in God and toward the ideals of ancient Greece and Rome for government and other beliefs.

> **Review Video: Black Death (An Overview)**
> Visit mometrix.com/academy and enter code: 431857

PROGRESSION OF THE CRUSADES AND MAJOR FIGURES INVOLVED

The Crusades began in the 11th century and continued into the 15th. The major goal of these various military ventures was to slow the progression of Muslim forces into Europe and to expel them from the **Holy Land**, where they had taken control of Jerusalem and Palestine. Alexius I, the Byzantine emperor, called for help from **Pope Urban** II when Palestine was taken. In 1095, the pope, hoping to reunite Eastern and Western Christianity, encouraged all Christians to help the cause. Amidst great bloodshed, this crusade recaptured **Jerusalem**, but over the next centuries, Jerusalem and other areas of the Holy Land changed hands numerous times. The **Second Crusade** (1147-1149) consisted of an unsuccessful attempt to retake Damascus. The **Third Crusade**, under Pope Gregory VIII, attempted to recapture Jerusalem but failed. The **Fourth Crusade**, under Pope Innocent III, attempted to come into the Holy Land via Egypt. The Crusades led to greater power for

Copyright © Mometrix Media. You have been licensed one copy of this document for personal use only. Any other reproduction or redistribution is strictly prohibited. All rights reserved.

the pope and the Catholic Church in general and also opened numerous trading and cultural routes between Europe and the East.

POLITICAL DEVELOPMENTS IN INDIA THROUGH THE 11TH CENTURY

After the Mauryan dynasty, the **Guptas** ruled India, maintaining a long period of peace and prosperity in the area. During this time, the Indian people invented the decimal system and the concept of zero. They produced cotton and calico, as well as other products in high demand in Europe and Asia, and developed a complex system of medicine. The Gupta Dynasty ended in the 6th century. First, the **Huns** invaded, and then the **Hephthalites** (an Asian nomadic tribe) destroyed the weakened empire. In the 14th century, **Tamerlane**, a Muslim who envisioned restoring Genghis Khan's empire, expanded India's borders and founded the **Mogul Empire**. His grandson Akbar promoted freedom of religion and built a widespread number of mosques, forts, and other buildings throughout the country.

DEVELOPMENT OF CHINESE AND JAPANESE GOVERNMENTS THROUGH THE 11TH CENTURY

After the Mongols, led by Genghis Khan and his grandson Kublai Khan, unified the Mongol Empire, **China** was led by the **Ming Dynasty** (1368-1644) and the **Manchu (also known as Qing) Dynasty** (1644-1912). Both dynasties were isolationist, ending China's interaction with other countries until the 18th century. The Ming Dynasty was known for its porcelain, while the Manchus focused on farming and road construction as the population grew.

Japan developed independently of China but borrowed the Buddhist religion, the Chinese writing system, and other elements of Chinese society. Ruled by the divine emperor, Japan basically functioned on a feudal system led by **daimyo**, or warlords, and soldiers known as **samurai**. Japan remained isolationist, not interacting significantly with the rest of the world until the 1800s.

MING DYNASTY

The Ming dynasty lasted in China from AD 1368 to 1644. This dynasty was established by a Buddhist monk, **Zhu Yuanzhang**, who quickly became obsessed with consolidating power in the central government and was known for the brutality with which he achieved his ends. It was during the **Ming dynasty** that China developed and introduced its famous civil service examinations, rigorous tests on the **Confucian classics**. The future of an ambitious Chinese youth depended on his performance on this exam. The capital was transferred from Nanjing to Beijing during this period, and the **Forbidden City** was constructed inside the new capital. The Ming period, despite its constant expansionary wars, also continued China's artistic resurgence; the porcelain of this period is especially admired.

DEVELOPMENTS IN AFRICA THROUGH THE 11TH CENTURY

Much of Africa was difficult to traverse early on, due to the large amount of desert and other inhospitable terrain. **Egypt** remained important, though most of the northern coast became Muslim as their armies spread through the area. **Ghana** rose as a trade center in the 9th century, lasting into the 12th century, primarily trading in gold, which it exchanged for Saharan salt. **Mali** rose somewhat later, with the trade center Timbuktu becoming an important exporter of goods such as iron, leather, and tin. Mali also dealt in agricultural trade, becoming one of the most significant trading centers in West Africa. The Muslim religion dominated, and technological advancement was sparse.

African culture was largely defined through migration, as Arab merchants and others settled on the continent, particularly along the east coast. Scholars from the Muslim nations gravitated to

Copyright © Mometrix Media. You have been licensed one copy of this document for personal use only. Any other reproduction or redistribution is strictly prohibited. All rights reserved.

Timbuktu, which in addition to its importance in trade, had also become a magnet for those seeking Islamic knowledge and education.

HISTORY OF ISLAM AND ITS ROLE IN BRINGING UNITY TO THE MIDDLE EAST

Born in AD 570, **Muhammad** began preaching around 613, leading his followers in a new religion called **Islam**, which means "submission to God's will." Before this time, the Arabian Peninsula was inhabited largely by Bedouins, nomads who battled amongst each other and lived in tribal organizations. But by the time Muhammad died in 632, most of Arabia had become Muslim to some extent.

Muhammad conquered **Mecca**, where a temple called the **Kaaba** had long served as a center of the nomadic religions. He declared this temple the most sacred of Islam, and Mecca as the holy city. His writings became the **Koran**, or **Qur'an**, divine revelations he said had been delivered to him by the angel Gabriel.

Muhammad's teachings gave the formerly tribal Arabian people a sense of unity that had not existed in the area before. After his death, the converted Muslims of Arabia conquered a vast territory, creating an empire and bringing advances in literature, technology, science, and art as Europe was declining under the scourge of the Black Death. Literature from this period includes the *Arabian Nights* and the *Rubaiyat* of Omar Khayyam.

Later in its development, Islam split into two factions; the **Shiite** and the **Sunni** Muslims. Conflict continues today between these groups.

OTTOMAN EMPIRE

By 1400, the Ottomans had grown in power in Anatolia and had begun attempts to take Constantinople. In 1453, they finally conquered the Byzantine capital and renamed it **Istanbul**. The **Ottoman Empire's** major strength, much like Rome before it, lay in its ability to unite widely disparate people through religious tolerance. This tolerance, which stemmed from the idea that Muslims, Christians, and Jews were fundamentally related and could coexist, enabled the Ottomans to develop a widely varied culture. They also believed in just laws and just government, with government centered in a monarch, known as the **sultan**.

RENAISSANCE

Renaissance literally means "rebirth." After the darkness of the Dark Ages and the Black Plague, interest rose again in the beliefs and politics of ancient Greece and Rome. Art, literature, music, science, and philosophy all burgeoned during the Renaissance.

Many of the ideas of the Renaissance began in **Florence, Italy** in the 14th century, spurred by the **Medici** family. Education for the upper classes expanded to include law, math, reading, writing, and classical Greek and Roman works. As the Renaissance progressed, the world was presented through art and literature in a realistic way that had never been explored before. This **realism** drove culture to new heights.

> **Review Video: Renaissance**
> Visit mometrix.com/academy and enter code: 123100

RENAISSANCE ARTISTS, AUTHORS, AND SCIENTISTS

Artists of the Renaissance included Leonardo da Vinci, also an inventor; Michelangelo, also an architect; and others who focused on realism in their work. In **literature**, major contributions came from humanist authors like Petrarch, Erasmus, Sir Thomas More, and Boccaccio, who believed man

Copyright © Mometrix Media. You have been licensed one copy of this document for personal use only. Any other reproduction or redistribution is strictly prohibited. All rights reserved.

should focus on reality rather than on the ethereal. Shakespeare, Cervantes, and Dante followed in their footsteps, and their works found a wide audience thanks to Gutenberg's development of the printing press.

Scientific developments of the Renaissance included the work of Copernicus, Galileo, and Kepler, who challenged the geocentric philosophies of the day by proving that the earth was not the center of the solar system.

TWO PHASES OF THE REFORMATION PERIOD

The Reformation consisted of both the Protestant and the Catholic Reformation. The **Protestant Reformation** rose in Germany when **Martin Luther** protested abuses of the Catholic Church. **John Calvin** led the movement in Switzerland, while in England, King Henry VIII made use of the Reformation's ideas to further his own political goals. The **Catholic Reformation**, or **Counter-Reformation**, occurred in response to the Protestant movement, leading to various changes in the Catholic Church. Some provided wider tolerance of different religious viewpoints, but others actually increased the persecution of those deemed to be heretics.

From a **religious** standpoint, the Reformation occurred due to abuses by the Catholic Church such as indulgences and dispensations, religious offices being offered up for sale, and an increasingly dissolute clergy. **Politically**, the Reformation was driven by increased power of various ruling monarchs, who wished to take all power to themselves rather than allowing power to remain with the church. They also had begun to chafe at papal taxes and the church's increasing wealth. The ideas of the Protestant Revolution removed power from the Catholic Church and the Pope himself, playing nicely into the hands of those monarchs, such as Henry VIII, who wanted out from under the church's control.

> **Review Video: Martin Luther and the Reformation**
> Visit mometrix.com/academy and enter code: 691828
>
> **Review Video: What was the Counter-Reformation?**
> Visit mometrix.com/academy and enter code: 950498
>
> **Review Video: Who Were the Protestants?**
> Visit mometrix.com/academy and enter code: 583582

DEVELOPMENTS OF THE SCIENTIFIC REVOLUTION

In addition to holding power in the political realm, church doctrine also governed scientific belief. During the **Scientific Revolution**, astronomers and other scientists began to amass evidence that challenged the church's scientific doctrines. Major figures of the Scientific Revolution included:

- **Nicolaus Copernicus**—wrote *On the Revolutions of the Celestial Spheres*, arguing that the earth revolved around the sun
- **Tycho Brahe**—cataloged astronomical observations
- **Johannes Kepler**—developed laws of planetary motion
- **Galileo Galilei**—defended the heliocentric theories of Copernicus and Kepler, discovered four moons of Jupiter, and died under house arrest by the church, charged with heresy
- **Isaac Newton**—discovered gravity; studied optics, calculus, and physics; and believed the workings of nature could be studied and proven through observation

> **Review Video: The Scientific Revolution**
> Visit mometrix.com/academy and enter code: 974600

Copyright © Mometrix Media. You have been licensed one copy of this document for personal use only. Any other reproduction or redistribution is strictly prohibited. All rights reserved.

MAJOR IDEAS OF THE ENLIGHTENMENT

During the Enlightenment, philosophers and scientists began to rely more and more on **observation** to support their ideas rather than building on past beliefs, particularly those held by the church. A focus on **ethics and logic** drove their work. Major philosophers of the **Enlightenment** included:

- **Rene Descartes**—he famously wrote, "I think, therefore I am." He believed strongly in logic and rules of observation.
- **David Hume**—he pioneered empiricism and skepticism, believing that truth could only be found through direct experience and that what others said to be true was always suspect.
- **Immanuel Kant**—he believed in self-examination and observation and that the root of morality lay within human beings.
- **Jean-Jacques Rousseau**—he developed the idea of the social contract, that government existed by the agreement of the people, and that the government was obligated to protect the people and their basic rights. His ideas influenced John Locke and Thomas Jefferson.

AMERICAN REVOLUTION VS. FRENCH REVOLUTION

Both the American and French Revolution came about as a protest against the excesses and overly controlling nature of their respective monarchs. In **America**, the British colonies had been left mostly to self-govern until the British monarchs began to increase control, spurring the colonies to revolt. In **France**, the nobility's excesses had led to increasingly difficult economic conditions, with inflation, heavy taxation, and food shortages creating great burdens on the lower classes. Both revolutions led to the development of republics to replace the monarchies that were displaced. However, the French Revolution eventually led to the rise of the dictator **Napoleon Bonaparte**, while the American Revolution produced a working **republic** from the beginning.

EVENTS AND FIGURES OF THE FRENCH REVOLUTION

In 1789, **King Louis XVI**, faced with a huge national debt, convened parliament. The **Third Estate**, or Commons, a division of the French parliament, then claimed power, and the king's resistance led to the storming of the **Bastille**, the royal prison. The people established a constitutional monarchy. When King Louis XVI and Marie Antoinette attempted to leave the country, they were executed on the guillotine. From 1793 to 1794, **Robespierre** and extreme radicals, the **Jacobins**, instituted a **Reign of Terror**, executing tens of thousands of nobles as well as anyone considered an enemy of the Revolution. Robespierre was then executed as well, and the **Directory** came into power, leading to a temporary return to bourgeois values. This governing body proved incompetent and corrupt, allowing **Napoleon Bonaparte** to come to power in 1799, first as a dictator, then as emperor. While the French Revolution threw off the power of a corrupt monarchy, its immediate results were likely not what the original perpetrators of the revolt had intended.

> **Review Video: The French Revolution: Napoleon Bonaparte**
> Visit mometrix.com/academy and enter code: 876330

INDUSTRIAL REVOLUTION

EFFECTS OF THE INDUSTRIAL REVOLUTION ON SOCIETY

The Industrial Revolution began in Great Britain in the 18th century, bringing coal- and steam-powered machinery into widespread use. Industry began a period of rapid growth with these developments. Goods that had previously been produced in small workshops or even in homes were produced more efficiently and in much larger quantities in **factories**. Where society had been largely agrarian-based, the focus swiftly shifted to an **industrial** outlook. As electricity and internal

Copyright © Mometrix Media. You have been licensed one copy of this document for personal use only. Any other reproduction or redistribution is strictly prohibited. All rights reserved.

combustion engines replaced coal and steam as energy sources, even more drastic and rapid changes occurred. Western European countries, in particular, turned to colonialism, taking control of portions of Africa and Asia to ensure access to the raw materials needed to produce factory goods. Specialized labor became very much in demand, and businesses grew rapidly, creating monopolies, increasing world trade, and developing large urban centers. Even agriculture changed fundamentally as the Industrial Revolution led to a second **Agricultural Revolution** with the addition of new technology to advance agricultural production.

> **Review Video: <u>Industrialization</u>**
> Visit mometrix.com/academy and enter code: 893924

FIRST AND SECOND PHASES OF THE INDUSTRIAL REVOLUTION

The **first phase** of the Industrial Revolution took place from roughly 1750 to 1830. The textile industry experienced major changes as more and more elements of the process became mechanized. Mining benefited from the steam engine. Transportation became easier and more widely available as waterways were improved and the railroad came into prominence. In the **second phase**, from 1830 to 1910, industries further improved in efficiency, and new industries were introduced as photography, various chemical processes, and electricity became more widely available to produce new goods or new, improved versions of old goods. Petroleum and hydroelectricity became major sources of power. During this time, the Industrial Revolution spread out of Western Europe and into the US and Japan.

POLITICAL, SOCIAL AND ECONOMIC SIDE EFFECTS OF THE INDUSTRIAL REVOLUTION

The Industrial Revolution led to widespread education, a wider franchise, and the development of mass communication in the political arena. **Economically**, conflicts arose between companies and their employees, as struggles for fair treatment and fair wages increased. Unions gained power and became more active. Government regulation over industries increased, but at the same time, growing businesses fought for the right to free enterprise. In the **social** sphere, populations increased and began to concentrate around centers of industry. Cities became larger and more densely populated. Scientific advancements led to more efficient agriculture, greater supply of goods, and increased knowledge of medicine and sanitation, leading to better overall health.

> **Review Video: <u>The Industrial Revolution</u>**
> Visit mometrix.com/academy and enter code: 372796

CAUSES AND PROGRESSION OF THE RUSSIAN REVOLUTION OF 1905

In Russia, rule lay in the hands of the **czars**, and the overall structure was **feudalistic**. Beneath the czars was a group of rich nobles, landowners whose lands were worked by peasants and serfs. The **Russo-Japanese War** (1904-1905) made conditions much worse for the lower classes. When peasants demonstrated outside the czar's Winter Palace, the palace guard fired upon the crowd. The demonstration had been organized by a trade union leader, and after the violent response, many unions and political parties blossomed and began to lead numerous strikes. When the economy ground to a halt, Czar Nicholas II signed a document known as the **October Manifesto**, which established a constitutional monarchy and gave legislative power to parliament. However, he violated the manifesto shortly thereafter, disbanding parliament and ignoring the civil liberties granted by the manifesto. This eventually led to the **Bolshevik Revolution**.

Copyright © Mometrix Media. You have been licensed one copy of this document for personal use only. Any other reproduction or redistribution is strictly prohibited. All rights reserved.

World History 1914 to Present

NATIONALISM AND ITS EFFECT ON SOCIETY THROUGH THE 18TH AND 19TH CENTURIES

Nationalism, put simply, is a strong belief in, identification with, and allegiance to a particular nation and people. **Nationalistic belief** unified various areas that had previously seen themselves as fragmented, which led to **patriotism** and, in some cases, **imperialism**. As nationalism grew, individual nations sought to grow, bringing in other, smaller states that shared similar characteristics such as language and cultural beliefs. Unfortunately, a major side effect of these growing nationalistic beliefs was often conflict and outright **war**.

In Europe, imperialism led countries to spread their influence into Africa and Asia. **Africa** was eventually divided among several European countries that wanted certain raw materials. **Asia** also came under European control, with the exception of China, Japan, and Siam (now Thailand). In the US, **Manifest Destiny** became the rallying cry as the country expanded west. Italy and Germany formed larger nations from a variety of smaller states.

> **Review Video: Historical Nationalism**
> Visit mometrix.com/academy and enter code: 510185
>
> **Review Video: What is Nationalism?**
> Visit mometrix.com/academy and enter code: 865693

EVENTS OF WORLD WAR I IN THE EUROPEAN THEATER

WWI began in 1914 with the assassination of **Archduke Franz Ferdinand**, heir to the throne of Austria-Hungary, by a Serbian national. This led to a conflict between Austria-Hungary and Serbia that quickly escalated into the First World War. Europe split into the **Allies**—Britain, France, and Russia, and later Italy, Japan, and the US, against the **Central Powers**—Austria-Hungary, Germany, the Ottoman Empire, and Bulgaria. As the war spread, countries beyond Europe became involved. The war left Europe deeply in debt, and particularly devastated the German economy. The ensuing **Great Depression** made matters worse, and economic devastation opened the door for communist, fascist, and socialist governments to gain power.

TRENCH WARFARE AND ITS USE IN WORLD WAR I

Fighting during WWI largely took place in a series of **trenches** built along the Eastern and Western Fronts. These trenches added up to more than 24,000 miles. This produced fronts that stretched over 400 miles, from the coast of Belgium to the border of Switzerland. The Allies made use of straightforward open-air trenches with a front line, supporting lines, and communications lines. By contrast, the German trenches sometimes included well-equipped underground living quarters.

BOLSHEVIK REVOLUTION

FACTORS LEADING TO THE BOLSHEVIK REVOLUTION OF 1917

Throughout its modern history, Russia had lagged behind other countries in development. The continued existence of a feudal system, combined with harsh conditions and the overall size of the country, led to massive food shortages and increasingly harsh conditions for the majority of the population. The tyrannical rule of the czars only made this worse, as did repeated losses in various military conflicts. Increasing poverty, decreasing supplies, and the czar's violation of the **October Manifesto,** which had given some political power and civil rights to the people, finally came to a head with the **Bolshevik Revolution.**

Copyright © Mometrix Media. You have been licensed one copy of this document for personal use only. Any other reproduction or redistribution is strictly prohibited. All rights reserved.

EVENTS OF THE BOLSHEVIK REVOLUTION

A **workers' strike in Petrograd** in 1917 set the revolutionary wheels in motion when the army sided with the workers. While parliament set up a provisional government made up of nobles, the workers and military joined to form their own governmental system known as **soviets**, which consisted of local councils elected by the people. The ensuing chaos opened the doors for formerly exiled leaders Vladimir Lenin, Joseph Stalin, and Leon Trotsky to move in and gain popular support as well as the support of the Red Guard. Overthrowing parliament, they took power, creating a **communist** state in Russia. This development led to the spread of communism throughout Eastern Europe and elsewhere, greatly affecting diplomatic policies throughout the world for several decades.

COMMUNISM VS. SOCIALISM

At their roots, socialism and communism both focus on public ownership and distribution of goods and services. However, **communism** works toward revolution by drawing on what it sees to be inevitable class antagonism, eventually overthrowing the upper classes and the systems of capitalism. **Socialism** makes use of democratic procedures, building on the existing order. This was particularly true of the utopian socialists, who saw industrial capitalism as oppressive, not allowing workers to prosper. While socialism struggled between the World Wars, communism took hold, especially in Eastern Europe. After WWII, **democratic socialism** became more common. Later, **capitalism** took a stronger hold again, and today most industrialized countries in the western world function under an economy that mixes elements of capitalism and socialism.

> **Review Video: Socialism**
> Visit mometrix.com/academy and enter code: 917677

CONDITIONS THAT LED TO THE RISE OF THE NAZI PARTY IN GERMANY

The **Great Depression** had a particularly devastating effect on Germany's economy, especially after the US was no longer able to supply reconstruction loans to help the country regain its footing. With unemployment rising rapidly, dissatisfaction with the government grew. Fascist and Communist parties rose, promising change and improvement.

Led by **Adolf Hitler**, the fascist **Nazi Party** eventually gained power in Parliament based on these promises and the votes of desperate German workers. When Hitler became chancellor, he launched numerous expansionist policies, violating the peace treaties that had ended WWI. His military buildup and conquering of neighboring countries sparked the aggression that soon led to WWII.

IMPORTANCE OF THE GERMAN BLITZKRIEG TO THE PROGRESSION OF WORLD WAR II

The blitzkrieg, or "lightning war," consisted of fast, powerful surprise attacks that disrupted communications, made it difficult if not impossible for the victims to retaliate, and demoralized Germany's foes. The "blitz," or the aerial bombing of England in 1940, was one example, with bombings occurring in London and other cities 57 nights in a row. The **Battle of Britain** in 1940 also brought intense raids by Germany's air force, the **Luftwaffe**, mostly targeting ports and British air force bases. Eventually, Britain's Royal Air Force blocked the Luftwaffe, ending Germany's hopes for conquering Britain.

BATTLE OF THE BULGE

Following the **D-Day Invasion**, Allied forces gained considerable ground and began a major campaign to push through Europe. In December of 1944, Hitler launched a counteroffensive, attempting to retake Antwerp, an important port. The ensuing battle became the largest land battle on the war's Western Front and was known as the Battle of the Ardennes, or the **Battle of the**

Copyright © Mometrix Media. You have been licensed one copy of this document for personal use only. Any other reproduction or redistribution is strictly prohibited. All rights reserved.

Bulge. The battle lasted from December 16, 1944, to January 25, 1945. The Germans pushed forward, making inroads into Allied lines, but in the end, the Allies brought the advance to a halt. The Germans were pushed back, with massive losses on both sides. However, those losses proved crippling to the German army.

HOLOCAUST

As Germany sank deeper and deeper into dire economic straits, the tendency was to look for a person or group of people to blame for the problems of the country. With distrust of the Jewish people already ingrained, it was easy for German authorities to set up the **Jews** as scapegoats for Germany's problems. Under the rule of Hitler and the Nazi party, the "Final Solution" for the supposed Jewish problem was devised. Millions of Jews, as well as Gypsies, homosexuals, communists, Catholics, the mentally ill, and others, simply named as criminals, were transported to concentration camps during the course of the war. At least six million were slaughtered in death camps such as **Auschwitz**, where horrible conditions and torture of prisoners were commonplace. The Allies were aware of rumors of mass slaughter throughout the war, but many discounted the reports. Only when troops went in to liberate the prisoners was the true horror of the concentration camps brought to light. The **Holocaust** resulted in massive loss of human life, but also in the loss and destruction of cultures. Because the genocide focused on specific ethnic groups, many traditions, histories, knowledge, and other cultural elements were lost, particularly among the Jewish and Gypsy populations. After World War II, the United Nations recognized **genocide** as a "crime against humanity." The UN passed the **Universal Declaration of Human Rights** in 1948 in order to further specify what rights the organization protected. Nazi war criminals faced justice during the **Nuremberg Trials**. There, individuals, rather than their governments, were held accountable for war crimes.

> **Review Video: The Holocaust**
> Visit mometrix.com/academy and enter code: 350695

WORLD WAR II AND THE ENSUING DIPLOMATIC CLIMATE THAT LED TO THE COLD WAR

With millions of military and civilian deaths and over 12 million persons displaced, **WWII** left large regions of Europe and Asia in disarray. **Communist** governments moved in with promises of renewed prosperity and economic stability. The **Soviet Union** backed communist regimes in much of Eastern Europe. In China, **Mao Zedong** led communist forces in the overthrow of the Chinese Nationalist Party and instituted a communist government in 1949. While the new communist governments restored a measure of stability to much of Eastern Europe, it brought its own problems, with dictatorial governments and an oppressive police force. The spread of communism also led to several years of tension between communist countries and the democratic West, as the West fought to slow the spread of oppressive regimes throughout the world. With both sides in possession of nuclear weapons, tensions rose. Each side feared the other would resort to nuclear attack. This standoff lasted until 1989, when the **Berlin Wall** fell. The Soviet Union was dissolved two years later.

ORIGINS OF THE UNITED NATIONS

The United Nations (**UN**) came into being toward the end of World War II. A successor to the less-than-successful League of Nations formed after World War I, the UN built and improved on those ideas. Since its inception, the UN has worked to bring the countries of the world together for **diplomatic solutions** to international problems, including sanctions and other restrictions. It has also initiated military action, calling for peacekeeping troops from member countries to move against countries violating UN policies. The **Korean War** was the first example of UN involvement in an international conflict.

Copyright © Mometrix Media. You have been licensed one copy of this document for personal use only. Any other reproduction or redistribution is strictly prohibited. All rights reserved.

EFFECTS OF DECOLONIZATION ON THE POST-WAR PERIOD

A rise of nationalism among European colonies led to many of them declaring independence. **India** and **Pakistan** became independent of Britain in 1947, and numerous African and Asian colonies declared independence as well. This period of **decolonization** lasted into the 1960s. Some colonies moved successfully into independence, but many, especially in Africa and Asia, struggled to create stable governments and economies and suffered from ethnic and religious conflicts, some of which continue today.

FACTORS AND SHIFTS IN POWER THAT LED TO THE KOREAN WAR

In 1910, Japan annexed Korea and maintained this control until 1945. After WWII, Soviet and US troops occupied Korea, with the **Soviet Union** controlling North Korea and the **US** controlling South Korea. In 1947, the UN ordered elections in Korea to unify the country, but the Soviet Union refused to allow them to take place in North Korea, instead setting up a communist government. In 1950, the US withdrew troops, and the North Korean troops moved to invade South Korea. The **Korean War** was the first war in which the UN—or any international organization—played a major role. The US, Australia, Canada, France, Netherlands, Great Britain, Turkey, China, the USSR, and other countries sent troops at various times, for both sides, throughout the war. In 1953, the war ended in a truce, but no peace agreement was ever achieved, and Korea remains divided.

EVENTS THAT LED TO THE VIETNAM WAR

Vietnam had previously been part of a French colony called French Indochina. The **Vietnam War** began with the **First Indochina War** from 1946 to 1954, in which France battled with the Democratic Republic of Vietnam, ruled by Ho Chi Minh.

In 1954, a siege at Dien Bien Phu ended in a Vietnamese victory. Vietnam was then divided into North and South, much like Korea. Communist forces controlled the North, and the South was controlled by South Vietnamese forces, supported by the US. Conflict ensued, leading to another war. US troops eventually led the fight, in support of South Vietnam. The war became a major political issue in the US, with many citizens protesting American involvement. In 1975, South Vietnam surrendered, and Vietnam became the **Socialist Republic of Vietnam**.

GLOBALISM

In the modern era, globalism has emerged as a popular political ideology. **Globalism** is based on the idea that all people and all nations are **interdependent**. Each nation is dependent on one or more other nations for production of and markets for goods, and for income generation. Today's ease of international travel and communication, including technological advances such as the airplane, has heightened this sense of interdependence. The global economy and the general idea of globalism have shaped many economic and political choices since the beginning of the 20th century. Many of today's issues, including environmental awareness, economic struggles, and continued warfare, often require the cooperation of many countries if they are to be dealt with effectively.

EFFECT OF GLOBALIZATION ON THE WAY COUNTRIES INTERACT WITH EACH OTHER

Countries worldwide often seek the same resources, leading to high demand, particularly for **nonrenewable resources**. This can result in heavy fluctuations in price. One major example is the demand for petroleum products such as oil and natural gas. Increased travel and communication make it possible to deal with diseases in remote locations; however, this also allows diseases to be spread via travelers.

A major factor contributing to increased globalization over the past few decades has been the **internet**. By allowing instantaneous communication with anyone nearly anywhere on the globe, the

Copyright © Mometrix Media. You have been licensed one copy of this document for personal use only. Any other reproduction or redistribution is strictly prohibited. All rights reserved.

internet has led to interaction between far-flung individuals and countries, and an ever-increasing awareness of events all over the world.

Review Video: Globalization
Visit mometrix.com/academy and enter code: 551962

ROLE OF THE MIDDLE EAST IN INTERNATIONAL RELATIONS AND ECONOMICS

The location on the globe, with ease of access to Europe and Asia, and its preponderance of oil deposits, makes the **Middle Eastern countries** crucial in many international issues, both diplomatic and economic. Because of its central location, the Middle East has been a hotbed for violence since before the beginning of recorded history. Conflicts over land, resources, and religious and political power continue in the area today, spurred by conflict over control of the area's vast oil fields as well as over territories that have been disputed for thousands of years.

MAJOR OCCURRENCES OF GENOCIDE IN MODERN HISTORY

The three major occurrences of genocide in modern history other than the Holocaust are:

- **Armenian genocide**—from 1914 to 1918, the Young Turks, heirs to the Ottoman Empire, slaughtered between 800,000 and 1.5 million Armenians. This constituted approximately half of the Armenian population at the time.
- **Russian purges under Stalin**—scholars have attributed deaths between 3 and 60 million, both directly and indirectly, to the policies and edicts of Joseph Stalin's regime. The deaths took place from 1921 to 1953, when Stalin died. In recent years, many scholars have settled on a number of deaths near 20 million, but this is still disputed today.
- **Rwandan genocide**—in 1994, hundreds of thousands of Tutsi, as well as Hutu who sympathized with them, were slaughtered during the Rwandan Civil War. The UN did not act or authorize intervention during these atrocities.

Copyright © Mometrix Media. You have been licensed one copy of this document for personal use only. Any other reproduction or redistribution is strictly prohibited. All rights reserved.

Geography

Geography

GEOGRAPHY

Geography is the study of Earth. Geographers study **physical characteristics** of Earth as well as man-made borders and boundaries. They also study the **distribution of life** on the planet, such as where certain species of animals can be found or how different forms of life interact. Major elements of the study of geography include:

- Locations
- Regional characteristics
- Spatial relations
- Natural and man-made forces that change elements of Earth

These elements are studied from regional, topical, physical, and human perspectives. Geography also focuses on the origins of Earth, as well as the history and backgrounds of different human populations.

PHYSICAL VS. CULTURAL GEOGRAPHY

Physical geography is the study of the physical characteristics of Earth: how they relate to each other, how they were formed, and how they develop. These characteristics include climate, land, and water, and also how they affect human population in various areas. Different landforms, in combination with various climates and other conditions, determine the characteristics of various cultures.

Cultural geography is the study of how the various aspects of physical geography affect individual cultures. Cultural geography also compares various cultures: how their lifestyles and customs are affected by their geographical location, climate, and other factors, as well as how they interact with their environment.

> **Review Video: Regional Geography**
> Visit mometrix.com/academy and enter code: 350378

DIVISIONS OF GEOGRAPHICAL STUDY AND TOOLS USED

The four divisions of geographical study and tools used are:

- **Topical**—the study of a single feature of Earth or one specific human activity that occurs worldwide.
- **Physical**—the various physical features of Earth, how they are created, the forces that change them, and how they are related to each other and to various human activities.
- **Regional**—specific characteristics of individual places and regions.
- **Human**—how human activity affects the environment. This includes the study of political, historical, social, and cultural activities.

Tools used in geographical study include special research methods like mapping, field studies, statistics, interviews, mathematics, and the use of various scientific instruments.

Copyright © Mometrix Media. You have been licensed one copy of this document for personal use only. Any other reproduction or redistribution is strictly prohibited. All rights reserved.

IMPORTANT ANCIENT GEOGRAPHERS

The following are three important ancient geographers and their contributions to the study of geography:

- **Eratosthenes** lived in ancient Greek times and mathematically calculated the circumference of Earth and the tilt of Earth's axis. He also created the first map of the world.
- **Strabo** wrote a description of the ancient world called *Geographica* in seventeen volumes.
- **Ptolemy**, primarily an astronomer, was an experienced mapmaker. He wrote a treatise entitled *Geography*, which was used by Christopher Columbus in his travels.

WAYS GEOGRAPHERS ANALYZE AREAS OF HUMAN POPULATION

In cities, towns, or other areas where many people have settled, geographers focus on the **distribution** of populations, neighborhoods, industrial areas, transportation, and other elements important to the society in question. For example, they would map out the locations of hospitals, airports, factories, police stations, schools, and housing groups. They would also make note of how these facilities are distributed in relation to the areas of habitation, such as the number of schools in a certain neighborhood or how many grocery stores are located in a specific suburban area. Another area of study and discussion is the distribution of **towns** themselves, from widely spaced rural towns to large cities that merge into each other to form a megalopolis.

ROLE OF A CARTOGRAPHER

A cartographer is a mapmaker. Mapmakers produce detailed illustrations of geographic areas to record where various features are located within that area. These illustrations can be compiled into maps, charts, graphs, and even globes. When constructing maps, **cartographers** must take into account the problem of **distortion**. Because Earth is round, a flat map does not accurately represent the correct proportions, especially if a very large geographical area is being depicted. Maps must be designed in such a way as to minimize this distortion and maximize accuracy. Accurately representing Earth's features on a flat surface is achieved through **projection**.

TYPES OF PROJECTION USED IN CREATING WORLD MAPS

The three major types of projection used in creating world maps are:

- **Cylindrical projection**—this is created by wrapping the globe of Earth in a cylindrical piece of paper, then using a light to project the globe onto the paper. The largest distortion occurs at the outermost edges.
- **Conical projection**—the paper is shaped like a cone and contacts the globe only at the cone's base. This type of projection is most useful for middle latitudes.
- **Flat-Plane projections**—also known as a gnomonic projection, this type of map is projected onto a flat piece of paper that only touches the globe at a single point. Flat-plane projections make it possible to map out Great-Circle routes, or the shortest route between one point and another on the globe, as a straight line.

SPECIFIC TYPES OF MAP PROJECTIONS

Four specific types of map projections that are commonly used today are:

- **Winkel tripel projection**—this is the most common projection used for world maps since it was accepted in 1998 by the National Geographic Society as a standard. The Winkel tripel projection balances size and shape, greatly reducing distortion.
- **Robinson projection**—east and west sections of the map are less distorted, but continental shapes are somewhat inaccurate.

Copyright © Mometrix Media. You have been licensed one copy of this document for personal use only. Any other reproduction or redistribution is strictly prohibited. All rights reserved.

- **Goode homolosine projection**—sizes and shapes are accurate, but distances are not. This projection basically represents a globe that has been cut into connected sections so that it can lie flat.
- **Mercator projection**—though distortion is high, particularly in areas farther from the equator, this cylindrical projection is commonly used by seafarers.

MAJOR ELEMENTS OF ANY MAP

The five major elements of any map are:

- **Title**—this tells basic information about the map, such as the area represented.
- **Legend**—also known as the key, the legend explains what symbols used on a particular map represent, such as symbols for major landmarks.
- **Grid**—this most commonly represents the geographic grid system, or latitude and longitude marks used to precisely locate specific locations.
- **Directions**—a compass rose or other symbol is used to indicate the cardinal directions.
- **Scale**—this shows the relation between a certain distance on the map and the actual distance. For example, one inch might represent one mile, or ten miles, or even more, depending on the size of the map.

> **Review Video: 5 Elements of Any Map**
> Visit mometrix.com/academy and enter code: 437727

EQUAL-AREA MAPS VS. CONFORMAL MAPS

An equal-area map is designed such that the proportional sizes of various areas are accurate. For example, if one landmass is one-fifth the size of another, the lines on the map will be shifted to accommodate for distortion so that the proportional size is accurate. In many maps, areas farther from the equator are greatly distorted; this type of map compensates for this phenomenon. A **conformal map** focuses on representing the correct shape of geographical areas, with less concern for comparative size.

CONSISTENT SCALE MAPS AND THEMATIC MAPS

With a consistent scale map, the same scale, such as one inch being equal to ten miles, is used throughout the entire map. This is most often used for maps of smaller areas, as maps that cover larger areas, such as the full globe, must make allowances for distortion. Maps of very large areas often make use of more than one scale, with scales closer to the center representing a larger area than those at the edges.

A **thematic map** is constructed to show very specific information about a chosen theme. For example, a thematic map might represent political information, such as how votes were distributed in an election, or could show population distribution or climatic features.

RELIEF MAPS

A relief map is constructed to show details of various **elevations** across the area of the map. Higher elevations are represented by different colors than lower elevations. **Relief maps** often also show additional details, such as the overall ruggedness or smoothness of an area. Mountains would be represented as ridged and rugged, while deserts would be shown as smooth.

Elevation in relief maps can also be represented by contour lines, or lines that connect points of the same elevation. Some relief maps even feature textures, reconstructing details in a sort of miniature model.

Copyright © Mometrix Media. You have been licensed one copy of this document for personal use only. Any other reproduction or redistribution is strictly prohibited. All rights reserved.

GEOGRAPHICAL FEATURES

- **Mountains** are elevated areas that measure 2,000 feet or more above sea level. Often steep and rugged, they usually occur in groups called chains or ranges. Six of the seven continents on Earth contain at least one range.
- **Hills** are of lower elevation than mountains, at about 500-2,000 feet. Hills are usually more rounded and are found throughout every continent.
- **Plains** are large, flat areas and are usually very fertile. The majority of Earth's population is supported by crops grown on vast plains.
- **Valleys** lie between hills and mountains. Depending on their location, their specific features can vary greatly, from fertile and habitable to rugged and inhospitable.
- **Plateaus** are elevated, but flat on top. Some plateaus are extremely dry, such as the Kenya Plateau, because surrounding mountains prevent them from receiving moisture.
- **Deserts** receive less than ten inches of rain per year. They are usually large areas, such as the Sahara Desert in Africa or the Australian Outback.
- **Deltas** occur at river mouths. Because the rivers carry sediment to the deltas, these areas are often very fertile.
- **Mesas** are flat, steep-sided mountains or hills. The term is sometimes used to refer to plateaus.
- **Basins** are areas of low elevation where rivers drain.
- **Foothills** are the transitional area between plains and mountains, usually consisting of hills that gradually increase in size as they approach a mountain range.
- **Marshes** and **swamps** are also lowlands, but they are very wet and largely covered in vegetation such as reeds and rushes.

GEOGRAPHICAL TERMS REFERRING TO BODIES OF WATER

- The **ocean** refers to the salt water that covers about two-thirds of Earth's surface.
- **Ocean basins** are named portions of the ocean. The five major ocean basins are the Atlantic, Pacific, Indian, Southern, and Arctic.
- **Seas** are generally also salt water, but are smaller than ocean basins and surrounded by land. Examples include the Mediterranean Sea, the Caribbean Sea, and the Caspian Sea.
- **Lakes** are bodies of fresh water found inland. Sixty percent of all lakes are located in Canada.
- **Rivers** are moving bodies of water that flow from higher elevations to lower. They usually start as rivulets or streams and grow until they finally empty into a sea or the ocean.
- **Canals**, such as the Panama Canal and the Suez Canal, are man-made waterways connecting two large bodies of water.

HOW COMMUNITIES DEVELOP

Communities, or groups of people who settle together in a specific area, typically gather where certain conditions exist. These conditions include:

- Easy access to resources such as food, water, and raw materials
- Ability to easily transport raw materials and goods, such as access to a waterway
- Room to house a sufficient workforce

People also tend to form groups with others who are similar to them. In a typical **community**, people can be found who share values, a common language, and common or similar cultural characteristics and religious beliefs. These factors will determine the overall composition of a community as it develops.

Copyright © Mometrix Media. You have been licensed one copy of this document for personal use only. Any other reproduction or redistribution is strictly prohibited. All rights reserved.

DIFFERENCES BETWEEN CITIES IN VARIOUS AREAS OF THE WORLD

Cities develop and grow as an area develops. Modern statistics show that over half of the world's people live in **cities**. That percentage is even higher in developed areas of the globe. Cities are currently growing more quickly in developing regions, and even established cities continue to experience growth throughout the world. In developing or developed areas, cities often are surrounded by a metropolitan area made up of both urban and suburban sections. In some places, cities have merged into each other and become a **megalopolis**—a single, huge city.

Cities develop differently in different areas of the world. The area available for cities to grow, as well as cultural and economic forces, drives how cities develop. For example, North American cities tend to cover wider areas. European cities tend to have better-developed transportation systems. In Latin America, the richest inhabitants can be found in the city centers, while in North America, wealthier inhabitants tend to live in suburban areas.

In other parts of the world, transportation and communication between cities are less developed. Technological innovations such as the cell phone have increased communication even in these areas. Urban areas must also maintain communication with rural areas in order to procure food, resources, and raw materials that cannot be produced within the city limits.

WEATHER VS. CLIMATE

Weather and climate are physical systems that affect geography. Though they deal with similar information, the way this information is measured and compiled is different.

Weather involves daily conditions in the atmosphere that affect temperature, precipitation (rain, snow, hail, or sleet), wind speed, air pressure, and other factors. Weather focuses on the short-term—what the conditions will be today, tomorrow, or over the next few days.

In contrast, **climate** aggregates information about daily and seasonal weather conditions in a region over a long period of time. The climate takes into account average monthly and yearly temperatures, average precipitation over long periods of time, and the growing season of an area. Climates are classified according to latitude, or how close they lie to Earth's equator. The three major divisions are:

- **Low Latitudes**, lying from 0 to approximately 23.5 degrees
- **Middle Latitudes**, found from approximately 23.5 to 66.5 degrees
- **High Latitudes**, found from approximately 66.5 degrees to the poles

> **Review Video: Climates**
> Visit mometrix.com/academy and enter code: 991320

CLIMATES FOUND IN THE LOW LATITUDES

Rainforests, savannas, and deserts occur in low latitudes:

- **Rainforest** climates, near the equator, experience high average temperatures and humidity, as well as relatively high rainfall.
- **Savannas** are found on either side of the rainforest region. Mostly grasslands, they typically experience dry winters and wet summers.
- Beyond the savannas lie the **desert** regions, with hot, dry climates, sparse rainfall, and temperature fluctuations of up to fifty degrees from day to night.

Copyright © Mometrix Media. You have been licensed one copy of this document for personal use only. Any other reproduction or redistribution is strictly prohibited. All rights reserved.

CLIMATE REGIONS FOUND IN THE MIDDLE LATITUDES

The climate regions found in the middle latitudes are:

- **Mediterranean**—the Mediterranean climate occurs between 30- and 40-degrees latitude, both north and south, on the western coasts of continents. Characteristics include a year-long growing season; hot, dry summers followed by mild winters; and sparse rainfall that occurs mostly during the winter months.
- **Humid-subtropical**—humid-subtropical regions are located in southeastern coastal areas. Winds that blow in over warm ocean currents produce long summers, mild winters, and a long growing season. These areas are highly productive and support a larger part of Earth's population than any other climate.
- **Humid-continental**—the humid continental climate produces the familiar four seasons typical of a good portion of the US. Some of the most productive farmlands in the world lie in these climates. Winters are cold, and summers are hot and humid.

MARINE, STEPPE, AND DESERT CLIMATES

The climate regions found in the middle latitudes are:

- **Marine**—marine climates are found near water or on islands. Ocean winds help make these areas mild and rainy. Summers are cooler than humid-subtropical summers, but winters also bring milder temperatures due to the warmth of the ocean winds.
- **Steppe**—steppe climates, or prairie climates, are found far inland on large continents. Summers are hot and winters are cold, but rainfall is sparser than in continental climates.
- **Desert**—desert climates occur where steppe climates receive even less rainfall. Examples include the Gobi Desert in Asia as well as desert areas of Australia and the southwestern US.

CLIMATES FOUND IN THE HIGH LATITUDES

The high latitudes consist of two major climate areas, the tundra and taiga:

- **Tundra** means "marshy plain." The ground is frozen throughout long, cold winters, but there is little snowfall. During the short summers, it becomes wet and marshy. Tundras are not amenable to crops, but many plants and animals have adapted to the conditions.
- **Taigas** lie south of tundra regions and include the largest forest areas in the world, as well as swamps and marshes. Large mineral deposits exist here, as well as many animals valued for their fur. In the winter, taiga regions are colder than the tundra, and summers are hotter. The growing season is short.

A **vertical climate** exists in high mountain ranges. Increasing elevation leads to varying temperatures, growing conditions, types of vegetation and animals, and occurrence of human habitation, often encompassing elements of various other climate regions.

FACTORS AFFECTING CLIMATE

Because Earth is tilted, its **rotation** brings about changes in **seasons**. Regions closer to the equator, and those nearest the poles, experience very little change in seasonal temperatures. Mid-range latitudes are most likely to experience distinct seasons. Large bodies of water also affect climate. Ocean currents and wind patterns can change the climate for an area that lies in a typically cold latitude, such as England, to a much more temperate climate. Mountains can affect both short-term weather and long-term climates. Some deserts occur because precipitation is stopped by the wall of a mountain range.

Copyright © Mometrix Media. You have been licensed one copy of this document for personal use only. Any other reproduction or redistribution is strictly prohibited. All rights reserved.

Over time, established **climate patterns** can shift and change. While the issue is hotly debated, it has been theorized that human activity has also led to climate change.

EFFECT OF HUMAN SYSTEMS
HUMAN SYSTEMS THAT GEOGRAPHERS INCORPORATE INTO THE STUDY OF EARTH

Human systems affect geography in the way in which they settle, form groups that grow into large-scale habitations, and even create permanent changes in the landscape. **Geographers** study movements of people, how they distribute goods among each other and to other settlements or cultures, and how ideas grow and spread. Migrations, wars, forced relocations, and trade can all spread cultural ideas, language, goods, and other practices to widespread areas. Throughout history, cultures have been changed due to a wide range of events, including major migrations and the conquering of one people by another. In addition, **human systems** can lead to various conflicts or alliances to control access to and the use of natural resources.

HUMAN SYSTEMS THAT FORM THE BASIS OF CULTURES IN NORTH AMERICA

North America consists of 23 countries, including (in decreasing population order) the United States of America, Mexico, Canada, Guatemala, Cuba, Haiti, and the Dominican Republic. The US and Canada support similarly diverse cultures, as both were formed from groups of native races and large numbers of immigrants. Many **North American cultures** come from a mixture of indigenous and colonial European influences. Agriculture is important to North American countries, while service industries and technology also play a large part in the economy. On average, North America supports a high standard of living and a high level of development and supports trade with countries throughout the world.

HUMAN SYSTEMS THAT SHAPE SOUTH AMERICA

Home to twelve sovereign states, including Brazil (largest in area and population), Colombia, Argentina, Venezuela, and Peru; two independent territories; and one internal territory, **South America** is largely defined by its prevailing languages. The majority of countries in South America speak Spanish or Portuguese. Most of South America has experienced a similar history, having been originally dominated by Native cultures and then conquered by European nations. The countries of South America have since gained independence, but there is a wide disparity between various countries' economic and political factors. Most South American countries rely on only one or two exports, usually agricultural, with suitable lands often controlled by rich families. Most societies in South America feature major separations between classes, both economically and socially. Challenges faced by developing South American countries include geographical limitations, economic issues, and sustainable development, including the need to preserve the existing rainforests.

HUMAN SYSTEMS INFLUENCING EUROPE

Europe contains a wide variety of cultures, ethnic groups, physical geographical features, climates, and resources, all of which have influenced the distribution of its varied population. **Europe**, in general, is industrialized and developed, with cultural differences giving each individual country its own unique characteristics. Greek and Roman influences played a major role in European culture, as did Christianity. European countries spread their beliefs and cultural elements throughout the world by means of migration and colonization. They have had a significant influence on nearly every other continent in the world. While Western Europe has been largely democratic, Eastern Europe functioned under communist rule for many years. The formation of the European Union (EU) in 1993 has increased stability and positive diplomatic relations among European nations. Like other industrialized regions, Europe is now focusing on various environmental issues.

Copyright © Mometrix Media. You have been licensed one copy of this document for personal use only. Any other reproduction or redistribution is strictly prohibited. All rights reserved.

HUMAN SYSTEMS THAT HAVE SHAPED RUSSIA

After numerous conflicts, Russia became a Communist state, known as the **USSR**. With the collapse of the USSR in 1991, the country has struggled in its transition to a market-driven economy. Attempts to build a workable system have led to the destruction of natural resources as well as problems with nuclear power, including accidents such as Chernobyl. To complete the transition to a market economy, Russia would need to improve its transportation and communication systems and find a way to more efficiently use its natural resources.

The population of Russia is not distributed evenly, with three-quarters of the population living west of the Ural Mountains. The people of Russia encompass over a hundred different ethnic groups. Over eighty percent of the population is ethnically Russian, and Russian is the official language of the country.

HUMAN SYSTEMS THAT HAVE SHAPED NORTH AFRICA AND SOUTHWEST AND CENTRAL ASIA

The largely desert climate of these areas has led most population centers to rise around sources of **water**, such as the Nile River. This area is the home of the **earliest known civilizations** and the origin of Christianity, Judaism, and Islam. After serving as the site of huge, independent civilizations in ancient times, North Africa and Southwest and Central Asia were largely parceled out as **European colonies** during the 18th and 19th centuries. The beginning of the 20th century saw many of these countries gain their independence. **Islam** has served as a unifying force for large portions of these areas, and many of the inhabitants speak Arabic. In spite of the arid climate, agriculture is a large business, but the most valuable resource is **oil**. Centuries of conflict throughout this area have led to ongoing political problems. These political problems have also contributed to environmental issues.

HUMAN SYSTEMS THAT SHAPE AND INFLUENCE THE CULTURE OF SUB-SAHARAN AFRICA

South of the Sahara Desert, **Africa** is divided into a number of culturally diverse nations. The inhabitants are unevenly distributed due to geographical limitations that prevent settlement in vast areas. **AIDS** has become a major plague throughout this part of Africa, killing millions, largely due to restrictive beliefs that prevent education about the disease, as well as abject poverty and unsettled political situations that make it impossible to manage the pandemic. The population of this area of Africa is widely diverse due to extensive **migration**. Many of the people still rely on **subsistence farming** for their welfare. Starvation and poverty are rampant due to drought and political instability. Some areas are far more stable than others due to the greater availability of resources. These areas have been able to begin the process of **industrialization**.

HUMAN SYSTEMS THAT DETERMINE THE CULTURAL MAKEUP OF SOUTH ASIA

South Asia is home to one of the first human civilizations, which grew up in the **Indus River Valley**. With a great deal of disparity between rural and urban life, South Asia has much to do to improve the quality of life for its lower classes. Two major religions, **Hinduism** and **Buddhism**, have their origins in this region. Parts of South Asia, most notably India, were subject to **British rule** for several decades and are still working to improve independent governments and social systems. Overall, South Asia is very culturally diverse, with a wide mix of religions and languages throughout. Many individuals are **farmers**, but a growing number have found prosperity in the spread of **high-tech industries**. Industrialization is growing in South Asia but continues to face environmental, social, religious, and economic challenges.

HUMAN SYSTEMS SHAPING THE CULTURE OF EAST ASIA

Governments in East Asia are varied, ranging from communist to democratic governments, with some governments that mix both approaches. **Isolationism** throughout the area limited the

Copyright © Mometrix Media. You have been licensed one copy of this document for personal use only. Any other reproduction or redistribution is strictly prohibited. All rights reserved.

countries' contact with other nations until the early 20th century. The unevenly distributed population of East Asia consists of over one and a half billion people with widely diverse ethnic backgrounds, religions, and languages. More residents live in **urban** areas than in **rural** areas, creating shortages of farmworkers at times. Japan, Taiwan, and South Korea are overall more urban, while China and Mongolia are more rural. Japan stands as the most industrial country in East Asia. Some areas of East Asia are suffering from major environmental issues. Japan has dealt with many of these problems and now has some of the strictest environmental laws in the world.

HUMAN SYSTEMS THAT HAVE INFLUENCED SOUTHEAST ASIA

Much of Southeast Asia was **colonized** by European countries during the 18th and 19th centuries, with the exception of Siam, now known as Thailand. All Southeast Asian countries are now independent, but the 20th century saw numerous conflicts between **communist** and **democratic** forces.

Southeast Asia has been heavily influenced by both Buddhist and Muslim religions. Industrialization is growing, with the population moving in large numbers from rural to urban areas. Some have moved to avoid conflict, oppression, and poverty.

Natural disasters, including volcanoes, typhoons, and flash flooding, are fairly common in Southeast Asia, creating extensive economic damage and societal disruption.

HUMAN SYSTEMS THAT AFFECT THE DEVELOPMENT AND CULTURE OF AUSTRALIA, OCEANA, AND ANTARCTICA

South Pacific cultures originally migrated from Southeast Asia, creating hunter-gatherer or sometimes settled agricultural communities. **European** countries moved in during later centuries, seeking the plentiful natural resources of the area. Today, some South Pacific islands remain under the control of foreign governments, and culture in these areas mixes modern, industrialized society with indigenous culture. Population is unevenly distributed, largely due to the inhabitability of many parts of the South Pacific, such as the extremely hot desert areas of Australia. **Agriculture** still drives much of the economy, with **tourism** growing. **Antarctica** remains the only continent that has not been claimed by any country. There are no permanent human habitations in Antarctica, but scientists and explorers visit the area on a temporary basis.

HUMAN-ENVIRONMENT INTERACTION

Geography also studies the ways people interact with, use, and change their **environment**. The effects, reasons, and consequences of these changes are studied, as are the ways the environment limits or influences human behavior. This kind of study can help determine the best course of action when a nation or group of people is considering making changes to the environment, such as building a dam or removing natural landscape to build or expand roads. Study of the **consequences** can help determine if these actions are manageable and how long-term, detrimental results can be mitigated.

PHYSICAL GEOGRAPHY AND CLIMATES
PHYSICAL GEOGRAPHY AND CLIMATE OF NORTH AMERICA

Together, the US and Canada make up the majority of North America and both have a similar distribution of geographical features: mountain ranges in both the east and the west, stretches of fertile plains through the center, and lakes and waterways. Both areas were shaped by **glaciers**, which also deposited highly fertile soil. Because they are so large, Canada and the US experience several varieties of **climate**, including continental climates with four seasons in median areas,

Copyright © Mometrix Media. You have been licensed one copy of this document for personal use only. Any other reproduction or redistribution is strictly prohibited. All rights reserved.

tropical climates in the southern part of the US, and arctic climes in the far north. The remaining area of North America includes Mexico, Central America, the Caribbean Isles, and Greenland.

PHYSICAL GEOGRAPHY AND CLIMATE OF SOUTH AMERICA

South America contains a wide variety of geographical features, including high **mountains** such as the Andes, wide **plains**, and high-altitude **plateaus**. The region contains numerous natural resources, but many of them have remained unused due to various obstacles, including political issues, geographic barriers, and lack of sufficient economic power. Climate zones in South America are largely **tropical**, with rainforests and savannas, but vertical climate zones and grasslands also exist in some places.

PHYSICAL GEOGRAPHY AND CLIMATE OF EUROPE

Europe spans a wide area with a variety of climate zones. In the east and south are **mountain** ranges, while the north is dominated by a **plains** region. The long coastline and the island nature of some countries, such as Britain, mean the climate is often warmer than other lands at similar latitudes, as the area is warmed by **ocean currents**. Many areas of western Europe have a moderate climate, while areas of the south are dominated by the classic Mediterranean climate. Europe carries a high level of natural resources. Numerous waterways help connect the inner regions with the coastal areas. Much of Europe is **industrialized**, and **agriculture** has been developed for thousands of years.

PHYSICAL GEOGRAPHY AND CLIMATE OF RUSSIA

Russia's area encompasses part of Asia and Europe. From the standpoint of square footage alone, **Russia** is the largest country in the world. Due to its size, Russia encompasses a wide variety of climatic regions, including **plains**, **plateaus**, **mountains**, and **tundra**.

Russia's **climate** can be quite harsh, with rivers that are frozen most of the year, making transportation of the country's rich natural resources more difficult. Siberia, in northern Russia, is dominated by **permafrost**. Native peoples in this area still follow a hunting and gathering lifestyle, living in portable yurts and subsisting largely on herds of reindeer or caribou. Other areas include taiga with extensive, dense woods in north-central Russia and more temperate steppes and grasslands in the southwest.

PHYSICAL GEOGRAPHY AND CLIMATE OF NORTH AFRICA, SOUTHWEST, AND CENTRAL ASIA

This area of the world is complex in its geographical structure and climate, incorporating seas, peninsulas, rivers, mountains, and numerous other features. **Earthquakes** are common, with tectonic plates in the area remaining active. Much of the world's **oil** lies in this area. The tendency of the large rivers of North Africa, especially the Nile, to follow a set pattern of **drought** and extreme **fertility**, led people to settle there from prehistoric times. As technology has advanced, people have tamed this river, making its activity more predictable and the land around it more productive. The extremely arid nature of many other parts of this area has also led to **human intervention** such as irrigation to increase agricultural production.

PHYSICAL GEOGRAPHY AND CLIMATE OF THE SOUTHERN PORTION OF AFRICA

South of the Sahara Desert, the high elevations and other geographical characteristics have made it very difficult for human travel or settlement to occur. The geography of the area is dominated by a series of **plateaus**. There are also mountain ranges and a large rift valley in the eastern part of the country. Contrasting the wide desert areas, sub-Saharan Africa contains numerous lakes, rivers, and world-famous waterfalls. The area has **tropical** climates, including rainforests, savannas, steppes, and desert areas. The main natural resources are minerals, including gems and water.

Copyright © Mometrix Media. You have been licensed one copy of this document for personal use only. Any other reproduction or redistribution is strictly prohibited. All rights reserved.

PHYSICAL GEOGRAPHY AND CLIMATE OF SOUTH ASIA

The longest **alluvial plain**, a plain caused by shifting floodplains of major rivers and river systems over time, exists in South Asia. South Asia boasts three major **river systems** in the Ganges, Indus, and Brahmaputra. It also has large deposits of **minerals**, including iron ore that is in great demand internationally. South Asia holds mountains, plains, plateaus, and numerous islands. The climates range from tropical to highlands and desert areas. South Asia also experiences monsoon winds that cause a long rainy season. Variations in climate, elevation, and human activity influence agricultural production.

GEOGRAPHY AND CLIMATE OF EAST ASIA

East Asia includes North and South Korea, Mongolia, China, Japan, and Taiwan. Mineral resources are plentiful but not evenly distributed throughout. The coastlines are long, and while the population is large, farmlands are sparse. As a result, the surrounding ocean has become a major source of sustenance. East Asia is large enough to encompass several climate regions. **Ocean currents** provide milder climates to coastal areas, while **monsoons** provide the majority of the rainfall for the region. **Typhoons** are somewhat common, as are **earthquakes**, **volcanoes**, and **tsunamis**. The latter occur because of the tectonic plates that meet beneath the continent and remain somewhat active.

GEOGRAPHY AND CLIMATE OF SOUTHEAST ASIA

Southeast Asia lies largely on the **equator**, and roughly half of the countries of the region are island nations. These countries include Indonesia, the Philippines, Vietnam, Thailand, Myanmar, and Malaysia (which is partially on the mainland and partially an island country). The island nations of Southeast Asia feature mountains that are considered part of the **Ring of Fire**, an area where tectonic plates remain active, leading to extensive volcanic activity as well as earthquakes and tsunamis. Southeast Asia boasts many rivers and abundant natural resources, including gems, fossil fuels, and minerals. There are basically two seasons: wet and dry. The wet season arrives with the **monsoons**. In general, Southeast Asia consists of **tropical rainforest climates**, but there are some mountain areas and tropical savannas.

GEOGRAPHY AND CLIMATE OF AUSTRALIA, OCEANIA, AND ANTARCTICA

In the far southern hemisphere of the globe, Australia and Oceania present their own climatic combinations. **Australia**, the only island on Earth that is also a continent, has extensive deserts as well as mountains and lowlands. The economy is driven by agriculture, including ranches and farms, and minerals. While the steppes bordering extremely arid inland areas are suitable for livestock, only the coastal areas receive sufficient rainfall for crops without using irrigation. **Oceania** refers to over 10,000 Pacific islands created by volcanic activity. Most of these have tropical climates with wet and dry seasons. **New Zealand**, Australia's nearest neighbor, boasts rich forests, mountain ranges, and relatively moderate temperatures, including rainfall throughout the year. **Antarctica** is covered with ice. Its major resource consists of scientific information. It supports some wildlife, such as penguins, and little vegetation, primarily mosses or lichens.

THEORY OF PLATE TECTONICS

According to the geological theory of plate tectonics, Earth's crust is made up of ten major and several minor **tectonic plates**. These plates are the solid areas of the crust. They float on top of Earth's mantle, which is made up of molten rock. Because the plates float on this liquid component of Earth's crust, they move, creating major changes in Earth's surface. These changes can happen very slowly over a long time period, such as in continental drift, or rapidly, such as when earthquakes occur. **Interaction** between the different continental plates can create mountain ranges, volcanic activity, major earthquakes, and deep rifts.

Copyright © Mometrix Media. You have been licensed one copy of this document for personal use only. Any other reproduction or redistribution is strictly prohibited. All rights reserved.

TYPES OF PLATE BOUNDARIES

Plate tectonics defines three types of plate boundaries, determined by how the edges of the plates interact. These **plate boundaries** are:

- **Convergent boundaries**—the bordering plates move toward one another. When they collide directly, this is known as continental collision, which can create very large, high mountain ranges such as the Himalayas and the Andes. If one plate slides under the other, this is called subduction. Subduction can lead to intense volcanic activity. One example is the Ring of Fire that lies along the northern Pacific coastlines.
- **Divergent boundaries**—plates move away from each other. This movement leads to rifts such as the Mid-Atlantic Ridge and East Africa's Great Rift Valley.
- **Transform boundaries**—plate boundaries slide in opposite directions against each other. Intense pressure builds up along transform boundaries as the plates grind along each other's edges, leading to earthquakes. Many major fault lines, including the San Andreas Fault, lie along transform boundaries.

EROSION, WEATHERING, TRANSPORTATION, AND DEPOSITION

Erosion involves movement of any loose material on Earth's surface. This can include soil, sand, or rock fragments. These loose fragments can be displaced by natural forces such as wind, water, ice, plant cover, and human factors. **Mechanical erosion** occurs due to natural forces. **Chemical erosion** occurs as a result of human intervention and activities. **Weathering** occurs when atmospheric elements affect Earth's surface. Water, heat, ice, and pressure all lead to weathering. **Transportation** refers to loose material being moved by wind, water, or ice. Glacial movement, for example, carries everything from pebbles to boulders, sometimes over long distances. **Deposition** is the result of transportation. When material is transported, it is eventually deposited, and builds up to create formations like moraines and sand dunes.

EFFECTS OF HUMAN INTERACTION AND CONFLICT ON GEOGRAPHICAL BOUNDARIES

Human societies and their interaction have led to divisions of territories into **countries** and various other subdivisions. While these divisions are at their root artificial, they are important to geographers in discussing various populations' interactions.

Geographical divisions often occur through conflict between different human populations. The reasons behind these divisions include:

- Control of resources
- Control of important trade routes
- Control of populations

Conflict often occurs due to religious, political, language, or race differences. Natural resources are finite and so often lead to conflict over how they are distributed among populations.

STATE SOVEREIGNTY

State sovereignty recognizes the division of geographical areas into areas controlled by various governments or groups of people. These groups control not only the territory but also all its natural resources and the inhabitants of the area. The entire planet Earth is divided into **political** or **administratively sovereign areas** recognized to be controlled by a particular government, with the exception of the continent of Antarctica.

Copyright © Mometrix Media. You have been licensed one copy of this document for personal use only. Any other reproduction or redistribution is strictly prohibited. All rights reserved.

ALLIANCES

Alliances form between different countries based on similar interests, political goals, cultural values, or military issues. Six existing **international alliances** include:

- North Atlantic Treaty Organization (NATO)
- Common Market
- European Union (EU)
- United Nations (UN)
- Caribbean Community
- Council of Arab Economic Unity

In addition, very large **companies** and **multi-national corporations** can create alliances and various kinds of competition based on the need to control resources, production, and the overall marketplace.

WAYS AGRICULTURAL REVOLUTION CHANGED SOCIETY

The agricultural revolution began approximately 6,000 years ago when the **plow** was invented in **Mesopotamia**. Using a plow drawn by animals, people were able to cultivate crops in large quantities rather than gathering available seeds and grains and planting them by hand. Because large-scale agriculture was labor-intensive, this led to the development of stable communities where people gathered to make farming possible. As **stable farming communities** replaced groups of nomadic hunter-gatherers, human society underwent profound changes. Societies became dependent on limited numbers of crops as well as subject to the vagaries of weather. Trading livestock and surplus agricultural output led to the growth of large-scale **commerce** and **trade routes**.

WAYS HUMAN POPULATIONS MODIFY THEIR SURROUNDING ENVIRONMENT

The agricultural revolution led human societies to begin changing their surroundings to accommodate their needs for shelter and room to cultivate food and to provide for domestic animals. Clearing ground for crops, redirecting waterways for irrigation purposes, and building permanent settlements all create major changes in the **environment**. Large-scale agriculture can lead to loose topsoil and damaging erosion. Building large cities leads to degraded air quality, water pollution from energy consumption, and many other side effects that can severely damage the environment. Recently, many countries have taken action by passing laws to **reduce human impact** on the environment and reduce the potentially damaging side effects. This is called **environmental policy**.

ECOLOGY

Ecology is the study of the way living creatures interact with their environment. **Biogeography** explores the way physical features of Earth affect living creatures.

Ecology bases its studies on three different levels of the environment:

- **Ecosystem**—this is a specific physical environment and all the organisms that live there.
- **Biome**—this is a group of ecosystems, usually consisting of a large area with similar flora and fauna as well as similar climate and soil. Examples of biomes include deserts, tropical rain forests, taigas, and tundra.
- **Habitat**—this is an area in which a specific species usually lives. The habitat includes the necessary soil, water, and resources for that particular species, as well as predators and other species that compete for the same resources.

Copyright © Mometrix Media. You have been licensed one copy of this document for personal use only. Any other reproduction or redistribution is strictly prohibited. All rights reserved.

TYPES OF INTERACTIONS OCCURRING BETWEEN SPECIES IN AN INDIVIDUAL HABITAT

Different interactions occur among species and members of single species within a habitat. These **interactions** fall into three categories:

- **Competition** — competition occurs when different animals, either of the same species or of different species, compete for the same resources. Robins can compete with other robins for available food, but other insectivores also compete for these same resources.
- **Predation** — predation occurs when one species depends on the other species for food, such as a fox who subsists on small mammals.
- **Symbiosis** — symbiosis occurs when two different species exist in the same environment without negatively affecting each other. Some symbiotic relationships are beneficial to one or both organisms without harm occurring to either.

IMPORTANCE OF AN ORGANISM'S ABILITY TO ADAPT

If a species is relocated from one habitat to another, it must **adapt** in order to survive. Some species are more capable of adapting than others. Those that cannot adapt will not survive. There are different ways a creature can adapt, including behavior modification and structural or physiological changes. Adaptation is also vital if an organism's environment changes around it. Although the creature has not been relocated, it finds itself in a new environment that requires changes in order to survive. The more readily an organism can adapt, the more likely it is to survive. The almost infinite ability of **humans** to adapt is a major reason why they are able to survive in almost any habitat in any area of the world.

BIODIVERSITY

Biodiversity refers to the variety of habitats that exist on the planet, as well as the variety of organisms that can exist within these habitats. A greater level of **biodiversity** makes it more likely that an individual habitat will flourish along with the species that depend upon it. Changes in habitat, including climate change, human intervention, or other factors, can reduce biodiversity by causing the extinction of certain species.

Copyright © Mometrix Media. You have been licensed one copy of this document for personal use only. Any other reproduction or redistribution is strictly prohibited. All rights reserved.

Illinois Geography

URBANIZATION

Urbanization is an increase in the proportion of human populations from **rural** areas to **cities**, plus how societies adapt to this change. As transportation and commuting take less money and time, educational, employment, and housing opportunities improve, and greater opportunities in economic competition, diversity, and proximity are available in cities, more people move there. Rural residents come seeking to change their social as well as economic status, as opportunities, money, and services are centralized in cities and businesses are more concentrated there. Tourism and trade generate revenue through bank systems and ports, also located in cities. Historically, small farmers and villagers have found it hard to obtain manufactured goods and services, and environmental changes that cannot be predicted or controlled have threatened their survival; these factors lead to rural flight, contributing to urbanization. Specialist services unavailable in rural areas are found in cities; senior citizens and others with specific healthcare needs may be required to move to cities for access to qualified hospitals and doctors. More plentiful, various, and better educational opportunities and social communities also attract people to cities.

GENERAL ECONOMIC, ENVIRONMENTAL, AND HEALTH EFFECTS

Economically, urban development can drastically raise expenses, frequently excluding local working-class citizens from the marketplace and leading to class segregation. Equity in urban development is often sacrificed for efficiency and speed. Unskilled and low-skilled migrant workers drawn to cities for employment but unable to find it end up living in slums. Infrastructure development and urban blight contribute to suburban development, even while urban density continues to increase. Diversity and proximity are opportunities of city life; congestion, monopoly, high overhead, and commuting intensify economic competition. **Environmentally**, urban heat islands raise temperatures and lower reabsorption of CO_2 emissions and soil moisture. Destructive subsistence farming (e.g., incorrectly applied slash-and-burn techniques) is decreased through rural emigration to cities; environmental stress from population growth is lowered as new city dweller birth rates instantly fall to replacement rates and continue falling. However, urban population growth and environmental change are projected to strain food resources, sanitation, and healthcare systems in the near future, with experts warning of environmental and humanitarian disaster potential by 2050 if changes are not made.

GENERAL POSITIVE AND NEGATIVE HEALTH EFFECTS ON HUMANS

In health, **mortality** from non-communicable lifestyle-related diseases (e.g., cancer, cardiovascular disease) has increased through urbanization. While the urban poor have disproportionately higher health problems, average health is better in urban areas than in rural areas. Although public sanitation, hygiene, and access to health care are all improvements associated with urbanization, these are also accompanied by changes in patterns of work, physical activity, and diet caused by urban living. As a result, the effects of urbanization on health patterns are **mixed**: it relieves some problems while exacerbating others. As one example, with urbanization children are at higher risk of being overweight or obese, but at lower risk of being malnourished or undernourished. The higher the income levels and rates of urbanization, the more markedly cholesterol levels and body mass index of citizens are raised. One factor of urbanization that may encourage less healthful dietary behaviors is easier access to processed and nontraditional foods. Overall, urban environments are associated with **greater major risk factors** for chronic diseases.

CENSUS STATISTICS ON URBAN POPULATIONS IN ILLINOIS

According to U.S Census Bureau statistics, in the state of Illinois the population was 23.5 percent **urban** in 1870, 30.6 percent in 1880, 44.9 percent in 1890, 54.3 percent in 1900, 61.7 percent in

118

Copyright © Mometrix Media. You have been licensed one copy of this document for personal use only. Any other reproduction or redistribution is strictly prohibited. All rights reserved.

1910, 67.9 percent in 1920, 73.9 percent in 1930, 73.6 percent in 1940, 77.6 percent in 1950, 80.7 percent in 1960, 83.2 percent in 1970, 83.3 percent in 1980, 86.4 percent in 1990, 87.8 percent in 2000, and 88.5 percent in 2010. The biggest city in Illinois is **Chicago**, which is also the third most populous city in America. The U.S Census Bureau reported its population as 2,695,598 in 2010. Seven other cities in Illinois have populations of over 100,000: Aurora (197,899 in 2010), a "satellite town" of Chicago; Rockford (152,871 in 2010), the largest Illinois city not in the Chicago suburbs and the third-largest city in the state; Joliet (147,433 in 2010), in metropolitan Chicago; Chicago suburb Naperville (141,853 in 2010), which shares a boundary along Rouge 59 with Aurora; Springfield (117,352 in 2010), the state capital; Peoria (115,007 in 2010), once the second-most populous, now seventh; and Chicago northwest suburb Elgin (108,188 in 2010).

NATURAL DISASTERS IN ILLINOIS DURING 20ᵀᴴ AND 21ˢᵀ CENTURIES

The **1967 Chicago blizzard** hit northeast Illinois and northwest Indiana on January 26-27 with a record 23 inches of snow in Chicago and its suburbs—still Chicago history's worst blizzard to this day. Thousands of commuters were stranded; approximately 50,000 cars and 800 Chicago Transit Authority buses were abandoned; both O'Hare and Midway Airports were closed; and schools were closed, with the city nearly shut down on January 27. Chicago's 1995 heat wave, with record temperatures in July up to 106° F, nighttime lows in the low 80s to upper 70s and high humidity, caused 739 deaths over five days, mostly of poor, elderly residents without air conditioning who kept their windows closed fearing crime. In April and May 2011, **Mississippi River floods,** caused by record rainfall from two major storm systems plus spring snowmelt, were the biggest and most destructive on that river in 100 years, affecting Illinois and six other states. Storms killed hundreds across these states, including Illinois. During April, four separate tornado systems caused **flash floods**. The Army Corps of Engineers blew a hole in a levee, flooding 130,000 acres of farmland in Mississippi County, Missouri, to save Cairo, Illinois, and the rest of the levee system from record flooding.

EARTHQUAKES AND MAJOR STORMS AND FLOODS AFFECTING ILLINOIS DURING 20ᵀᴴ AND 21ˢᵀ CENTURIES

Years with **earthquakes** in Illinois include 1838, 1891, 1909, 1917, 1968, 1972, 1987, 2004, 2008, 2010, 2013, and more. The **Chicago blizzard** of January 13-14, 1979, set a new Chicago one-day snow record (16.5 inches), totaling 18.8 inches in two days. Frozen Ell and Metra system tracks in January-February caused beyond-capacity commuter crowding on buses; this, combined with detours around giant snowdrifts, delayed snowplow deployment, and continuing snowfall that impeded plowing, made 30-45-minute commutes take several hours. Most of the snow remained for two months, causing continuing transit delays and garbage collection problems. Journalists and the public blamed inadequate city response on the mayor, who was then defeated in February's primary election. In 1993, **Mississippi River flooding** affected the towns of Valmeyer and Fults near Columbia, Illinois, where levees broke; Grafton was flooded for 195 days and Quincy for 152 days. In 1957, **Hurricane Audrey** caused record rainfall, flooding, and ten deaths in Paris, Illinois. In December 2007, **snow and ice storms** disrupted Chicago operations, causing one highway death and many injuries; 400 flights at O'Hare Airport and 28 at Midway Airport were canceled; and power outages affected 140,000 Illinois residents.

Copyright © Mometrix Media. You have been licensed one copy of this document for personal use only. Any other reproduction or redistribution is strictly prohibited. All rights reserved.

Political Science and Economics

Economics

ECONOMICS

Economics is the study of the ways specific societies **allocate** resources to individuals and groups within that society. Also important are the choices society makes regarding what efforts or initiatives are funded and which are not. Since resources in any society are finite, allocation becomes a vivid reflection of that society's values. In general, the economic system that drives an individual society is based on:

- What goods are produced
- How those goods are produced
- Who acquires the goods or benefits from them

Economics consists of two main categories: **macroeconomics**, which studies larger systems, and **microeconomics**, which studies smaller systems.

MARKET ECONOMY

A market economy is based on supply and demand. **Demand** has to do with what customers want and need, as well as what quantity those consumers are able to purchase based on other economic factors. **Supply** refers to how much can be produced to meet demand, or how much suppliers are willing and able to sell. Where the needs of consumers meet the needs of suppliers is referred to as a market equilibrium price. This price varies depending on many factors, including the overall health of a society's economy and the overall beliefs and considerations of individuals in society. The following is a list of terms defined in the context of a market economy:

- **Elasticity**—this is based on how the quantity of a particular product responds to the price demanded for that product. If quantity responds quickly to changes in price, the supply/demand for that product is said to be elastic. If it does not respond quickly, then the supply/demand is inelastic.
- **Market efficiency**—this occurs when a market is capable of producing output high enough to meet consumer demand.
- **Comparative advantage**—in the field of international trade, this refers to a country focusing on a specific product that it can produce more efficiently and more cheaply, or at a lower opportunity cost, than another country, thus giving it a comparative advantage in production.

> **Review Video: Basics of Market Economy**
> Visit mometrix.com/academy and enter code: 791556

PLANNED ECONOMY VS. MARKET ECONOMY

In a **market economy**, supply and demand are determined by consumers. In a **planned economy**, a public entity or planning authority makes the decisions about what resources will be produced, how they will be produced, and who will be able to benefit from them. The means of production, such as factories, are also owned by a public entity rather than by private interests. In **market socialism**, the economic structure falls somewhere between the market economy and the planned

Copyright © Mometrix Media. You have been licensed one copy of this document for personal use only. Any other reproduction or redistribution is strictly prohibited. All rights reserved.

economy. Planning authorities determine the allocation of resources at higher economic levels, while consumer goods are driven by a market economy.

MICROECONOMICS

While economics generally studies how resources are allocated, **microeconomics** focuses on economic factors such as the way consumers behave, how income is distributed, and output and input markets. Studies are limited to the industry or firm level rather than an entire country or society. Among the elements studied in microeconomics are factors of production, costs of production, and factor income. These factors determine production decisions of individual firms, based on resources and costs.

> **Review Video: Microeconomics**
> Visit mometrix.com/academy and enter code: 779207

CLASSIFICATION OF VARIOUS MARKETS BY ECONOMISTS

The conditions prevailing in a given market are used to **classify** markets. Conditions considered include:

- Existence of competition
- Number and size of suppliers
- Influence of suppliers over price
- Variety of available products
- Ease of entering the market

Once these questions are answered, an economist can classify a certain market according to its structure and the nature of competition within the market.

> **Review Video: Classification of Markets**
> Visit mometrix.com/academy and enter code: 904798

MARKET FAILURE

When any of the elements for a successfully competitive market are missing, this can lead to a **market failure**. Certain elements are necessary to create what economists call "**perfect competition**." If one of these factors is weak or lacking, the market is classified as having "**imperfect competition**." Worse than imperfect competition, though, is a market failure. There are five major types of market failure:

- Inadequate competition
- Inadequate information
- Immobile resources
- Negative externalities, or side effects
- Failure to provide public goods

Externalities are side effects of a market that affect third parties. These effects can be either negative or positive.

> **Review Video: Market Failure**
> Visit mometrix.com/academy and enter code: 889023

Copyright © Mometrix Media. You have been licensed one copy of this document for personal use only. Any other reproduction or redistribution is strictly prohibited. All rights reserved.

Factors of Production and Costs of Production

Every good and service requires certain resources, or **inputs**. These inputs are referred to as **factors of production**. Every good and service requires four factors of production:

- Labor
- Capital
- Land
- Entrepreneurship

These factors can be fixed or variable and can produce fixed or variable costs. Examples of **fixed costs** include land and equipment. **Variable costs** include labor. The total of fixed and variable costs makes up the cost of production.

Factor Income

Factors of production each have an associated **factor income**. Factors that earn income include:

- **Labor**—earns wages
- **Capital**—earns interest
- **Land**—earns rent
- **Entrepreneurship**—earns profit

Each factor's income is determined by its **contribution**. In a market economy, this income is not guaranteed to be equal. How scarce the factor is and the weight of its contribution to the overall production process determines the final factor income.

Kinds of Market Structures in an Output Market.

The four kinds of market structures in an output market are:

- **Perfect competition**—all existing firms sell an identical product. The firms are not able to control the final price. In addition, there is nothing that makes it difficult to become involved in or leave the industry. Anything that would prevent entering or leaving an industry is called a barrier to entry. An example of this market structure is agriculture.
- **Monopoly**—a single seller controls the product and its price. Barriers to entry, such as prohibitively high fixed cost structures, prevent other sellers from entering the market.
- **Monopolistic competition**—a number of firms sell similar products, but they are not identical, such as different brands of clothes or food. Barriers to entry are low.
- **Oligopoly**—only a few firms control the production and distribution of products, such as automobiles. Barriers to entry are high, preventing large numbers of firms from entering the market.

Types of Monopolies

Four types of monopolies are:

- **Natural monopoly**—a single supplier has a distinct advantage over the others.
- **Geographic monopoly**—only one business offers the product in a certain area.
- **Technological monopoly**—a single company controls the technology necessary to supply the product.
- **Government monopoly**—a government agency is the only provider of a specific good or service.

Copyright © Mometrix Media. You have been licensed one copy of this document for personal use only. Any other reproduction or redistribution is strictly prohibited. All rights reserved.

ACTIONS TAKEN BY THE US GOVERNMENT TO CONTROL MONOPOLIES

The US government has passed several acts to regulate businesses, including:

- **Sherman Antitrust Act (1890)**—this prohibited trusts, monopolies, and any other situations that eliminated competition.
- **Clayton Antitrust Act (1914)**—this prohibited price discrimination.
- **Robinson-Patman Act (1936)**—this strengthened provisions of the Clayton Antitrust Act, requiring businesses to offer the same pricing on products to any customer.

The government has also taken other actions to ensure competition, including requirements for public disclosure. The **Securities and Exchange Commission (SEC)** requires companies that provide public stock to provide financial reports on a regular basis. Because of the nature of their business, banks are further regulated and required to provide various information to the government.

MARKETING AND UTILITY

Marketing consists of all of the activity necessary to convince consumers to acquire goods. One major way to move products into the hands of consumers is to convince them that any single product will satisfy a need. The ability of a product or service to satisfy the need of a consumer is called **utility**. There are four types of utility:

- **Form utility**—a product's desirability lies in its physical characteristics.
- **Place utility**—a product's desirability is connected to its location and convenience.
- **Time utility**—a product's desirability is determined by its availability at a certain time.
- **Ownership utility**—a product's desirability is increased because ownership of the product passes to the consumer.

Marketing behavior will stress any or all of these types of utility when marketing to the consumer.

PRODUCERS DETERMINING WHAT CUSTOMERS DESIRE FOR THEIR PRODUCTS

Successful marketing depends not only on convincing customers they need the product but also on focusing the marketing towards those who already have a need or desire for the product. Before releasing a product into the general marketplace, many producers will **test** markets to determine which will be the most receptive to the product. There are three steps usually taken to evaluate a product's market:

- **Market research**—this involves researching a market to determine if it will be receptive to the product.
- **Market surveys**—a part of market research, market surveys ask consumers specific questions to help determine the marketability of a product to a specific group.
- **Test marketing**—this includes releasing the product into a small geographical area to see how it sells. Often test marketing is followed by wider marketing if the product does well.

MAJOR ELEMENTS OF A MARKETING PLAN

The four major elements of a marketing plan are:

- **Product**—this includes any elements pertaining directly to the product, such as packaging, presentation, or services to include along with it.
- **Price**—this calculates the cost of production, distribution, advertising, etc., as well as the desired profit to determine the final price.

Copyright © Mometrix Media. You have been licensed one copy of this document for personal use only. Any other reproduction or redistribution is strictly prohibited. All rights reserved.

- **Place**—this determines which outlets will be used to sell the product, whether traditional outlets such as brick and mortar stores or through direct mail or internet marketing.
- **Promotion**—this involves ways to let consumers know the product is available, through advertising and other means.

Once these elements have all been determined, the producer can proceed with production and distribution of his product.

DISTRIBUTION CHANNELS

Distribution channels determine the route a product takes on its journey from producer to consumer, and can also influence the final price and availability of the product. There are two major forms of distributions: wholesale and retail. A **wholesale distributor** buys in large quantities and then resells smaller amounts to other businesses. **Retailers** sell directly to the consumers rather than to businesses. In the modern marketplace, additional distribution channels have grown up with the rise of markets such as club warehouse stores as well as purchasing through catalogs or over the internet. Most of these newer distribution channels bring products more directly to the consumer, eliminating the need for middlemen.

DISTRIBUTION OF INCOME IN A SOCIETY

Distribution of income in any society ranges from poorest to richest. In most societies, income is not distributed evenly. To determine **income distribution**, family incomes are ranked from lowest to highest. These rankings are divided into five sections called **quintiles**, which are compared to each other. The uneven distribution of income is often linked to higher levels of education and ability in the upper classes but can also be due to other factors such as discrimination and existing monopolies. The **income gap** in America continues to grow, largely due to growth in the service industry, changes in the American family unit, and reduced influence of labor unions. **Poverty** is defined by comparing incomes to poverty guidelines. Poverty guidelines determine the level of income necessary for a family to function. Those below the poverty line are often eligible for assistance from government agencies.

MACROECONOMICS

Macroeconomics examines economies on a much larger level than microeconomics. While **microeconomics** studies economics on a firm or industry level, **macroeconomics** looks at economic trends and structures on a national level. Variables studied in macroeconomics include:

- Output
- Consumption
- Investment
- Government spending
- Net exports

The overall economic condition of a nation is defined as the **Gross Domestic Product**, or GDP. GDP measures a nation's economic output over a limited time period, such as a year.

> **Review Video: <u>Microeconomics and Macroeconomics</u>**
> Visit mometrix.com/academy and enter code: 538837
>
> **Review Video: <u>Gross Domestic Product</u>**
> Visit mometrix.com/academy and enter code: 409020

Copyright © Mometrix Media. You have been licensed one copy of this document for personal use only. Any other reproduction or redistribution is strictly prohibited. All rights reserved.

TYPES OF CONSUMER BEHAVIOR

The two major types of consumer behavior as defined in macroeconomics are:

- **Marginal propensity to consume (MPC)** defines the tendency of consumers to increase spending in conjunction with increases in income. In general, individuals with greater income will buy more. As individuals increase their income through job changes or growth of experience, they will also increase spending.
- **Utility** is a term that describes the satisfaction experienced by a consumer in relation to acquiring and using a good or service. Providers of goods and services will stress utility to convince consumers they want the products being presented.

WAYS TO MEASURE THE GROSS DOMESTIC PRODUCT OF A COUNTRY

The two major ways to measure the Gross Domestic Product of a country are:

- The **expenditures approach** calculates the GDP based on how much money is spent in each individual sector.
- The **income approach** calculates the GDP based on how much money is earned in each sector.

Both methods yield the same results, and both of these calculation methods are based on four **economic sectors** that make up a country's macro-economy:

- Consumers
- Business
- Government
- Foreign sector

TYPES OF EARNINGS GENERATED BY AN ECONOMY CONSIDERED TO CALCULATE GDP

Several factors must be considered in order to accurately calculate the GDP using the incomes approach. **Income factors** are:

- Wages paid to laborers, or compensation of employees (CE)
- Rental income derived from land
- Interest income derived from invested capital
- Entrepreneurial income

Entrepreneurial income consists of two forms. **Proprietor's income** is income that comes back to the entrepreneur himself. **Corporate profit** is income that goes back into the corporation as a whole. Corporate profit is divided by the corporation into corporate profits taxes, dividends, and retained earnings. Two other figures must be subtracted in the incomes approach. These are **indirect business taxes**, including property and sales taxes, and **depreciation**.

EFFECTS OF POPULATION OF A COUNTRY ON THE GROSS DOMESTIC PRODUCT

Changes in population can affect the calculation of a nation's **GDP**, particularly since GDP and GNP (Gross National Product) are generally measured per capita. If a country's economic production is low but the population is high, the income per individual will be lower than if the income is high and the population is lower. Also, if the population grows quickly and the income grows slowly, individual income will remain low or even drop drastically.

Copyright © Mometrix Media. You have been licensed one copy of this document for personal use only. Any other reproduction or redistribution is strictly prohibited. All rights reserved.

Population growth can also affect overall **economic growth**. Economic growth requires both that consumers purchase goods and workers produce them. A population that does not grow quickly enough will not supply enough workers to support rapid economic growth.

IDEAL BALANCE TO BE OBTAINED IN AN ECONOMY

Ideally, an economy functions efficiently, with the **aggregate supply**, or the amount of national output, equal to the **aggregate demand**, or the amount of the output that is purchased. In these cases, the economy is stable and prosperous. However, economies more typically go through **phases**. These phases are:

- **Boom**—GDP is high and the economy prospers
- **Recession**—GDP falls and unemployment rises
- **Trough**—the recession reaches its lowest point
- **Recovery**—unemployment lessens, prices rise, and the economy begins to stabilize again

These phases tend to repeat in cycles that are not necessarily predictable or regular.

UNEMPLOYMENT AND INFLATION

When demand outstrips supply, prices are driven artificially high, or are **inflated**. This occurs when too much spending causes an imbalance in the economy. In general, inflation occurs because an economy is growing too quickly. When there is too little spending, and supply has moved far beyond demand, a **surplus** of product results. Companies cut back on production and reduce the number of employees, and **unemployment** rises as people lose their jobs. This imbalance occurs when an economy becomes sluggish. In general, both these economic instability situations are caused by an imbalance between supply and demand. Government intervention may be necessary to stabilize an economy when either inflation or unemployment becomes too serious.

DIFFERENT FORMS OF UNEMPLOYMENT

- **Frictional**—when workers change jobs and are unemployed while waiting for new jobs
- **Structural**—when economic shifts reduce the need for workers
- **Cyclical**—when natural business cycles bring about loss of jobs
- **Seasonal**—when seasonal cycles reduce the need for certain jobs
- **Technological**—when advances in technology result in the elimination of certain jobs

Any of these factors can increase unemployment in certain sectors.

Inflation is classified by the overall rate at which it occurs:

- **Creeping inflation**—this is an inflation rate of about 1%-3% annually.
- **Walking inflation**—this is an inflation rate of 3%-10% annually.
- **Galloping inflation**—this is a high inflation rate of more than 10% but less than 1,000% annually.
- **Hyperinflation**—this is an inflation rate of over 1,000% per year. Hyperinflation usually leads to complete monetary collapse in a society, as individuals cannot generate sufficient income to purchase necessary goods.

Review Video: <u>Forms of Unemployment</u>
Visit mometrix.com/academy and enter code: 774028

Copyright © Mometrix Media. You have been licensed one copy of this document for personal use only. Any other reproduction or redistribution is strictly prohibited. All rights reserved.

GOVERNMENT INTERVENTION POLICIES THAT CAN HELP MITIGATE INFLATION AND UNEMPLOYMENT

When an economy becomes too imbalanced, either due to excessive spending or not enough spending, **government intervention** often becomes necessary to put the economy back on track. Government fiscal policy can take several forms, including:

- Contractionary policy
- Expansionary policy
- Monetary policy

Contractionary policies help counteract inflation. These include increasing taxes and decreasing government spending to slow spending in the overall economy. **Expansionary policies** increase government spending and lower taxes in order to reduce unemployment and increase the level of spending in the economy overall. **Monetary policy** can take several forms and affects the amount of funds available to banks for making loans.

STUDY AND QUANTIFICATION OF POPULATIONS AND POPULATION GROWTH

Populations are studied by **size**, rates of **growth** due to immigration, the overall **fertility rate**, and **life expectancy**. For example, though the population of the United States is considerably larger than it was two hundred years ago, the rate of population growth has decreased greatly, from about three percent per year to less than one percent per year.

In the US, the fertility rate is fairly low, with most choosing not to have large families, and life expectancy is high, creating a projected imbalance between older and younger people in the near future. In addition, immigration and the mixing of racially diverse cultures are projected to increase the percentages of Asians, Hispanics, and African Americans.

FUNCTIONS AND TYPES OF MONEY

Money is used in three major ways:

- As an accounting unit
- As a store of value
- As an exchange medium

In general, money must be acceptable throughout a society in exchange for debts or to purchase goods and services. Money should be relatively scarce, its value should remain stable, and it should be easily carried, durable, and easy to divide up. There are three basic types of money: commodity, representative, and fiat. **Commodity money** includes gems or precious metals. **Representative money** can be exchanged for items such as gold or silver that have inherent value. **Fiat money**, or legal tender, has no inherent value but has been declared to function as money by the government. It is often backed by gold or silver but not necessarily on a one-to-one ratio.

TYPES OF MONEY AVAILABLE IN THE US AND ECONOMISTS' MEASURE OF IT

Money in the US is not just currency. When economists calculate the amount of money available, they must take into account other factors, such as deposits that have been placed in checking accounts, debit cards, and "near moneys," such as savings accounts, that can be quickly converted into cash. Currency, checkable deposits and traveler's checks, referred to as **M1**, are added up, and then **M2** is calculated by adding savings deposits, CDs, and various other monetary deposits. The final result is the total quantity of available money.

Copyright © Mometrix Media. You have been licensed one copy of this document for personal use only. Any other reproduction or redistribution is strictly prohibited. All rights reserved.

ASPECTS OF MONETARY POLICY AND THE ROLE OF THE FEDERAL RESERVE SYSTEM

The Federal Reserve System, also known as the **Fed**, implements all monetary policy in the US. Monetary policy regulates the amount of money available in the American banking system. The Fed can decrease or increase the amount of available money for loans, thus helping regulate the national economy. Monetary policies implemented by the Fed are part of expansionary or contractionary monetary policies that help counteract inflation or unemployment. The **discount rate** is an interest rate charged by the Fed when banks borrow money from them. A lower discount rate leads banks to borrow more money, leading to increased spending. A higher discount rate has the opposite effect.

> **Review Video: Monetary Policy**
> Visit mometrix.com/academy and enter code: 662298

HOW BANKS FUNCTION

Banks earn their income by **loaning** out money and charging **interest** on those loans. If less money is available, fewer loans can be made, which affects the amount of spending in the overall economy. While banks function by making loans, they are not allowed to loan out all the money they hold in deposit. The amount of money they must maintain in reserve is known as the **reserve ratio**. If the reserve ratio is raised, less money is available for loans and spending decreases. A lower reserve ratio increases available funds and increases spending. This ratio is determined by the Federal Reserve System.

OPEN MARKET OPERATIONS

The Federal Reserve System can also expand or contract the overall money supply through **open market operations**. In this case, the Fed can buy or sell **bonds** it has purchased from banks or individuals. When the Fed buys bonds, more money is put into circulation, creating an expansionary situation to stimulate the economy. When the Fed sells bonds, money is withdrawn from the system, creating a **contractionary** situation to slow an economy suffering from inflation. Because of international financial markets, however, American banks often borrow and lend money in markets outside the US. By shifting their attention to international markets, domestic banks and other businesses can circumvent whatever contractionary policies the Fed may have put into place.

MAJOR CHARACTERISTICS OF INTERNATIONAL TRADE

International trade can take advantage of broader markets, bringing a wider variety of products within easy reach. By contrast, it can also allow individual countries to specialize in particular products that they can produce easily, such as those for which they have easy access to raw materials. Other products, more difficult to make domestically, can be acquired through trade with other nations. **International trade** requires efficient use of **native resources** as well as sufficient **disposable income** to purchase native and imported products. Many countries in the world engage extensively in international trade, but others still face major economic challenges.

MAJOR CHARACTERISTICS OF A DEVELOPING NATION

The five major characteristics of a developing nation are:

- Low GDP
- Rapid growth of population
- Economy that depends on subsistence agriculture

Copyright © Mometrix Media. You have been licensed one copy of this document for personal use only. Any other reproduction or redistribution is strictly prohibited. All rights reserved.

- Poor conditions, including high infant mortality rates, high disease rates, poor sanitation, and insufficient housing
- Low literacy rate

Developing nations often function under oppressive governments that do not provide private property rights and withhold education and other rights from women. They also often feature an extreme disparity between upper and lower classes, with little opportunity for the lower classes to improve their position.

STAGES OF ECONOMIC DEVELOPMENT

Economic development occurs in three stages that are defined by the activities that drive the economy:

- Agricultural stage
- Manufacturing stage
- Service sector stage

In developing countries, it is often difficult to acquire the necessary funding to provide equipment and training to move into the advanced stages of economic development. Some can receive help from developed countries via foreign aid and investment or international organizations such as the **International Monetary Fund** or the **World Bank**. Having developed countries provide monetary, technical, or military assistance can help developing countries move forward to the next stage in their development.

OBSTACLES DEVELOPING NATIONS FACE REGARDING ECONOMIC GROWTH

Developing nations typically struggle to overcome obstacles that prevent or slow economic development. Major **obstacles** can include:

- Rapid, uncontrolled population growth
- Trade restrictions
- Misused resources, often perpetrated by the government
- Traditional beliefs that can slow or reject change

Corrupt, oppressive governments often hamper the economic growth of developing nations, creating huge **economic disparities** and making it impossible for individuals to advance, in turn preventing overall growth. Governments sometimes export currency, called **capital flight**, which is detrimental to a country's economic development. In general, countries are more likely to experience economic growth if their governments encourage entrepreneurship and provide private property rights.

PROBLEMS WHEN INDUSTRIALIZATION OCCURS TOO QUICKLY

Rapid growth throughout the world leaves some nations behind and sometimes spurs their governments to move forward too quickly into **industrialization** and **artificially rapid economic growth**. While slow or nonexistent economic growth causes problems in a country, overly rapid industrialization carries its own issues. Four major problems encountered due to rapid industrialization are:

- Use of technology not suited to the products or services being supplied
- Poor investment of capital

Copyright © Mometrix Media. You have been licensed one copy of this document for personal use only. Any other reproduction or redistribution is strictly prohibited. All rights reserved.

- Lack of time for the population to adapt to new paradigms
- Lack of time to experience all stages of development and adjust to each stage

Economic failures in Indonesia were largely due to rapid growth that was poorly handled.

IMPORTANCE OF E-COMMERCE IN TODAY'S MARKETPLACE

The growth of the internet has brought many changes to our society, not the least of which is the modern way of business. Where supply channels used to move in certain necessary ways, many of these channels are now bypassed as **e-commerce** makes it possible for nearly any individual to set up a direct market to consumers, as well as direct interaction with suppliers. Competition is fierce. In many instances, e-commerce can provide nearly instantaneous gratification, with a wide variety of products. Whoever provides the best product most quickly often rises to the top of a marketplace. How this added element to the marketplace will affect the economy in the future remains to be seen. Many industries are still struggling with the best ways to adapt to the rapid, continuous changes.

KNOWLEDGE ECONOMY AND POSSIBLE EFFECT ON FUTURE ECONOMIC GROWTH

The knowledge economy is a growing sector in the economy of developed countries, and includes the trade and development of:

- Data
- Intellectual property
- Technology, especially in the area of communications

Knowledge as a resource is steadily becoming more and more important. What is now being called the **Information Age** may prove to bring about changes in life and culture as significant as those brought on by the Agricultural and Industrial Revolutions.

CYBERNOMICS

Related to the knowledge economy is what has been dubbed "**cybernomics**," or economics driven by e-commerce and other computer-based markets and products. Marketing has changed drastically with the growth of cyber communication, allowing suppliers to connect one-on-one with their customers. Other issues coming to the fore regarding cybernomics include:

- Secure online trade
- Intellectual property rights
- Rights to privacy
- Bringing developing nations into the fold

As these issues are debated and new laws and policies developed, the face of many industries continues to undergo drastic change. Many of the old ways of doing business no longer work, leaving industries scrambling to function profitably within the new system.

Copyright © Mometrix Media. You have been licensed one copy of this document for personal use only. Any other reproduction or redistribution is strictly prohibited. All rights reserved.

US Government and Citizenship

POLITICAL SCIENCE AND ITS TIES TO OTHER MAJOR DISCIPLINES

Political science focuses on studying different governments and how they compare to each other, general political theory, ways political theory is put into action, how nations and governments interact with each other, and a general study of governmental structure and function. Other elements of **political science** include the study of elections, governmental administration at various levels, development and action of political parties, and how values such as freedom, power, justice, and equality are expressed in different political cultures. Political science also encompasses elements of other disciplines, including:

- **History**—how historical events have shaped political thought and process
- **Sociology**—the effects of various stages of social development on the growth and development of government and politics
- **Anthropology**—the effects of governmental process on the culture of an individual group and its relationships with other groups
- **Economics**—how government policies regulate the distribution of products and how they can control and/or influence the economy in general

GENERAL POLITICAL THEORY

Based on general political theory, the four major purposes of any given government are:

- **Ensuring national security**—the government protects against international, domestic, and terrorist attacks and also ensures ongoing security through negotiating and establishing relationships with other governments.
- **Providing public services**—the government should "promote the general welfare," as stated in the Preamble to the US Constitution, by providing whatever is needed to its citizens.
- **Ensuring social order**—the government supplies means of settling conflicts among citizens as well as making laws to govern the nation, state, or city.
- **Making decisions regarding the economy**—laws help form the economic policy of the country, regarding both domestic and international trade and related issues. The government also has the ability to distribute goods and wealth to some extent among its citizens.

MAIN THEORIES REGARDING THE ORIGIN OF THE STATE

There are four main theories regarding the origin of the state:

- **Evolutionary**—the state evolved from the family, with the head of state the equivalent of the family's patriarch or matriarch.
- **Force**—one person or group of people brought everyone in an area under their control, forming the first government.
- **Divine Right**—certain people were chosen by the prevailing deity to be the rulers of the nation, which is itself created by the deity or deities.
- **Social Contract**—there is no natural order. The people allow themselves to be governed to maintain social order, while the state, in turn, promises to protect the people they govern. If the government fails to protect its people, the people have the right to seek new leaders.

Copyright © Mometrix Media. You have been licensed one copy of this document for personal use only. Any other reproduction or redistribution is strictly prohibited. All rights reserved.

INFLUENCES OF PHILOSOPHERS ON POLITICAL STUDY

Ancient Greek philosophers **Aristotle** and **Plato** believed political science would lead to order in political matters and that this scientifically organized order would create stable, just societies.

Thomas Aquinas adapted the ideas of Aristotle to a Christian perspective. His ideas stated that individuals should have certain rights but also certain duties, and that these rights and duties should determine the type and extent of government rule. In stating that laws should limit the role of government, he laid the groundwork for ideas that would eventually become modern constitutionalism.

Niccolò Machiavelli, author of *The Prince*, was a proponent of politics based on power. He is often considered the founder of modern political science.

Thomas Hobbes, author of *Leviathan* (1651), believed that individuals' lives were focused solely on a quest for power and that the state must work to control this urge. Hobbes felt that people were completely unable to live harmoniously without the intervention of a powerful, undivided government.

CONTRIBUTIONS OF JOHN LOCKE, MONTESQUIEU, AND ROUSSEAU TO POLITICAL SCIENCE

John Locke published *Two Treatises of Government* in 1689. This work argued against the ideas of Thomas Hobbes. He put forth the theory of *tabula rasa*—that people are born with minds like blank slates. Individual minds are molded by experience, not innate knowledge or intuition. He also believed that all men should be independent and equal. Many of Locke's ideas found their way into the Constitution of the United States.

The two French philosophers, **Montesquieu** and **Rousseau**, heavily influenced the French Revolution (1789-1799). They believed government policies and ideas should change to alleviate existing problems, an idea referred to as "liberalism." Rousseau, in particular, directly influenced the Revolution with writings such as *The Social Contract* (1762) and *Declaration of the Rights of Man and of the Citizen* (1789). Other ideas Rousseau and Montesquieu espoused included:

- Individual freedom and community welfare are of equal importance
- Man's innate goodness leads to natural harmony
- Reason develops with the rise of civilized society
- Individual citizens carry certain obligations to the existing government

POLITICAL IDEOLOGIES OF DAVID HUME, JEREMY BENTHAM, JOHN STUART MILL, JOHANN GOTTLIEB FICHTE, AND FRIEDRICH HEGEL

David Hume and **Jeremy Bentham** believed politics should have as its main goal maintaining "the greatest happiness for the greatest number." Hume also believed in empiricism, or that ideas should not be believed until the proof has been observed. He was a natural skeptic and always sought out the truth of matters rather than believing what he was told.

John Stuart Mill, a British philosopher as well as an economist, believed in progressive policies such as women's suffrage, emancipation, and the development of labor unions and farming cooperatives.

Johann Fichte and **Georg Hegel**, German philosophers in the late 18th and early 19th centuries, supported a form of liberalism grounded largely in socialism and a sense of nationalism.

Copyright © Mometrix Media. You have been licensed one copy of this document for personal use only. Any other reproduction or redistribution is strictly prohibited. All rights reserved.

MAIN POLITICAL ORIENTATIONS

The four main political orientations are:

- **Liberal**—liberals believe that government should work to increase equality, even at the expense of some freedoms. Government should assist those in need, focusing on enforced social justice and free basic services for everyone.
- **Conservative**—a conservative believes that government should be limited in most cases. The government should allow its citizens to help one another and solve their own problems rather than enforcing solutions. Business should not be overregulated, allowing a free market.
- **Moderate**—this ideology incorporates some liberal and some conservative values, generally falling somewhere between in overall belief.
- **Libertarian**—libertarians believe that the government's role should be limited to protecting the life and liberty of citizens. Government should not be involved in any citizen's life unless that citizen is encroaching upon the rights of another.

MAJOR PRINCIPLES OF GOVERNMENT AS OUTLINED IN THE UNITED STATES CONSTITUTION

The six major principles of government as outlined in the United States Constitution are:

- **Federalism**—the power of the government does not belong entirely to the national government but is divided between federal and state governments.
- **Popular sovereignty**—the government is determined by the people and gains its authority and power from the people.
- **Separation of powers**—the government is divided into three branches (executive, legislative, and judicial) with each having its own set of powers.
- **Judicial review**—courts at all levels of government can declare laws invalid if they contradict the constitutions of individual states, or the US Constitution, with the Supreme Court serving as the final judicial authority on decisions of this kind.
- **Checks and balances**—no single branch can act without input from another, and each branch has the power to "check" any other, as well as balance other branches' powers.
- **Limited government**—governmental powers are limited, and certain individual rights are defined as inviolable by the government.

> **Review Video: Supreme Court**
> Visit mometrix.com/academy and enter code: 270434

TYPES OF POWERS DELEGATED TO THE NATIONAL GOVERNMENT BY THE US CONSTITUTION

The structure of the US government divides power between national and state governments. Powers delegated to the federal government by the Constitution are:

- **Expressed powers**—powers directly defined in the Constitution, including power to declare war, regulate commerce, make money, and collect taxes
- **Implied powers**—powers the national government must have in order to carry out the expressed powers
- **Inherent powers**—powers inherent to any government, not expressly defined in the Constitution

Some of these powers, such as collection and levying of taxes, are also granted to the individual state governments.

Copyright © Mometrix Media. You have been licensed one copy of this document for personal use only. Any other reproduction or redistribution is strictly prohibited. All rights reserved.

PRIMARY POSITIONS OF FEDERALISM AND DEVELOPMENT THROUGH THE YEARS IN THE US

The way federalism should be practiced has been the subject of debate since the writing of the Constitution. There were—and still are—two main factions regarding this issue:

- **States' rights**—those favoring the states' rights position feel that the state governments should take the lead in performing local actions to manage various problems.
- **Nationalist**—those favoring a nationalist position feel the national government should take the lead to deal with those same matters.

The flexibility of the Constitution has allowed the US government to shift and adapt as the needs of the country have changed. Power has often shifted from the state governments to the national government and back again, and both levels of government have developed various ways to influence each other.

EFFECTS OF FEDERALISM ON POLICY-MAKING AND THE BALANCE OF POLITICS IN THE US

Federalism has three major effects on **public policy** in the US:

- Determining whether the local, state, or national government originates policy
- Affecting how policies are made
- Ensuring policy-making functions under a set of limitations

Federalism also influences the **political balance of power** in the US by:

- Making it difficult, if not impossible, for a single political party to seize total power
- Ensuring that individuals can participate in the political system at various levels
- Making it possible for individuals working within the system to be able to affect policy at some level, whether local or more widespread

THREE BRANCHES OF THE US FEDERAL GOVERNMENT

The following are the three branches of the US Federal government and the individuals that belong to each branch:

- **Legislative Branch**—this consists of the two houses of Congress: the House of Representatives and the Senate. All members of the Legislative Branch are elected officials.
- **Executive Branch**—this branch is made up of the president, vice president, presidential advisors, and other various cabinet members. Advisors and cabinet members are appointed by the president, but they must be approved by Congress.
- **Judicial Branch**—the federal court system, headed by the Supreme Court.

> **Review Video: Three Branches of Government**
> Visit mometrix.com/academy and enter code: 718704

MAJOR RESPONSIBILITIES OF THE THREE BRANCHES OF THE FEDERAL GOVERNMENT

The three branches of the federal government each have specific roles and responsibilities:

- The **Legislative Branch** is largely concerned with lawmaking. All laws must be approved by Congress before they go into effect. They are also responsible for regulating money and trade, approving presidential appointments, and establishing organizations like the postal service and federal courts. Congress can also propose amendments to the Constitution, and can impeach, or bring charges against, the president. Only Congress can declare war.

Copyright © Mometrix Media. You have been licensed one copy of this document for personal use only. Any other reproduction or redistribution is strictly prohibited. All rights reserved.

- The **Executive Branch** carries out laws, treaties, and war declarations enacted by Congress. The president can also veto bills approved by Congress, and serves as commander in chief of the US military. The president appoints cabinet members, ambassadors to foreign countries, and federal judges.
- The **Judicial Branch** makes decisions on challenges as to whether laws passed by Congress meet the requirements of the US Constitution. The Supreme Court may also choose to review decisions made by lower courts to determine their constitutionality.

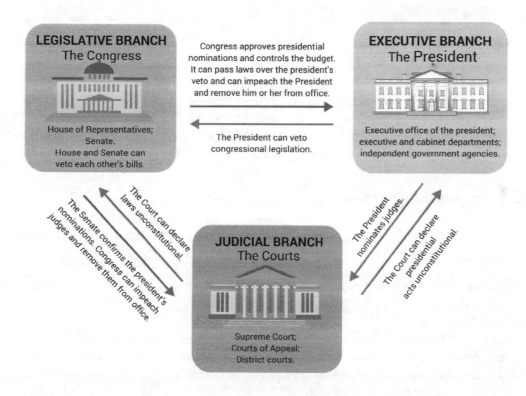

US CITIZENSHIP

QUALIFICATIONS OF A US CITIZEN/HOW CITIZENSHIP MAY BE LOST

Anyone born in the US, born abroad to a US citizen, or who has gone through a process of naturalization is considered a **citizen** of the United States. It is possible to lose US citizenship as a result of conviction of certain crimes such as treason. Citizenship may also be lost if a citizen pledges an oath to another country or serves in the military of a country engaged in hostilities with the US. A US citizen can also choose to hold dual citizenship, work as an expatriate in another country without losing US citizenship, or even to renounce citizenship if he or she so chooses.

RIGHTS, DUTIES, AND RESPONSIBILITIES GRANTED TO OR EXPECTED FROM CITIZENS

Citizens are granted certain rights under the US government. The most important of these are defined in the **Bill of Rights**, and include freedom of speech, religion, assembly, and a variety of other rights the government is not allowed to remove. A US citizen also has a number of **duties**:

- Paying taxes
- Loyalty to the government (though the US does not prosecute those who criticize or seek to change the government)
- Support and defense of the Constitution

Copyright © Mometrix Media. You have been licensed one copy of this document for personal use only. Any other reproduction or redistribution is strictly prohibited. All rights reserved.

- Serving in the Armed Forces when required by law
- Obeying laws as set forth by the various levels of government.

Responsibilities of a US citizen include:

- Voting in elections
- Respecting one another's rights and not infringing on them
- Staying informed about various political and national issues
- Respecting one another's beliefs

BILL OF RIGHTS
IMPORTANCE OF THE BILL OF RIGHTS

The first ten amendments of the US Constitution are known as the **Bill of Rights**. These amendments prevent the government from infringing upon certain freedoms that the Founding Fathers felt were natural rights that already belonged to all people. These rights included freedom of speech, freedom of religion, freedom of assembly, and the right to bear arms. Many of the rights were formulated in direct response to the way the colonists felt they had been mistreated by the British government.

RIGHTS GRANTED IN THE BILL OF RIGHTS

The first ten amendments were passed by Congress in 1789. Three-fourths of the existing thirteen states had ratified them by December of 1791, making them official additions to the Constitution. The rights granted in the Bill of Rights are:

- **First Amendment**—freedom of religion, speech, freedom of the press, and the right to assemble and to petition the government
- **Second Amendment**—the right to bear arms
- **Third Amendment**—Congress cannot force individuals to house troops
- **Fourth Amendment**—protection from unreasonable search and seizure
- **Fifth Amendment**—no individual is required to testify against himself, and no individual may be tried twice for the same crime
- **Sixth Amendment**—the right to criminal trial by jury and the right to legal counsel
- **Seventh Amendment**—the right to civil trial by jury
- **Eighth Amendment**—protection from excessive bail or cruel and unusual punishment
- **Ninth Amendment**—prevents rights not explicitly named in the Constitution from being taken away because they are not named
- **Tenth Amendment**—any rights not directly delegated to the national government, or not directly prohibited by the government from the states, belong to the states or to the people

> **Review Video: Bill of Rights**
> Visit mometrix.com/academy and enter code: 585149

SITUATIONS WHERE THE GOVERNMENT RESTRICTS OR REGULATES FIRST AMENDMENT FREEDOMS

In some cases, the government restricts certain elements of First Amendment rights. Some examples include:

- **Freedom of religion**—when a religion espouses illegal activities, the government often restricts these forms of religious expression. Examples include polygamy, animal sacrifice, and use of illicit drugs or illegal substances.

Copyright © Mometrix Media. You have been licensed one copy of this document for personal use only. Any other reproduction or redistribution is strictly prohibited. All rights reserved.

- **Freedom of speech**—this can be restricted if exercise of free speech endangers other people.
- **Freedom of the press**—laws prevent the press from publishing falsehoods.

In **emergency situations** such as wartime, stricter restrictions are sometimes placed on these rights, especially rights to free speech and assembly, and freedom of the press, in order to protect national security.

CONSTITUTION'S ADDRESS OF THE RIGHTS OF THOSE ACCUSED OF CRIMES

The US Constitution makes allowances for the **rights of criminals**, or anyone who has transgressed established laws. There must be laws to protect citizens from criminals, but those accused of crimes must also be protected and their basic rights as individuals preserved. In addition, the Constitution protects individuals from the power of authorities to prevent police forces and other enforcement organizations from becoming oppressive. The fourth, fifth, sixth, and eighth amendments specifically address these rights.

SUPREME COURT'S PROVISION OF EQUAL PROTECTION UNDER THE LAW FOR ALL INDIVIDUALS

When the Founding Fathers wrote in the Declaration of Independence that "all men are created equal," they actually were referring to men, and, in fact, defined citizens as white men who owned land. However, as the country has developed and changed, the definition has expanded to more wholly include all people.

"**Equality**" does not mean all people are inherently the same, but it does mean they all should be granted the same rights and should be treated the same by the government. Amendments to the Constitution have granted citizenship and voting rights to all Americans regardless of race or gender. The Supreme Court evaluates various laws and court decisions to determine if they properly represent the idea of **equal protection**. One sample case was Brown v. Board of Education in 1954, which declared separate-but-equal treatment to be unconstitutional.

CIVIL LIBERTY CHALLENGES ADDRESSED IN CURRENT POLITICAL DISCUSSIONS

The **civil rights movements** of the 1960s and the ongoing struggle for the rights of women and other minorities have sparked **challenges to existing law**. In addition, debate has raged over how much information the government should be required to divulge to the public. Major issues in the 21st century political climate include:

- Continued debate over women's rights, especially regarding equal pay for equal work
- Debate over affirmative action to encourage hiring of minorities
- Debate over civil rights of homosexuals, including marriage and military service
- Decisions as to whether minorities should be compensated for past discriminatory practices
- Balance between the public's right to know and the government's need to maintain national security
- Balance between the public's right to privacy and national security

Copyright © Mometrix Media. You have been licensed one copy of this document for personal use only. Any other reproduction or redistribution is strictly prohibited. All rights reserved.

CIVIL LIBERTIES VS. CIVIL RIGHTS

While the terms *civil liberties* and *civil rights* are often used interchangeably, in actuality, their definitions are slightly different. The two concepts work together, however, to define the basics of a free state:

- **"Civil liberties"** define the constitutional freedoms guaranteed to citizens. Examples include freedoms such as free speech, privacy, or free thought.
- **"Civil rights"** are guarantees of or protections of civil liberties. One comparison can be found in the case of freedom of religion. The civil liberty is that one has the freedom to practice the religion of his or her choice, whereas the civil right would protect that individual from being denied a job on the basis of their religion.

SUFFRAGE, FRANCHISE, AND THE CHANGE OF VOTING RIGHTS OVER THE COURSE OF AMERICAN HISTORY

Suffrage and franchise both refer to the right to **vote**. As the US developed as a nation, there was much debate over which individuals should hold this right. In the early years, only white male landowners were granted suffrage. By the 19th century, most states had franchised, or granted the right to vote, to all adult white males. The **Fifteenth Amendment** of 1870 granted suffrage to formerly enslaved men. The **Nineteenth Amendment** gave women the right to vote in 1920, and in 1971 the **Twenty-sixth Amendment** expanded voting rights to include any US citizen over the age of eighteen. However, those who have not been granted full citizenship and citizens who have committed certain crimes do not have voting rights.

WAYS IN WHICH THE VOTING PROCESS HAS CHANGED OVER THE YEARS

The first elections in the US were held by **public ballot**. However, election abuses soon became common, since public ballot made it easy to intimidate, threaten, or otherwise influence the votes of individuals or groups of individuals. New practices were put into play, including **registering voters** before elections took place and using a **secret or Australian ballot**. In 1892, the introduction of the **voting machine** further privatized the voting process, since it allowed complete privacy for voting. Today, debate continues about the accuracy of various voting methods, including high-tech voting machines and even low-tech punch cards.

EFFECT OF POLITICAL PARTIES ON THE FUNCTIONING OF AN INDIVIDUAL GOVERNMENT

Different types and numbers of political parties can have a significant effect on how a government is run. If there is a **single party**, or a one-party system, the government is defined by that one party, and all policy is based on that party's beliefs. In a **two-party system**, two parties with different viewpoints compete for power and influence. The US is basically a two-party system, with checks and balances to make it difficult for one party to gain complete power over the other. There are also **multiparty systems**, with three or more parties. In multiparty systems, various parties will often come to agreements in order to form a majority and shift the balance of power.

Copyright © Mometrix Media. You have been licensed one copy of this document for personal use only. Any other reproduction or redistribution is strictly prohibited. All rights reserved.

DEVELOPMENT OF POLITICAL PARTIES IN THE US.

George Washington was adamantly against the establishment of **political parties**, based on the abuses perpetrated by such parties in Britain. However, political parties developed in US politics almost from the beginning. Major parties throughout US history have included:

- **Federalists and Democratic-Republicans**—these parties formed in the late 1700s and disagreed on the balance of power between national and state government.
- **Democrats and Whigs**—these developed in the 1830s, and many political topics of the time centered on national economic issues.
- **Democrats and Republicans**—the Republican Party developed before the Civil War, after the collapse of the Whig party, and the two parties debated issues centering on slavery and economic issues, such as taxation.

While third parties sometimes enter the picture in US politics, the government is basically a two-party system, dominated by the Democrats and Republicans.

FUNCTIONS OF POLITICAL PARTIES

Political parties form organizations at all levels of government. Activities of individual parties include:

- Recruiting and backing candidates for offices
- Discussing various issues with the public, increasing public awareness
- Working toward compromise on difficult issues
- Staffing government offices and providing administrative support

At the administrative level, parties work to ensure that viable candidates are available for elections and that offices and staff are in place to support candidates as they run for office and afterward, when they are elected.

PROCESSES OF SELECTING POLITICAL CANDIDATES

Historically, in the quest for political office, a potential candidate has followed one of the following four processes:

- **Nominating convention**—an official meeting of the members of a party for the express purpose of nominating candidates for upcoming elections. The Democratic National Convention and the Republican National Convention, convened to announce candidates for the presidency, are examples of this kind of gathering.
- **Caucus**—a meeting, usually attended by a party's leaders. Some states still use caucuses, but not all.
- **Primary election**—the most common method of choosing candidates today, the primary is a publicly held election to choose candidates.
- **Petition**—signatures gathered to place a candidate on the ballot. Petitions can also be used to place legislation on a ballot.

WAYS THE AVERAGE CITIZEN PARTICIPATES IN THE POLITICAL PROCESS

In addition to voting for elected officials, American citizens are able to participate in the political process through several other avenues. These include:

- Participating in local government
- Participating in caucuses for large elections

Copyright © Mometrix Media. You have been licensed one copy of this document for personal use only. Any other reproduction or redistribution is strictly prohibited. All rights reserved.

- Volunteering to help political parties
- Running for election to local, state, or national offices

Individuals can also donate money to political causes or support political groups that focus on specific causes such as abortion, wildlife conservation, or women's rights. These groups often make use of **representatives** who lobby legislators to act in support of their efforts.

WAYS IN WHICH POLITICAL CAMPAIGN GAINS FUNDING

Political campaigns are very expensive. In addition to the basic necessities of a campaign office, including office supplies, office space, etc., a large quantity of the money that funds a political campaign goes toward **advertising**. Money to fund a political campaign can come from several sources, including:

- The candidate's personal funds
- Donations by individuals
- Special interest groups

The most significant source of campaign funding is **special interest groups**. Groups in favor of certain policies will donate money to candidates they believe will support those policies. Special interest groups also do their own advertising in support of candidates they endorse.

Review Video: <u>Political Campaigns</u>
Visit mometrix.com/academy and enter code: 838608

IMPORTANCE OF FREE PRESS AND THE MEDIA

The right to free speech guaranteed in the first amendment to the Constitution allows the media to report on **government and political activities** without fear of retribution. Because the media has access to information about the government, the government's policies and actions, and debates and discussions that occur in Congress, it can keep the public informed about the inner workings of the government. The media can also draw attention to injustices, imbalances of power, and other transgressions the government or government officials might commit. However, media outlets may, like special interest groups, align themselves with certain political viewpoints and skew their reports to fit that viewpoint. The rise of the **internet** has made media reporting even more complex, as news can be found from an infinite variety of sources, both reliable and unreliable.

FORMS OF GOVERNMENT

ANARCHISM, COMMUNISM, AND DICTATORSHIP

Anarchists believe that all government should be eliminated and that individuals should rule themselves. Historically, anarchists have used violence and assassination to further their beliefs.

Communism is based on class conflict, revolution, and a one-party state. Ideally, a communist government would involve a single government for the entire world. Communist government controls the production and flow of goods and services rather than leaving this to companies or individuals.

Dictatorship involves rule by a single individual. If rule is enforced by a small group, this is referred to as an oligarchy. Dictators tend to rule with a violent hand, using a highly repressive police force to ensure control over the populace.

Copyright © Mometrix Media. You have been licensed one copy of this document for personal use only. Any other reproduction or redistribution is strictly prohibited. All rights reserved.

FASCISM AND MONARCHY

Fascism centers on a single leader and is, ideologically, an oppositional belief to communism. **Fascism** includes a single-party state and centralized control. The power of the fascist leader lies in the "cult of personality," and the fascist state often focuses on expansion and conquering of other nations. **Monarchy** was the major form of government for Europe through most of its history.

A monarchy is led by a king or a queen. This position is hereditary, and the rulers are not elected. In modern times, constitutional monarchy has developed, where the king and queen still exist, but most of the governmental decisions are made by democratic institutions such as a parliament.

PRESIDENTIAL SYSTEM AND SOCIALISM

A presidential system, like a parliamentary system, has a legislature and political parties, but there is no difference between the head of state and the head of government. Instead of separating these functions, an elected president performs both. Election of the president can be direct or indirect, and the president may not necessarily belong to the largest political party. In **socialism**, the state controls the production of goods, though it does not necessarily own all means of production. The state also provides a variety of social services to citizens and helps guide the economy. A democratic form of government often exists in socialist countries.

Review Video: Socialism
Visit mometrix.com/academy and enter code: 917677

TOTALITARIAN AND AUTHORITARIAN SYSTEMS

A totalitarian system believes everything should be under the control of the government—from resource production, to the press, to religion, and other social institutions. All aspects of life under a totalitarian system must conform to the ideals of the government. **Authoritarian** governments practice widespread state authority but do not necessarily dismantle all public institutions. If a church, for example, exists as an organization but poses no threat to the authority of the state, an authoritarian government might leave it as it is. While all totalitarian governments are by definition authoritarian, a government can be authoritarian without becoming totalitarian.

Review Video: Totalitarianism vs. Authoritarianism
Visit mometrix.com/academy and enter code: 104046

PARLIAMENTARY AND DEMOCRATIC SYSTEMS

In a parliamentary system, government involves a legislature and a variety of political parties. The head of government, usually a prime minister, is typically the head of the dominant party. A head of state can be elected, or this position can be taken by a monarch, as in Great Britain's constitutional monarchy system.

In a **democratic system** of government, the people elect their government representatives. The word *democracy* is a Greek term that means "rule of the people." There are two forms of democracy: direct and indirect. In a direct democracy, each issue or election is decided by a vote where each individual is counted separately. An indirect democracy employs a legislature that votes on issues that affect large numbers of people whom the legislative members represent. Democracy can exist as a parliamentary system or a presidential system. The US is a presidential, indirect democracy.

Copyright © Mometrix Media. You have been licensed one copy of this document for personal use only. Any other reproduction or redistribution is strictly prohibited. All rights reserved.

REALISM, LIBERALISM, INSTITUTIONALISM, AND CONSTRUCTIVISM IN INTERNATIONAL RELATIONS

The theory of realism states that nations are by nature aggressive and work in their own self-interest. Relations between nations are determined by military and economic strength. The nation is seen as the highest authority. **Liberalism** believes states can cooperate and that they act based on capability rather than power. This term was originally coined to describe Woodrow Wilson's theories on international cooperation. In **institutionalism**, institutions provide structure and incentive for cooperation among nations. Institutions are defined as a set of rules used to make international decisions. These institutions also help distribute power and determine how nations will interact. **Constructivism**, like liberalism, is based on international cooperation but recognizes that perceptions countries have of each other can affect their relations.

> **Review Video: Social Liberalism**
> Visit mometrix.com/academy and enter code: 624507

EFFECTS OF FOREIGN POLICY ON A COUNTRY'S POSITION IN WORLD AFFAIRS

Foreign policy is a set of goals, policies, and strategies that determine how an individual nation will interact with other countries. These strategies shift, sometimes quickly and drastically, according to actions or changes occurring in the other countries. However, a nation's **foreign policy** is often based on a certain set of ideals and national needs. Examples of US foreign policy include isolationism versus internationalism. In the 1800s, the US leaned more toward isolationism, exhibiting a reluctance to become involved in foreign affairs. The World Wars led to a period of internationalism, as the US entered these wars in support of other countries and joined the United Nations. Today's foreign policy tends more toward **interdependence**, or **globalism**, recognizing the widespread effects of issues like economic health.

MAJOR FIGURES INVOLVED IN DETERMINING AND ENACTING US FOREIGN POLICY

US foreign policy is largely determined by Congress and the president, influenced by the secretary of state, secretary of defense, and the national security adviser. Executive officials carry out policies. The main departments in charge of these day-to-day issues are the **US Department of State**, also referred to as the State Department. The Department of State carries out policy, negotiates treaties, maintains diplomatic relations, assists citizens traveling in foreign countries, and ensures that the president is properly informed of any international issues. The **Department of Defense**, the largest executive department in the US, supervises the armed forces and provides assistance to the president in his role as commander-in-chief.

MAJOR TYPES OF INTERNATIONAL ORGANIZATIONS

Two types of international organizations are:

- **Intergovernmental organizations (IGOs)**. These organizations are made up of members from various national governments. The UN is an example of an intergovernmental organization. Treaties among the member nations determine the functions and powers of these groups.
- **Nongovernmental organizations (NGOs)**. An NGO lies outside the scope of any government and is usually supported through private donations. An example of an NGO is the International Red Cross, which works with governments all over the world when their countries are in crisis but is formally affiliated with no particular country or government.

Copyright © Mometrix Media. You have been licensed one copy of this document for personal use only. Any other reproduction or redistribution is strictly prohibited. All rights reserved.

ROLE OF DIPLOMATS IN INTERNATIONAL RELATIONS

Diplomats are individuals who reside in foreign countries in order to maintain communications between that country and their home country. They help negotiate trade agreements and environmental policies, as well as conveying official information to foreign governments. They also help to resolve conflicts between the countries, often working to sort out issues without making the conflicts official in any way. **Diplomats**, or **ambassadors**, are appointed in the US by the president. Appointments must be approved by Congress.

ROLE OF THE UNITED NATIONS IN INTERNATIONAL RELATIONS AND DIPLOMACY

The United Nations (**UN**) helps form international policies by hosting representatives of various countries who then provide input into policy decisions. Countries that are members of the UN must agree to abide by all final UN resolutions, but this is not always the case in practice, as dissent is not uncommon. If countries do not follow UN resolutions, the UN can decide on sanctions against those countries, often economic sanctions, such as trade restriction. The UN can also send military forces to problem areas, with "peacekeeping" troops brought in from member nations. An example of this function is the Korean War, the first war in which an international organization played a major role.

Copyright © Mometrix Media. You have been licensed one copy of this document for personal use only. Any other reproduction or redistribution is strictly prohibited. All rights reserved.

Illinois Government

ADOPTION AND RATIFICATION OF STATE CONSTITUTIONS IN ILLINOIS

The State of Illinois adopted its first **constitution** in 1818 upon Illinois' admission into the Union. Newer constitutions were ratified in 1848 and 1870. The **fourth Illinois State Constitution** was ratified at a special election held in 1970, and this is the current version. The parts of this constitution consist of one preamble, fourteen articles, and one schedule. These parts are: Preamble, similar to the Preamble of the United States Constitution;

- Article I – Bill of Rights
- Article II – The Powers of the State
- Article III – Suffrage and Elections
- Article IV – The Legislature
- Article V – The Executive
- Article VI – The Judiciary
- Article VII – Local Government
- Article VIII – Finance
- Article IX – Revenue
- Article X – Education
- Article XI – Environment
- Article XII – Militia
- Article XIII – General Provisions
- Article XIV – Constitutional Revision; and the Transition

Schedule detailing when each of the changes in provisions made by the newest Constitution would go into effect.

ILLINOIS STATE CONSTITUTION'S ARTICLE I, BILL OF RIGHTS

The following are the rights provided for in each section of the Illinois State Constitution's **Article I, Bill of Rights**:

1. Inherent and Inalienable Rights, reflecting the U.S. Constitution

2. Due process and equal protection under the law

3. Religious Freedom

4. Freedom of Speech

5. Right to Assemble and Petition

6. Searches, Seizures, Privacy and Interceptions

7. Indictment and Preliminary Hearing

8. Rights after Indictment

8.1. Crime Victim's Rights

9. Bail and Habeas Corpus

10. Self-Incrimination and Double Jeopardy

144

Copyright © Mometrix Media. You have been licensed one copy of this document for personal use only. Any other reproduction or redistribution is strictly prohibited. All rights reserved.

11. Limitation of Penalties after Conviction

12. Right to Remedy and Justice

13. Trial by Jury

14. Imprisonment for Debt

15. Right of Eminent Domain

16. Ex Post Facto Laws and Impairing Contracts

17. No Discrimination in Employment and the Sale or Rental of Property

18. No Discrimination on the Basis of Sex

19. No Discrimination against the Handicapped

20. Individual Dignity

21. Quartering of Soldiers

22. Right to Arms

23. Fundamental Principles

24. Rights Retained (Many of these reflect rights in the U.S. Constitution, including amendments as of 1970.)

ILLINOIS STATE CONSTITUTION'S ARTICLE II – THE POWERS OF THE STATE

Article II, The Powers of the State, has two sections. Section 1, **Separation of Powers**, reads: "The legislative, executive, and judicial branches are separate. No branch shall exercise powers properly belonging to another." This reflects the same separation of powers established in the United States Constitution. The State of Illinois has the same three branches as the federal government. Section 2, **Powers of Government**, states: "The enumeration in this Constitution of specified powers and functions shall not be construed as a limitation of powers of state government." This can be interpreted to mean that, while the state constitution names specific powers of state government and certain functions it performs, the powers of state government include but are not necessarily limited to those named in the state constitution. One may infer from this that the state government has the power to perform additional functions and take other actions not detailed in its constitution.

BASIC PRINCIPLES EXPRESSED IN ILLINOIS STATE CONSTITUTION

The **Preamble** to the Illinois State Constitution thanks God for the civil, political, and religious liberties realized by the people of Illinois, and it also asks for the blessing of their endeavors. These **endeavors** include the following: to provide for the safety, welfare, and health of the people; to sustain a government that is organized and representative of the state's population; to eradicate inequity and poverty among its citizens; to ensure justice, both socially and economically; to give individuals opportunities for their most complete development; to keep peace on a domestic level; to provide for the defense of the people; and to ensure liberty and freedom to the people of Illinois and their future generations. The wording of the Illinois State Constitution's preamble is identical to that of the U.S. Constitution's preamble in certain phrases, for example, "to ensure domestic tranquility" and "provide for the common defense."

Copyright © Mometrix Media. You have been licensed one copy of this document for personal use only. Any other reproduction or redistribution is strictly prohibited. All rights reserved.

JUDICIAL BRANCH OF ILLINOIS STATE GOVERNMENT

The judicial branch of the Illinois State Government has two main divisions, the Courts Commission and the State Supreme Court. Included under the **Courts Commission** are the Judicial Inquiry Board and the Court of Claims. Included under the **State Supreme Court** are the Appellate Court; the Circuit Courts; and the Administrative Office of the Illinois Courts. The **Administrative Office** of the Illinois Courts is responsible for the administration of the following groups and individuals: the Board of Admissions to the Bar (for attorneys); the Attorney Registration and Disciplinary Commission; the State Appellate Defender; and the State's Attorneys Appellate Prosecutor. The judicial branch has the fewest divisions in Illinois State Government. The legislative branch has three main divisions, with eleven subordinate committees, commissions, bureaus, or units. The executive branch is the largest, with many departments, and all other state government boards, commissions, committees, councils, authorities, and so forth under it.

ILLINOIS STATE GOVERNMENT'S LEGISLATIVE BRANCH

The legislative branch of the Illinois State Government is divided into three main parts: the **House of Representatives**, the **Senate**, and the **Auditor General**. The State House of Representatives and State Senate make up the **State General Assembly**. The Clerk of the House, its committees, and its staff are under the State House of Representatives. The Secretary of the Senate, its committees, and its staff are under the State Senate. Under all three main divisions is the **Joint Committee on Legislative Support Services**. Under this committee are the following units, each one in charge of the legislative support services reflected in their names: the Joint Committee on Administrative Rules; the Legislative Information System; the Legislative Audit Commission; the Legislative Printing Unit; the Economic and Fiscal Commission; the Legislative Reference Bureau; the Commission on Intergovernmental Cooperation; the Legislative Research Unit; the Pension Laws Commission; and the Legislative Space Needs Commission.

EXECUTIVE BRANCH OF ILLINOIS STATE GOVERNMENT

The executive branch is divided into the secretary of state, treasurer, governor, lieutenant governor, comptroller, and the attorney general. The Board of Ethics, the Bureau of the Budget, and the Office of Citizens Assistance answer directly to the **governor**. Also under the governor are twenty-four **civil administrative code departments**. These are: the State Board of Education; the Department on Aging; the Departments of Agriculture, Central Management Services, Children and Family Services, Commerce and Community Affairs, Corrections, Employment Security, Financial Institutions, Human Rights, Human Services, Insurance, Labor, Military Affairs, Natural Resources, Nuclear Safety, Professional Regulation, Public Aid, Public Health, Revenue, Transportation, and Veterans Affairs; and the Illinois State Police and State Lottery. The Departments of Children and Family Services, Mental Health, Public Aid, and Public Aid are parts of the Department of Human Services. In addition to these civil administrative code departments, there are many other Commissions/Boards/Agencies under the executive branch.

REGULATORY AGENCIES

The executive branch contains fourteen **regulatory agencies**, which are not included as Civil Administrative Code Departments. These regulatory agencies are the State Board of Elections, for regulating state elections to prevent illegal and unethical practices; the Office of Banks and Real Estate, for enforcing real estate law; the Commerce Commission, for controlling state commercial practices; the Health Care Cost Containment Council, for controlling excessive state government spending on health care; the Industrial Commission, for regulating state industries; the Liquor Control Commission; the Racing, Gaming, and Lottery Control Boards, for regulation of gambling; the Banking Board; the Board of Savings Institutions; the Hospital Licensing Board, for the

Copyright © Mometrix Media. You have been licensed one copy of this document for personal use only. Any other reproduction or redistribution is strictly prohibited. All rights reserved.

administration and regulation of the licensure of hospitals; the Medical Licensing Board, for the administration and regulation of licensure to physicians, nurses, and other medical practitioners; and the Miners Examining Board, for administering and regulating the qualification of miners to work in the state.

FINANCING AUTHORITIES WITHIN ILLINOIS STATE GOVERNMENT

Under the executive branch of Illinois State Government, the **Housing Development Authority** is a financing authority that administers funding for such things as mortgage loans for homeowners. As farming is such an important part of the Illinois state economy, the **Farm Development Authority** administers funding that is allocated to support farming in the state, and the **Rural Bond Bank** provides business loans to farmers to help them establish, develop, maintain, and run their farms. The **Medical District Commission** is a financing authority that is in charge of financing for each of the state's medical districts, and the **Health Facilities Authority** is another financing authority that manages funding for hospitals and other medical facilities in the state. The executive branch also has the **Sports Facilities Authority** that manages finances for the state's various sporting facilities. The **Export Development Authority** administers funds supporting exporting Illinois goods to other states and countries.

FIRST STEP IN ILLINOIS STATE CONSTITUTION'S PROVISIONS FOR RECALLING A GOVERNOR

The state constitution stipulates that **recall of a governor** requires a petition signed by electors numbering at least 15 percent of all votes that governor received in the election. A minimum of 100 of these signatures must come from each of a minimum of twenty-five different counties. This petition must be signed no later than 150 days after the petitioners have filed an affidavit with the State Board of Elections, notifying the board of their intent to distribute such a petition to recall the governor. The constitution requires this affidavit be filed no earlier than six months after the governor's term of office began. The person proposing the recall petition must sign the affidavit, as well as a minimum twenty members of the State House of Representatives and ten members of the state senate. The signatures from the House and Senate, respectively, must not include more than half from one party.

CURRENT POWER AND STRUCTURE OF THE ILLINOIS STATE LEGISLATURE

A 1980 amendment provides that the House and Senate are elected by **electors** from fifty-nine legislative districts and 118 representative districts. Laws are enacted only by **bill**. Either of the two houses may initiate a bill; either may amend or reject a bill from the other house. A majority vote from members of each house is required for a bill to become law. A bill's final passage is by record vote of yeas and nays recorded on the journal. Bills passed must be presented to the governor within thirty calendar days. To veto a bill, the governor returns it to the initiating house with objections within sixty calendar days of presentation. Objections are entered on one house's journal; if three-fifths of that house passes the bill within fifteen calendar days, and the other house does the same within fifteen calendar days of receiving it, it becomes law despite the veto.

PROVISIONS INTERGOVERNMENTAL COOPERATION BY ILLINOIS STATE CONSTITUTIONAL LAW

Article VII, Local Government, of the Illinois State Constitution, Section 10, **Intergovernmental Cooperation**, provides the following: Units of local government and school districts are allowed to contract and associate with the state, with other states and their local governments and school districts, with the United States Government; with individuals, associations, and corporations, in any ways that are not prohibited by any laws or ordinances. Governmental entities doing this are allowed to use their revenue, credit, and/or other resources to pay debts and expenses associated with such intergovernmental actions. This section of the law stipulates that employees and officers

Copyright © Mometrix Media. You have been licensed one copy of this document for personal use only. Any other reproduction or redistribution is strictly prohibited. All rights reserved.

of local government units and school districts do not have to give up their positions to participate in intergovernmental activities authorized by their employing units. It also provides that the state will use its monetary and technical resources to support intergovernmental activity and promote cooperation among governments and the private sector.

IRON TRIANGLES IN GOVERNMENT

Iron triangles refer to relationships among government agencies, legislative oversight committees/subcommittees, and special interest lobbies. Members in these relationships reciprocally support one another, but are closed against outside influences attempting to change policies achieved by long-term "insider" negotiations. For example, if a new president or a new majority in Congress tries to reform or downsize government agencies, these agencies' bureaucrats may rely on their congressional colleagues to prevent it. Reciprocally, senators and representatives running oversight committees depend on friends in the agencies to maintain their "pet" programs and pork-barrel projects. Lobbies give information and campaign support, and influence public opinion, for agencies and committees. In return, lobbies' special interests are protected in new laws or appointments by agency and committee members. These "triangles" are "strong as iron" because proponents of more general societal interests usually cannot affect policymaking if those interests contradict the special interests of politicians, bureaucrats, and lobbyists.

RECENTLY PROPOSED TAX INCREASE IN ILLINOIS

In January of 2011, an **increase to income taxes** was proposed. According to the Illinois Policy Institute, a couple with two children and a combined income of $80,000 already pay an average of $2,160.00 in income taxes, and would have to pay $1,527.00 more under this increase. The Institute reports that in job creation and competition, Illinois currently is ranked near the bottom among the states. Proponents of repealing the new tax hike warn it could lower personal income by $17.3 billion over the coming 3-5 years, corresponding to a loss of $2,734 per household and of 217,519 jobs in the private sector. These outcomes could devastate Illinois' already suffering economy. Both Democrats and Republicans in Congress agreed with President Obama about the necessity of providing Federal tax relief, but Illinois' 67 percent increase in personal income tax will subtract nearly twice the savings made by the bipartisan federal tax cut.

PROBLEMS WITH TAXATION, BUSINESS COMPETITION, POPULATION, AND SPENDING IN ILLINOIS

Illinois' new **corporate income tax rate** of 7 percent, added to 2.5 percent tax on personal property replacement, means Illinois' corporate tax rate is among the highest worldwide, exceeding those of France, Germany, and Russia. New taxes will change Illinois' rank in the Tax Foundation's State Business Tax Climate Index from 23 to 36; its individual income tax rank from 9 to 14; and its corporate tax rank from 27 to 45. Competition will be damaged by businesses starting/expanding in other states, removing more jobs from Illinois. A new 67 percent tax increase reinforces Illinois' reputation as a high-tax state, with lower growth rates in population, personal income, and employment. This tax hike is supposed to end in 2015, but experience shows "temporary" increases in Illinois usually become permanent, for example, those for the Illinois Tollway. Experts also note that regardless of revenue, spending continues to escalate, and necessary reforms have not been instituted.

EFFECTS OF PUBLIC POLICY ON MIGRATION PATTERNS OF PEOPLE FROM ILLINOIS

The Illinois Policy Institute states that **public policy** influences people's **residential choices**, remarking that "Migration between the U.S. States is the ultimate expression of 'voting with your feet.'" From 1991-2009, there were 1,227,347 Illinois residents that moved to other states, equaling 1.22 residents every ten minutes. An average $1.8 billion in annual net income moved out

Copyright © Mometrix Media. You have been licensed one copy of this document for personal use only. Any other reproduction or redistribution is strictly prohibited. All rights reserved.

of Illinois from 1995-2007 for a total $23.5 billion loss, representing $2.4 billion in lost tax revenues. The state also loses all future income from residents moving out, representing an estimated $16.9 billion in state and local tax revenue and $163.6 billion in net income lost. The motivations for moving include lower taxes, lower residence costs, lower union dues, lower population densities, and warmer weather. Especially significant is that the largest proportion of migration by Illinois residents is to Florida, which not only has warmer weather, but also has no estate tax and no individual income tax.

LIBERTY LEADERS

Citing the success of national volunteer organizations such as MoveOn.org, the Illinois Policy Institute offers a state organization, **Liberty Leaders**, which was launched in 2008. Members attend and participate in local board meetings. They write letters to the editor of local newspapers to inform and influence public opinion. They telephone elected officials asking them to vote for/against specific laws and support policies they believe will protect/promote liberty in Illinois. They function as teachers, instructing their local communities in practical methods of reestablishing transparency and accountability in local governments. They organize to address a variety of issues, including educational reform, budget management, et cetera. Adam Andrzejewski, founder of non-profit FortheGoodofIllinois.org, ran for governor in 2010 on a platform of accountability and transparency. Liberty Leader Michael Tams ran for and won the office of Lisle Township Board Trustee in 2009. Liberty Leader Mike Gorman ran for and won the presidency of the village of Riverside.

REQUIREMENTS FOR VOTER REGISTRATION IN ILLINOIS

In Illinois, an individual must be a United States citizen, must be 18 years old by election day, and must have been a resident of their precinct for a minimum of thirty days before election day in order to **register to vote**. Voter registration is available all year except for twenty-seven days before an election and two days after an election, or one day after an election in Chicago. Some labor unions or groups, some civic groups, and some corporations may be entitled to register their members to vote. Individuals can register to vote at schools, public libraries, military recruitment offices, township offices, the offices of precinct committee members, city and village offices, county clerks' offices, and offices of the Board of Elections Commissioners. They may also register when applying for driver's licenses, services from the Department of Healthcare and Family Services, or services from the Department of Employment Security.

INFLUENCE OF PUBLIC OPINION ON GOVERNMENT POLICY

Various studies have been conducted on the general question of whether **public opinion** influences **policymaking**. They have all found that public opinion does indeed affect policy. However, one study by Casey Borch and David Weakliem (2005) additionally investigated whether or not different groups among the public have varying amounts of influence on policies. As in others' studies, this one used a statistical regression method to compare measures of policy with measures of public opinion on corresponding issues, and with control variables. To generalize extant research, Borch and Weakliem weighted averages of individual opinions in the sample. They compared the averages with models giving different weights to different groups' opinions to see if influences among groups were unequal. They found relatively strong support for their hypothesis that the opinions of highly educated people had more influence than those of the less educated. Their hypothesis that blacks' opinions had less influence than whites' opinions received weaker support.

Copyright © Mometrix Media. You have been licensed one copy of this document for personal use only. Any other reproduction or redistribution is strictly prohibited. All rights reserved.

OCTOBER 2010 ILLINOIS STATE SUPREME COURT DECISION IN FAVOR OF CHICAGO JOHN WALSH

In 2007, accountant and president of his condominium association **John Walsh** spoke in a public meeting at his alderman's office in Chicago about problems with developers of his condo. A reporter interviewed and quoted him. The developers sued Walsh for **defamation**. For the first time, the Illinois State Supreme Court analyzed the **2007 Illinois Citizen Participation Act** and unanimously ruled in October 2010 that Walsh was immune from liability under this law, which protects a citizen's constitutional right to participate in government. The court interpreted the law broadly regarding scope of immunity, deciding citizens have the right to complain not just to city councils, but also to the press. Though speaking at public meetings is American, "strategic lawsuits against public participation," or SLAPP suits, have been brought to discourage civic activists. In reaction, almost half the states, including Illinois, regulate such suits. The developers had to pay Walsh's legal expenses.

RESOURCES OFFERED BY THE IGFOA

The **Illinois Government Finance Officers Association** (IGFOA) furthers its mission of promoting excellence in government finance by providing numerous member benefits. It presents low-cost seminars, statewide and in neighboring states cooperatively with other GFOAs, in cash management, debt administration, governmental accounting, capital planning, and budgeting; and updates the complexities of public pensions at the Illinois Public Pension Institute. It offers an ethics workshop and workshops/seminars on changing federal and state regulations, procedures, and developing technologies. It sends a weekly job opening newsletter and affords networking among finance professionals. Its legislative committee monitors actions of the Illinois General Assembly, state administrative agencies, and represents interests of members and local governments to them. Its Technical Accounting Review Committee monitors actions/rulings of the Governmental Accounting Standards Board (GASB), informs members of these, and represents members in testimony to the GASB on proposed standards. It provides an online financial services guide. The IGFOA has several chapters and additional committees.

LGDF IN ILLINOIS

According to the Illinois Municipal League (IML), the **Local Government Distributive Fund** (LGDF) must be protected against decreases in funding as an important source of revenue for cities, towns, and villages. Local government units receive 10 percent of the state's shared revenues. The LGDF distributes these funds on a per capita basis to municipalities and unincorporated parts of counties. The IML has conducted surveys of Illinois municipalities and found that some of them depend upon the LGDF's disbursements for up to 45 percent of their operations budgets. The IML also reported as of 2010 that in many Illinois cities, unpaid LGDF bills had accumulated for five months as the state had not been making monthly payments to the LGDF on time. The IML noted that the state needed to begin making timely payments. Illinois municipal residents rely on services funded by the LGDF, such as clearing snow, caring for grass, and the provision of police and fire protection services.

STATUS OF PENSIONS FOR PUBLIC SAFETY EMPLOYEES FOR LOCAL GOVERNMENTS IN ILLINOIS

The Illinois Municipal League (IML) reports that **pensions for public safety employees** represent financial challenges for local governments. Officials have expressed concern they may be unable to sustain pension benefits at present levels in the near future. Of particular concern are future benefits for newer public safety employees who will retire later. The IML collaborated with the Illinois General Assembly in 2008 to pass significant **pension reforms**. The members of the IML

Copyright © Mometrix Media. You have been licensed one copy of this document for personal use only. Any other reproduction or redistribution is strictly prohibited. All rights reserved.

viewed these reforms as an initial step to raise consciousness and understand laws better prior to their being enacted. Almost all of the Illinois pension systems were further reformed by legislation that the general assembly passed and the governor signed in 2010. While the Downstate Police and Fire Pension Funds were not included in these reforms, the IML states that the Illinois House of Representatives Police and Fire Pension Reform Sub-Committee have since met to discuss more reforms.

IMPACT OF UNFUNDED GOVERNMENT MANDATES UPON LOCAL GOVERNMENTS IN ILLINOIS

At times, the federal and state governments issue **directives** that will affect local governments financially without providing appropriations to cover the expenses that will be incurred by compliance with such mandates. This can result in a decrease in services and/or an increase in taxation. **Unfunded proposals** by the federal government are resented by state government officials, and those issued by state governments are likewise resented by local government officials, since proposals without accompanying funding compound their economic burdens. It is not unusual for interest groups to make proposals to the Illinois General Assembly, some worthwhile. However, the Illinois Municipal League warns groups should be responsible to include funding sources for such proposals. An example of an unfunded mandate is the Freedom of Information Act. The IML determines that local officials having to address requests under this Act are its only real practitioners and should be consulted about improving it.

FINANCIAL ISSUE IN LOCAL ILLINOIS GOVERNMENT RELATED TO IMPROVING LOCAL ROADS

The local government units in Illinois are responsible for maintaining more than 88 percent of the **public roads**. The Illinois Municipal League (IML) reports that a considerable amount of work on the local transportation systems in Illinois is needed. The **Capital Infrastructure Improvement Program** was passed by the Illinois General Assembly and signed into law by Governor Pat Quinn in 2009. Under this program, $500 million in funds to maintain and repair local roads was included. By late in August of 2010, more than $660 million worth of **Transportation Series D Bonds** had been sold. The revenue from the sale of these bonds could be used for work to improve both state and local roadways. But none of these monies has been designated specifically for local road work. As a result, none of the funds available for road improvement has been released, and no improvement to local roads has been made.

LOCAL CONTROL AND POWERS OF HOME RULE

The Illinois Municipal League (IML) finds that elected government officials are closest to their constituencies on the **local level**, and that therefore, maintaining local government control affords local officials the freedom to make decisions on this level, where those decisions will be most applicable to the needs and interests of the local people. This gives local government officials the best chances to serve their constituents. The IML asks local government officials to urge all candidates for the state's general assembly to eschew any laws that undermine the authority of local officials to make decisions on behalf of their local constituents. Almost 200 municipalities in Illinois are home rule municipalities, meaning they have the authority for self-governance in customizing their legislation to meet citizen needs and serve their communities. The IML feels local officials know what is best for their communities, and thus that state officials should not restrict their authority.

REFORMS MADE TO MEDICAID PROGRAM IN ILLINOIS IN JANUARY OF 2011

On January 25, 2011, Illinois Governor Pat Quinn signed into law a set of major reforms to the state's **Medicaid program** as a bipartisan effort of Illinois legislators. Quinn referred to the enactment of these reforms as a "landmark achievement." He stated the Medicaid reforms are part of his plan for stabilizing the budget. The **budget deficit** in Illinois is projected to reach $15 billion

Copyright © Mometrix Media. You have been licensed one copy of this document for personal use only. Any other reproduction or redistribution is strictly prohibited. All rights reserved.

within the year. The governor's office expects Medicaid reform to save an estimated $624 to $774 million within five years. Medicaid's yearly budget equals roughly 1/3 of Illinois' budget for general revenue funds. Of 2.8 million Illinois people receiving Medicaid, the new law requires half to be on managed care by 2015, a plan that many critics find will be difficult. The law also aims to save money by decreasing institutionalization of persons with disabilities, paying Medicaid bills earlier to save late penalties, and reducing Medicaid fraud.

NSTU

The **Northwest Suburban Taxpayers United** (NSTU) organization was founded in December 2010. Its founder, **Roland Ley**, found that while his property value was lower than before, his November property tax bill was higher. He and others discovered upon contacting the tax assessor's office that it determines property values but does not control tax levies or the amounts each taxing entity charges. In response, Ley contacted other taxpayers and organized the NSTU in Barrington, Elk Grove, Hanover, Schaumburg, and Wheeling townships. With over eighty governing units included in these townships, Ley says the NSTU is recruiting members, as hundreds or thousands will be required to monitor all units and report their findings to the group and communities. NSTU members feel taxpayers have a responsibility to become more involved with local governments. Organizing as a Political Action Committee (PAC), NSTU has goals including ending local schools tenures, limiting fund balances, and freezing compensation.

ALCOHOL PROHIBITION IN KNOXVILLE, ILLINOIS

The city of Knoxville, Illinois has had a ban on the sale of **alcohol** for seventy-seven years. While prohibition nationwide was enacted in 1907 and repealed by the 21st Amendment to the United States Constitution in 1933, Knoxville is an example of a town that made its own local laws, prohibiting alcohol sales after national prohibition ended. As reported in the Galesburg Register-Mail, in January 2011 Knoxville residents filed petitions with the city to repeal the alcohol ban. The total of 529 signatures constituted thirty-five more than the legally required minimum. This proposal was not contested and was placed on the ballot for the April general election. With a majority vote to discontinue the ban, the city council would issue an ordinance permitting businesses to sell alcoholic beverages, and can also restrict the number of businesses it permits. With several offices running uncontested, this issue could become central to the election.

FREEDOM OF INFORMATION ACT AND OPINIONS OF LOCAL GOVERNMENT OFFICIALS IN ILLINOIS

The Freedom of Information Act is a Federal law which has recently undergone a number of amendments of a pervasive and complicated nature. Officials in local Illinois governments have expressed concern about a lack of clarity in the interpretation of this amended law. They are also worried about the amendments causing increases in both monetary expenses for local government and workloads for its employees. In addition, they see a problem with shorter response times required for requests. The Illinois Municipal League and other local government organizations are collaborating to determine which changes to the **Freedom of Information Act** are the most important ones to be made. The Illinois Municipal League has published a list of thirteen areas wherein they propose changes to the Freedom of Information Act aimed at reducing confusion, abuse, costs, dangers to individual citizens, red tape, inappropriate requirements and standards, and facilitating public access to available information.

CHANGES NEEDED TO ELIMINATE THE ABUSE OF COMMERCIAL REQUESTS

According to the Illinois Municipal League, requests that are being made for **commercial purposes** under the aegis of the Freedom of Information Act only cause significant, unneeded demands on communities by incurring considerable expense without advancing this law's purposes of

152

Copyright © Mometrix Media. You have been licensed one copy of this document for personal use only. Any other reproduction or redistribution is strictly prohibited. All rights reserved.

increasing government accountability and the participation of citizens in the democratic process. Working with other local government groups, the Illinois Municipal League advocates that the Illinois State General Assembly should **prohibit the use of the Freedom of Information Act for commercial reasons**. They call for the General Assembly further to add to the definition of a "commercial purpose" to mean not only the sale of a product or service, but also the "furtherance of a commercial enterprise." In addition, they recommend that the Illinois State government should give the public a way to address such circumstances wherein requests are incorrectly made for commercial purposes under the Freedom of Information Act.

ELIMINATING OR PREVENTING CONFUSION AROUND REQUESTS

When someone makes a request under the Freedom of Information Act, the current request process does not just allow **confusion**; it perpetrates it by prohibiting the relevant public body from talking about the request with the requester. Thus public bodies are not allowed to clear up any questions about the details of a request. The Illinois Municipal League opines that the Illinois General Assembly should permit public bodies to ask "reasonable questions" about requests made under the Freedom of Information Act. They find that such questions would enable them to **clarify** these requests. They would also enable them to reduce the breadth of unreasonable or unrealistic requests. Asking questions directly of requesters would enable public bodies to ascertain whether requests are being made inappropriately for commercial purposes. It would further enable them to find out if fee waivers are applicable, and would enable them to negotiate time extensions as needed.

TOLLING RESPONSE TIME FOR REQUESTS WHEN ADVISORY OPINIONS FROM ATTORNEY GENERAL ARE SOLICITED

Under the Freedom of Information Act, public entities are authorized to ask for **advisory opinions** from their state attorney general when they see the need. If this statute were practicable, it could prevent much confusion over how to interpret the federal regulations under this law. However, the requirement for response time to requests under the Freedom of Information Act is five days. According to the Illinois Municipal League, public bodies that request an advisory opinion about a request would never be able to receive a response from the attorney general within the five days allotted. Therefore, the Illinois Municipal League, reflecting the opinions of its own members and of other local government organizations, has raised the point that the general assembly should provide for tolling the five-day response time when any public body asks the attorney general for an advisory opinion on a request under the Freedom of Information Act.

RATIONALE TO EXEMPT IDENTIFYING INFORMATION OF PROGRAM PARTICIPANTS

The **Freedom of Information Act** (FOIA) was designed to make more governmental information available to the public to ensure government accountability, transparency, and citizens' participation in our democracy. Following new amendments to this law, groups representing local Illinois government officials such as the **Illinois Municipal League** (IML) are advocating for changes to clarify and improve the amended law. The IML points out that it is a chief responsibility of all public bodies to protect their citizens' personal information, and that the Freedom of Information Act "should not be used as a loophole" to disclose information, as this could endanger citizens without affording any public benefit to justify such danger. As an example, the FOIA should not be used to make public bodies disclose the identities of "latch-key" children participating in after-school recreational/educational programs, which could threaten their safety. They feel the General Assembly should exempt such name or identity information.

Copyright © Mometrix Media. You have been licensed one copy of this document for personal use only. Any other reproduction or redistribution is strictly prohibited. All rights reserved.

PERSONNEL RECORDS

The FOIA previously had exempted **personnel files** from being open records, but recent amendments removed this exemption. Because of the sensitive private and personal information in personnel records, and the precedent that open-records laws nationwide tend to recognize this, the Illinois Municipal League and other local groups want their general assembly to **exempt from disclosure** such records as: letters of reference or recommendations regarding the "character or qualifications" of identifiable persons; performance reviews or ratings; results of civil service or other tests given by public agencies; job applications submitted to public bodies; information on workplace support service programs; written criticisms or complaints about employees; grievance documents, including over sexual harassment or discrimination; information on reprimands, discipline, remediation, demotion, or discharge (not to include an agency's final action which resulted in a demotion or discharge); academic transcripts; or any other information in a personnel file "that a person would consider private."

FINANCIAL IMPACT UPON TAXPAYERS

The Freedom of Information Act (FOIA) is a law that is known as an **unfunded mandate**. The federal government has enacted this law but has not provided funding appropriations for enforcing it at the local level, even though local governments are still responsible for this administration. The Illinois Municipal League (IML) points out that for every request filed under the FOIA, public employees must research, gather, and review documents. In addition to this expense of work time spent by government workers, if attorneys must also review documents to address legal issues, their billable hours are also charged to the government. Such costs are transmitted to the taxpayers. The IML suggests as one possibility that if one requester's fees accumulate to over $1,000 in one calendar year, the public body could charge a fee for any additional request to cover the full cost of searching for, reviewing, reproducing, and providing records.

DIFFICULTY OF DENIAL PROCESS

As a publication by the Illinois Municipal League (IML) makes clear, the Freedom of Information Act (FOIA) stipulates if a request for records is made of a public body that denies the request, this **denial** must give a "detailed factual basis" for denying the request, citing "supporting legal authority." However, as the IML's publication points out, this requirement makes use of circular reasoning: Giving such factual details to show why disclosing records would violate an individual's privacy would itself violate the individual's privacy! In addition, the requirement of a "citation to supporting legal authority" means an attorney would have to prepare a legal brief for every single denial. This would cause compliance with the FOIA to cost public bodies far more, increasing the cost to taxpayers accordingly. The Illinois Municipal League expresses the feeling of its members and those of other local government groups that these requirements should be removed.

EVIDENTIARY STANDARD FOR DENIALS OF RECORD REQUESTS

The recently amended Freedom of Information Act (FOIA) requires any public body that denies a request for records to prove its denial was **justified** by providing "clear and convincing evidence." The Illinois Municipal League (IML) is an organization that represents local government officials and collaborates with other local government associations, including endeavors to influence federal laws, regulations, and policies wherever they see the need. The IML has published discussion points for the changes its members feel are needed to the current FOIA. In these, its authors make the point that a standard of clear and convincing evidence is applicable to issues involving factual information. When facts are involved, this standard provides that the evidence convinces the trier that a claim is probably true. However, the IML notes most issues with the FOIA are not factual but involve interpretation of laws. They recommend the General Assembly remove this standard as inappropriate.

Copyright © Mometrix Media. You have been licensed one copy of this document for personal use only. Any other reproduction or redistribution is strictly prohibited. All rights reserved.

CONFLICT WITH FEDERAL AND STATE LAWS BANNING INFORMATION DISCLOSURE

The Illinois Municipal League (IML) makes note of the fact that while the Freedom of Information Act requires more disclosure of government records, many other federal and state laws have been passed concurrently that **prohibit disclosure**. This offense is often punishable by large fines or even criminal penalties. These opposing laws can put public bodies and officials between a rock and a hard place: If they supply information requested of them, they risk penalties for improper disclosure; but if they withhold the information by denying the request, they then risk penalties for violation of the Freedom of Information Act. The IML feels that public bodies should be given more clarity regarding which government records may or may not be disclosed. This group recommends that the Illinois General Assembly require the attorney general's office to identify all federal and state laws banning disclosure and publish them, with binding opinions, on the attorney general's website.

FINANCIAL CONSIDERATIONS

The Freedom of Information Act (FOIA) stipulates that local responses to this statute are a "primary duty" of public bodies, and that this statute "should be construed notwithstanding fiscal obligations" according to the Illinois Municipal League (IML). The IML notes, however, that FOIA responses are "the only 'primary duty' for communities identified under the statute." The group logically points out that local governments provide many other services in addition to responding to requests for records, and these other services can be just as important, if not more so. Regarding the requirement of construing the law "as if money were no object," the IML realistically observes that anyone acquainted with the workings of local governments "knows that money is always an object." It finds ignoring **financial considerations** not only unrealistic, but "bad policy." It recommends that the general assembly remove these requirements, which would constitute acknowledging the costs of the FOIA.

Copyright © Mometrix Media. You have been licensed one copy of this document for personal use only. Any other reproduction or redistribution is strictly prohibited. All rights reserved.

Psychology, Sociology, and Anthropology

IMPORTANCE OF SOCIALIZATION TO INDIVIDUALS WITHIN A SPECIFIC CULTURE

Individuals learn how to function within a specific culture, group, or society via a process called **socialization**. Social contact with other human beings is vitally important to early development so that children can grow up to function in society as expected.

During the early years, children receive socialization from their families, siblings, peers, and schoolmates, as well as from exposure to mass media when applicable. Observing the behavior of others and adapting it to their own use helps children learn to interact with others. This process continues throughout life as individuals learn to adapt to various situations and interact with new groups.

PROCESSES BRINGING ABOUT CULTURAL CHANGE AND TRAITS THAT APPEAR IN ALL CULTURES

Three major processes bring about the majority of changes in a culture:

1. **Discovery**—finding things that already exist, such as fire, a major cultural transformer
2. **Invention**—creating new equipment, machinery, etc., that changes the way tasks are accomplished
3. **Diffusion**—borrowing elements from other cultures

Over 70 **traits** have been identified that are found in nearly every culture to some level. These traits can be divided into four categories that determine the basic structure, mores, norms, and other characteristics of a culture:

- Language and cognition
- Society
- Myth, ritual, and aesthetics
- Technology

CULTURE

Culture refers to all learned human behaviors and behavioral patterns and is made up of:

- **Cultural universals**—traits shared by all human beings, such as language
- **Culture**—all traditions that define a society
- **Subculture**—groups within a culture that share specific traits

While culture serves as a survival mechanism by bringing people together in groups and helping individuals identify with each other, it also undergoes frequent and sometimes profound **change** as groups respond to new technologies, knowledge, or contact with other cultures.

CHARACTERISTICS AND IMPORTANCE OF RELIGION IN AN ANTHROPOLOGICAL SENSE

Strictly defined, **religion** consists of a belief system and usually a set of rituals involving worship of a supernatural force or forces that have some effect on both everyday life and the overall structure and functioning of the world around us. Religion provides meaning and explanation for various life events and profoundly affects a culture's **worldviews**. Religion provides emotional support for individuals and a sense of **community** within a group that has shared religious views. Religious

Copyright © Mometrix Media. You have been licensed one copy of this document for personal use only. Any other reproduction or redistribution is strictly prohibited. All rights reserved.

organization also provides structured sets of **moral norms** and motivation to abide by these norms and rules.

Increased **secularization**, particularly in developed countries, has reduced the role of religion in everyday life, leading individuals to find other systems to fill these basic human needs.

BEHAVIORISM

John B. Watson, an American, developed the idea of **behaviorism**. In his theory, growth, learning, and training would always win out over any possible inborn tendencies. He believed that any person, regardless of origin, could learn to perform any type of art, craft, or enterprise with sufficient training and experience.

SCIENCE OF SOCIOLOGY

Sociology is a scientific discipline that focuses on the study of societies. Human societies are made up of institutions, groups, and individuals. How all these levels of organization **interact** is the major interest of sociologists. The way individuals organize themselves, how they interact with each other, and the attitudes and beliefs different groups develop all define those groups' cultural backgrounds. Groups of people in the same geographical area often develop similar organizational structures, beliefs, and attitudes.

MAJOR STUDY AREAS COVERED BY SOCIOLOGY

The five major study areas covered by sociology are:

1. **Population studies**—these studies involve observing social patterns of groups of people who live in the same area.
2. **Social behaviors**—sociologists study how general behaviors change over time, as well as attitudes such as morale, need for conformity, and other elements of social interaction.
3. **Cultural influences**—the influences of culture on social groups include art, religion, language, and overall knowledge and learning.
4. **Social change**—this involves the ways societies change over time, including major events such as wars and revolutions, or the way technology changes how people interact.
5. **Social institutions**—large groups of people are organized to fit specific niches in society, such as churches, hospitals, government, businesses, and schools. These organizations change over time and according to the overall needs and beliefs of an individual society.

HOW SOCIOLOGISTS GATHER AND TEST DATA

The three major methods of gathering data for sociological studies are:

1. **Surveys**—gathering information via direct questioning of members of the social group being studied
2. **Controlled experiments**—performing experiments that change an element of society
3. **Field observations**—living among members of a particular group or culture and observing how they interact and live their everyday lives

MAJOR CLASSIFICATIONS OF SOCIAL GROUPS

Social groups are defined based on how they come into being, how they develop, and how they interact with wider society. The five major classifications are:

1. **Primary groups**—focused on members' need for support, such as a family or friend grouping
2. **Secondary groups**—form around the need to complete a task

Copyright © Mometrix Media. You have been licensed one copy of this document for personal use only. Any other reproduction or redistribution is strictly prohibited. All rights reserved.

3. **Reference groups**—help form an individual's identity
4. **In-groups and out-groups**—oppose each other or exclude members of other groups
5. **Social networks**—provide multiple links to an often large number of other individuals

MAJOR TYPES OF SOCIAL INTERACTION

Five main forms of social interaction help define social groups:

1. Cooperation
2. Coercion
3. Conflict
4. Conformity
5. Social exchange

All of these elements can bring a group into existence, break it apart, or transform it.

MAJOR SOCIAL INSTITUTIONS THAT CHARACTERIZE AND MEET THE NEEDS OF ANY SOCIETY

Six major social institutions that characterize and meet the needs of any society are:

1. **Family**—this is the basic unit of any society and the most important social institution in all sociological study.
2. **Education**—in many societies, the values and norms of culture are communicated through institutionalized education as well as via the family.
3. **Political institutions**—political institutions in a society determine the distribution of power.
4. **Economic institutions**—these institutions determine the distribution of wealth.
5. **Religion**—this provides mores and beliefs that help unify a culture. Unfortunately, many religions also function in an in-group/out-group capacity.
6. **Sport**—this reflects values of society, promotes unity, and provides an outlet for aggression.

VARIOUS PATTERNS USED BY SOCIOLOGISTS TO DEFINE RELATIONSHIPS INVOLVING RACE AND ETHNICITY

In general, relationships within cultures involving race and ethnicity are defined by either assimilation or conflict. **Assimilation** in the US can involve:

- **Anglo-conformity**—immigrants and racial minorities conform to the expectations of Anglo-American society, whether by choice, necessity, or force.
- **Cultural pluralism**—this involves the acceptance of varieties of racial and ethnic groups.
- **Accommodation**—this is mutual adaptation between majority and minority groups.
- **Melting pot**—the mixing together of various ethnic groups will bring about a new cultural group.

Patterns of **conflict** include:

- **Population transfer**—one group is required or forced to leave by another group.
- **Subjugation**—one group exercises control over the other.
- **Genocide**—one group slaughters another.

WAYS GENDER AND AGE LEAD TO DISCRIMINATION

In spite of legislation, education, and other attempts to bring about a higher level of equality, **discrimination** still exists against women and the elderly, particularly as it involves law, politics, and economic standing. Discrimination against **women** is particularly profound in most developing

Copyright © Mometrix Media. You have been licensed one copy of this document for personal use only. Any other reproduction or redistribution is strictly prohibited. All rights reserved.

countries. It is believed that increasing the standing of women in a society is a major element in increasing the overall livelihood of that society.

While some societies value the **elderly** for their knowledge and experience, others discriminate against older people because of their decreased physical ability and ability to contribute economically. In the US, the poverty level for the elderly still stands at about ten percent. As lifespan increases, all societies must find a way to accommodate the needs of the elderly population.

IMPORTANCE OF AUGUSTE COMTE

Auguste Comte, a French philosopher, first used the term *sociology* to describe the study of human organizations and culture. His major theory was **positivism**. Positivism relies entirely on physical and sensory data to describe and evaluate human experience, completely discounting anything metaphysical. **Social behavior**, according to Comte, could be measured scientifically, as could major events that occurred in different populations. Comte is considered to be the first sociologist in the Western world.

INFLUENCE OF ÉMILE DURKHEIM ON SOCIOLOGY AND SOCIOLOGICAL STUDY

Through Durkheim's efforts, sociology eventually came to be considered a discipline in major universities. Heavily influenced by Comte's views of positivism, Durkheim felt the larger world was influenced by group beliefs, attitudes, and cultural aspects rather than by individuals. He performed in-depth studies on the cause of higher suicide rates among certain social groups. In the course of this study, he discussed **anomie**, a condition when people are affected by larger changes in society, such as unemployment or alienation of social groups, and receive little moral guidance from society.

PHILOSOPHY OF KARL MARX AND FRIEDRICH ENGELS

According to Marx and Engels, society worldwide could be boiled down to a constant struggle between **classes**. This socioeconomic battle, as explained in *The Communist Manifesto*, would eventually lead to a revolution by the working class, since work itself is a social organization that involves large groups of people.

HERBERT SPENCER

Herbert Spencer is credited with the idea known as **Social Darwinism**. Though he and Darwin were technically rivals, Spencer applied Darwin's idea of "**survival of the fittest**" (a term actually coined by Spencer) to the way society develops. According to Spencer, **competition** is the major driving force behind the development and changes inherent in human society.

MAX WEBER

Weber's major thesis stated that the differing **religions** of the East and West led to differences in societal development. Weber believed **Protestantism** as a religion influenced the development of **capitalism** in the West. He also stated that the organization of the state felt **violence** was a legitimate means of protecting citizenry or enforcing rule. Police action, military action, and violence of individuals against each other in order to protect themselves or property demonstrate the state's propensity to solve problems through violence.

SCIENCE OF ANTHROPOLOGY

While archaeology studies the physical remains of populations, **anthropology,** in contrast, is the study of human culture, its development, and how various cultural groups are similar or different. Anthropologists often engage in direct study of cultures by living among them, observing and participating in everyday activities. This is referred to as "**participant observation**." Anthropologists also perform cross-cultural and comparative research.

Copyright © Mometrix Media. You have been licensed one copy of this document for personal use only. Any other reproduction or redistribution is strictly prohibited. All rights reserved.

Anthropology can be divided into four major areas of study. Each one addresses a slightly different approach to culture and how it affects human beings, as well as how culture develops over time:

- **Archaeology**—this is the study of materials and physical items left behind by human settlements
- **Social-cultural anthropology**—focuses on cultural standards, beliefs, values, and norms
- **Biological anthropology**—this is the study of specific genetic characteristics of different populations
- **Linguistics**— this is the study of the development of languages over time

SUBSISTENCE PATTERNS AND ITS MAJOR CLASSIFICATIONS

The term *subsistence pattern* refers to ways in which societies obtain the necessities of life, such as food and shelter. The **subsistence pattern** of a society often directly correlates to its economy, population size, political systems, and overall technological development. Certain subsistence patterns can only support lower levels of societal development, while others can support a much more developed culture. The four major subsistence patterns are:

1. **Foraging**—the hunter-gatherer lifestyle
2. Pastoralism—herding
3. **Horticulture**—small-scale farming
4. Intensive agriculture—large-scale farming

Hunter-gatherer societies by nature are nomadic and do not tend to support highly developed cultures. Intensive agriculture, in contrast, can support a large population to a high subsistence level, allowing for the development of a sophisticated, modern culture.

MARGARET MEAD

Margaret Mead studied sexual beliefs and norms among **South Pacific** and **Southeast Asian** cultures. She acquired a PhD from Columbia University, and her work popularized sociology. She also studied how children were treated and brought up in different cultures and how breastfeeding was viewed in different population groups. Among other works, she wrote a book called *Coming of Age in Samoa* about the culture of these Pacific Islanders.

MARY AND LOUIS LEAKEY AND DISCOVERIES AT OLDUVAI GORGE

The Leakeys made major discoveries regarding the **origin of the human species** during their excavations in Olduvai Gorge in Tanzania, Africa, excavating wide varieties of stone tools and other artifacts dating back as far as two million years. Mary Leakey discovered footprints belonging to early humans at **Laetoli**, a palaeontological site in Tanzania, and developed a system to classify early human tools. The Leakeys also discovered prehistoric remains of humans, including early humans dating to nearly four million years ago, fifteen new species, and one new genus of early human ancestors. They also discovered the first fossil ape skull, and only three similar specimens exist to this day. Their findings fundamentally changed theories regarding the development and evolution of ancient humans.

PSYCHOLOGY

Psychology is the study of **human behavior** and how the **mind** works. Some psychologists pursue scientific psychology, while others focus on applied psychology. Psychologists correlate human behavior and can make use of this data to predict behavior or determine why a particular behavior has occurred. Psychologists also help work with people who have specific problems with relationships or with how they perceive the world. By observing patterns and recording them in

160

Copyright © Mometrix Media. You have been licensed one copy of this document for personal use only. Any other reproduction or redistribution is strictly prohibited. All rights reserved.

detail, psychologists can apply these patterns to predictions about human behavior in individuals, groups, cultures, and even countries.

TECHNIQUES USED BY PSYCHOLOGISTS IN RESEARCH

Psychological researchers study their discipline in various ways. Based on what they are studying, they generally use one of the following methods:

- **Naturalistic observation**—much as with sociological study, psychologists observe people and their natural behavior without interfering.
- **Survey method**—surveys are distributed among a wide range of people, and the answers are correlated.
- **Case studies**—specific individuals or groups are studied in depth over a period of time, sometimes for many years.
- **Experimental method**—this involves experimental and control groups and the use of specific experiments to prove or disprove a theory.
- **Correlational design**—this is concerned with relationships between variables, such as whether one factor causes or influences another.

IMPORTANCE OF ARISTOTLE TO THE SCIENCE OF PSYCHOLOGY

Aristotle is often cited as founding the science of **psychology** through his overall interest in the working of the human mind. His beliefs stated that the mind was part of the body, while the psyche functioned as a receiver of knowledge. He felt psychology's major focus was to uncover the soul. Later philosophers and scientists built on these ideas to eventually develop the modern science of psychology.

NATIVISM

Nativism is a theory that states that there is a certain **body of knowledge** all people are born with. This knowledge requires no learning or experience on the part of the individual. **René Descartes**, a French philosopher, developed this concept. He believed the body and mind affected each other profoundly, largely because they are separate from each other. The physical site of this interaction took place in the **pineal gland** (a small gland in the brain), according to his theory. Descartes developed several theories in the fields of philosophy and psychology that are still studied in modern universities.

EMPIRICISM

Empiricism is in direct opposition to Descartes' theory of nativism, theorizing that all knowledge is acquired through **life experience**, impressing itself on a mind and brain that are **blank** at the time of birth. Major proponents of empiricism were Thomas Hobbes, John Locke, David Hume, and George Berkeley.

JOHANNES P. MÜLLER, HERMANN L. F. VON HELMHOLTZ, WILLIAM JAMES, AND WILHELM WUNDT

Johannes P. Müller and Hermann L. F. von Helmholtz conducted scientific, organized studies of sensation and perception. As the first psychologists to attempt this kind of study, they showed that it was possible to study actual physical processes that work to produce mental activity.

William James was the founder of the world's first psychology laboratory. **Wilhelm Wundt**, a student of Helmholtz, published the first experimental psychology journal and is known as the father of modern psychology. Together, James and Wundt helped bring psychology into its own,

Copyright © Mometrix Media. You have been licensed one copy of this document for personal use only. Any other reproduction or redistribution is strictly prohibited. All rights reserved.

separating it from philosophy. The method of psychological study called introspection grew out of their work.

SIGMUND FREUD

An Austrian doctor, Freud developed a number of theories regarding human mental processes and behavior. He believed the **subconscious** to hold numerous repressed experiences and feelings that drive behavior without the individual's awareness, and that these subconscious motivators could lead to severe personality problems and disorders. He particularly stressed sexual desire as a motivating force. Freud developed the method of **psychoanalysis** to help discover the hidden impulses driving individual behavior. Freud's psychoanalytic theory proposed three major components to an individual's psychological makeup:

- **Id**—driven by instinct and basic drives
- **Ego**—most conscious and producing self-awareness
- **Superego**—strives for perfection and appropriate behavior

The **ego** acts as mediator between the **id** and **superego**, which function in opposition to each other.

> **Review Video: Who was Sigmund Freud?**
> Visit mometrix.com/academy and enter code: 473747

CARL JUNG

A student of Freud, Jung eventually developed different theories regarding the workings of the human mind. With an intense interest in both Eastern and Western philosophy, he incorporated ideas from both into his psychological explorations. He developed the theories of **extroversion** and **introversion**, as well as proposing the existence of the **collective unconscious** and the occurrence of **synchronicity**.

IVAN PAVLOV AND B. F. SKINNER

Ivan Pavlov and B. F. Skinner both built on Watson's theories of behaviorism. This work came about largely as a counter to the growing importance of introspective techniques to psychological study. Believing **environment** strongly influenced individual behavior, Pavlov and Skinner searched for connections between outside stimuli and behavioral patterns. Pavlov's experiments proved the existence of **conditioned response**. His most famous experiment conditioned dogs to salivate at the sound of a ringing bell. Skinner went on to build further on these ideas, developing the "Skinner box," a device used to develop and study conditioned response in rats.

GESTALT PSYCHOLOGY, SOCIAL PSYCHOLOGY, AND MODERN PSYCHOLOGY

Gestalt psychology is a theory developed by **Max Wertheimer**. In **Gestalt theory**, events are not considered individually but as part of a larger pattern. **Social psychology** is the study of how social conditions affect individuals. **Modern psychology**, as it has developed, combines earlier schools of psychology, including Freudian, Jungian, behaviorism, cognitive, humanistic, and stimulus-response theories.

Copyright © Mometrix Media. You have been licensed one copy of this document for personal use only. Any other reproduction or redistribution is strictly prohibited. All rights reserved.

DIVISIONS OF THE HUMAN LIFESPAN

Developmental psychologists divide the human lifespan into stages and list certain developmental milestones that generally take place during these stages:

- **Infancy and childhood**—this is the most rapid period of human development, during which the child learns to experience its world, relate to other people, and perform tasks necessary to function in its native culture. Debate exists as to which characteristics are inborn and which are learned.
- **Adolescence**—this period represents the shift from child to adult. Changes are rapid and can involve major physical and emotional shifts.
- **Adulthood**—individuals take on new responsibilities, become self-sufficient, and often form their own families and other social networks.
- **Old age**—priorities shift again as children become adults and no longer require support and supervision.

TYPES OF LEARNING

Psychologists define learning as a **permanent change in behavior**. Learning is divided into three basic categories, based on how the behavioral change is acquired:

- **Classical conditioning**—this is a learning process in which a specific stimulus is associated with a specific response over time.
- **Operant conditioning**—this is a learning process in which behavior is punished or rewarded, leading to a desired long-term behavior.
- **Social learning**—this refers to learning based on observation of others and modeling others' behavior.

These three learning processes work together to produce the wide variety of human behavior.

FACTORS INVOLVED IN SOCIAL PSYCHOLOGY AND EFFECTS ON VARIOUS GROUPS OF PEOPLE

Social psychology studies how people **interact** as well as why and how they decide whom to interact with. The ways people react with each other are defined in several ways, including:

- **Social perception**—this describes how we perceive others and their behavior as we make judgments based on our own experiences and prejudices.
- **Personal relationships**—close relationships develop among people for various reasons, including the desire to reproduce and form a family unit.
- **Group behavior**—people gather into groups with similar beliefs, needs, or other characteristics. Sometimes group behavior differs greatly from behavior that would be practiced by individuals.
- **Attitudes**—individual attitudes toward others develop over time based on individual history, experience, knowledge, and other factors. Attitudes can change over time, but some are deeply ingrained and can lead to prejudice.

Copyright © Mometrix Media. You have been licensed one copy of this document for personal use only. Any other reproduction or redistribution is strictly prohibited. All rights reserved.

ILTS Practice Test

Want to take this practice test in an online interactive format?
Check out the bonus page, which includes interactive practice questions and much more: **http://www.mometrix.com/bonus948/iltsmgsocsci**

1. Some countries in the Americas still have large populations of indigenous or partly indigenous peoples. Of the following, which pair of countries does not have comparatively as large of an indigenous population as the other countries?
   a. Guatemala and Peru
   b. Ecuador and Bolivia
   c. Paraguay and Mexico
   d. Argentina and Uruguay

2. Which of the following statements is *not* true regarding English expansionism in the 16th century?
   a. England's defeat of the Spanish Armada in 1588 brought a decisive end to their war with Spain.
   b. King Henry VIII's desire to divorce Catherine of Aragon strengthened English expansionism.
   c. Queen Elizabeth's support for the Protestant Reformation strengthened English expansionism.
   d. Sir Francis Drake and other English sea captains plundered the goods that the Spaniards took from indigenous peoples.

3. Which of the following is *not* correct regarding the Virginia Companies?
   a. One of these companies, the Virginia Company of Plymouth, made its base in North America.
   b. One of these companies, the Virginia Company of London, made its base in Massachusetts.
   c. One company had a charter to colonize America between the Hudson and Cape Fear rivers.
   d. One company had a charter to colonize America from the Potomac River to north Maine.

4. Which of the following conquistadores unwittingly gave smallpox to the indigenous peoples and destroyed the Aztec empire in Mexico?
   a. Balboa
   b. Ponce de Leon
   c. Cortes
   d. De Vaca

5. Which statement best describes the significance of the Peter Zenger trial in colonial America?
   a. It was the earliest American case on the right to bear arms.
   b. It established a precedent for freedom of the press.
   c. It was the earliest American case on right of peaceable assembly.
   d. It established a precedent for freedom of religion.

164

Copyright © Mometrix Media. You have been licensed one copy of this document for personal use only. Any other reproduction or redistribution is strictly prohibited. All rights reserved.

6. Which of these factors was *not* a direct contributor to the beginning of the American Revolution?

a. The attitudes of American colonists toward Great Britain following the French and Indian War *F. & I. War was in 1763 & colonists liked Britain back then*

b. The attitudes of leaders in Great Britain toward the American colonies and imperialism

c. James Otis's court argument against Great Britain's Writs of Assistance as breaking natural law

d. Lord Grenville's Proclamation of 1763, the Sugar Act, the Currency Act, and especially the Stamp Act

7. Which of the following statements is *not* true regarding the Tea Act of 1773?

a. The British East India Company was suffering financially because Americans were buying tea smuggled from Holland.

b. Parliament granted concessions to the British East India Company to ship tea straight to America, bypassing England.

c. Colonists found that even with added taxes, tea directly shipped by the British East India Company cost less, and they bought it.

d. American colonists refused to buy less expensive tea from the British East India Company on the principle of taxation.

8. Which of the following is true concerning the formation of new state governments in the new United States of America following freedom from British rule?

a. By the end of 1777, new constitutions had been created for twelve of the American states.

b. The states of Connecticut and Massachusetts retained their colonial charters, minus the British parts.

c. The state of Massachusetts required a special convention for its constitution, setting a good example.

d. The state of Massachusetts did not formally begin to use its new constitution until 1778.

9. Which of the following is *not* a true statement regarding the Louisiana Purchase?

a. Jefferson sent a delegation to Paris to endeavor to purchase only the city of New Orleans from Napoleon.

b. Napoleon, anticipating U.S. intrusions into Louisiana, offered to sell the U.S. the entire Louisiana territory.

c. The American delegation accepted Napoleon's offer, though they were only authorized to buy New Orleans.

d. The Louisiana Purchase, once it was completed, increased the territory of the U.S. by 50% overnight.

10. Which of these was *not* a factor that contributed to the duel in which Aaron Burr killed Alexander Hamilton?

a. Some Federalists who opposed U.S. Western expansion were attempting to organize a movement to secede from the Union.

b. Alexander Hamilton challenged Aaron Burr to a duel because he objected to U.S. expansion into the West, which Burr supported. *Hamilton did not object to expansion & Burr did not support*

c. Secessionist Federalists tried to enlist Aaron Burr's support for their cause by backing him in his run for Governor of New York.

d. Alexander Hamilton was the leader of the group that opposed Aaron Burr's campaign to run for New York Governor.

Copyright © Mometrix Media. You have been licensed one copy of this document for personal use only. Any other reproduction or redistribution is strictly prohibited. All rights reserved.

11. **Which of the following did *not* occur during the War of 1812?**

 a. Early in the war, the U.S. executed a three-pronged invasion of Canada and succeeded on two of three fronts. *but did not succeed on 2 fronts*

 b. Early in the war, Americans won naval battles against the British, but were soon beaten back by the British.

 c. Admiral Oliver Hazard Perry's fleet defeated the British navy on Lake Erie in September, 1813.

 d. William Henry Harrison invaded Canada and defeated the British and the Native Americans in the Battle of the Thames.

12. **Which of the following was *not* an immediate effect of rapid urban growth in the 1800s?**

 a. Poor sanitation conditions in the cities

 b. Epidemics of diseases in the cities

 c. Inadequate police and fire protection

 d. Widespread urban political corruption

13. **Which of the following laws was instrumental in spurring westward migration to the Great Plains between 1860 and 1880?**

 a. The Homestead Act

 b. The Timber Culture Act

 c. The Desert Land Act

 d. All of these laws were instrumental in spurring westward migration to the Great Plains during that period.

14. **What did *not* contribute to ending America's neutrality in World War I?**

 a. Germany's telegram to Mexico that proposed they form an alliance if the US entered the war

 b. Germany's declaration of a war on Russia after Archduke Ferdinand's assassination

 c. Germany's sinking the British ship *Lusitania*, which killed 128 American passengers

 d. Germany's declaration of unrestricted submarine warfare on all ships in the war zone

15. **Of the following international diplomatic conferences, which one made US-Soviet differences apparent?**

 a. The Potsdam conference

 b. The conference at Yalta

 c. Dumbarton Oaks conference

 d. The Tehran conference

16. **Which statement about relations between the Middle East and the US and Europe in the 1950s is *not* correct?**

 a. President Nasser of Egypt refused to align with the US in the Cold War.

 b. President Eisenhower removed US funding from the Aswan Dam in 1956.

 c. President Nasser nationalized the Suez Canal, which was owned by England.

 d. In 1956, Egypt attacked Israel, and England and France joined in the war.

166

Copyright © Mometrix Media. You have been licensed one copy of this document for personal use only. Any other reproduction or redistribution is strictly prohibited. All rights reserved.

17. Of the following, which person or group was *not* instrumental in postwar advancement of civil rights and desegregation during the 1940s and 1950s?

   a. The President
   b. The Supreme Court
   c. The Congress
   d. The NAACP

18. Of the programs enacted by President Lyndon B. Johnson's administration, which was most closely related to John F. Kennedy's legacy?

   a. The Economic Opportunity Act
   b. The Civil Rights Act
   c. The Great Society program
   d. Clean Air Act

19. Which statement regarding US international trade policy in the 1990s is *not* correct?

   a. In 1994, the General Agreement on Tariffs and Trade (GATT) was approved by Congress.
   b. The GATT was between 57 countries who agreed they would remove or reduce many of their tariffs.
   c. The GATT created the World Trade Organization (WTO) to settle international trade differences.
   d. The NAFTA (North American Free Trade Agreement), ratified in 1994, had originally been set up by George H.W. Bush's administration.

20. Which statement about factors related to the growth of the US economy between 1945 and 1970 is *not* correct?

   a. The Baby Boom's greatly increased birth rates contributed to economic growth during this time.
   b. The reduction in military spending after World War II contributed to the stronger US economy.
   c. Government programs and growing affluence nearly quadrupled college enrollments in 20 years.
   d. Increased mobility and bigger families caused fast suburban expansion, especially in the Sunbelt.

21. Which of the following statements regarding immigration to America during the 1980s is *not* true?

   a. Twice as many immigrants came to America during the 1980s than during the 1970s.
   b. Latin Americans comprised the largest proportion of immigrants to America in the 1980s.
   c. Most immigrants to the US in the 1980s were Latin American, Asian, and Caribbean.
   d. The 1986 Immigration Reform and Control Act reduced illegal Mexican immigration.

22. Which is *not* correct regarding black activism during the 1960s?

   a. There was a riot in the Los Angeles ghetto of Watts in 1965.
   b. There was a riot involving black activists in Newark, New Jersey, after the Watts riot.
   c. The Mississippi Freedom Democrats unseated that state's delegation at the convention.
   d. There was a riot involving black activists in Detroit, Michigan, after the riot in Watts.

Copyright © Mometrix Media. You have been licensed one copy of this document for personal use only. Any other reproduction or redistribution is strictly prohibited. All rights reserved.

23. **What was the earliest written language in Mesopotamia?**
    a. Sumerian
    b. Elamite
    c. Akkadian
    d. Aramaic

24. **During which of these periods were pyramids *not* built in Egypt?**
    a. The Old Kingdom
    b. The Middle Kingdom
    c. The New Kingdom
    d. The Third Dynasty

25. **Which of the following is *not* true about the Crusades?**
    a. Their purpose was for European rulers to retake the Middle East from Muslims
    b. The Crusades succeeded at European kings' goal of reclaiming the "holy land"
    c. The Crusades accelerated the already incipient decline of the Byzantine Empire
    d. Egypt saw a return as a major Middle Eastern power as a result of the Crusades

26. **Which of the following is NOT true about the Italian Renaissance?**
    a. The Black Death killed 1/3 of the population of Europe.
    b. The lower classes benefited from the need for laborers.
    c. The middle classes developed from a need for services.
    d. The upper class invested in banks.

27. **Which of the following is *not* correct regarding assumptions of mercantilism?**
    a. The money and the wealth of a nation are identical properties
    b. In order to prosper, a nation should try to increase its imports — *imports is spending*
    c. In order to prosper, a nation should try to increase its exports
    d. Economic protectionism by national governments is advisable

28. **Which of the following is *not* true about the English Civil Wars between 1641 and 1651?**
    a. These wars all were waged between Royalists and Parliamentarians
    b. The outcome of this series of civil wars was victory for Parliament
    c. These wars legalized Parliament's consent as requisite to monarchy
    d. Two of the wars in this time involved supporters of King Charles I

29. **Which of the following choices is/are *not* considered among causes of the French Revolution?**
    a. Famines causing malnutrition and starvation
    b. War debt, court spending, and a bad monetary system
    c. Resentment against the Catholic Church's rule
    d. Resentment against the Protestant Reformation

Copyright © Mometrix Media. You have been licensed one copy of this document for personal use only. Any other reproduction or redistribution is strictly prohibited. All rights reserved.

30. Which statement best describes the role played by the French economy in causing the 1789 French Revolution?

a. France's very large national debt led to heavy tax burdens on the French peasantry.
b. Nearly sixty percent of annual national expenditures financed luxuries for the French nobility.
c. Reforms in the guild system allowed many peasants to rise to the middle class.
d. The king's attempt to curtail free trade led skilled journeymen to rebel against the monarchy.

31. Which of the following statements is accurate regarding the end of the First World War?

a. The Treaty of Versailles brought peace among all countries involved in the war
b. The Treaty of Versailles contained a clause for establishing the United Nations
c. President Woodrow Wilson had proposed forming a coalition of world nations
d. President Wilson succeeded in getting the USA to ratify the League of Nations

32. How did Russia's participation in World War I influence the Russian Revolution?

a. Civilian suffering and military setbacks served as a catalyst for revolutionary forces.
b. Nicholas III capitalized on battlefield successes to temporarily silence critics.
c. The government eased laws banning collective action by factory workers to appease social discontent about the war.
d. Anti-government protesters temporarily ceased protesting to show patriotism in a difficult war.

33. During the decolonization of the Cold War years, which of the following events occurred chronologically latest?

a. The Eastern Bloc and Satellite states became independent from the Soviet Union
b. Canada became totally independent from British Parliament via the Canada Act
c. The Bahamas, in the Caribbean, became independent from the United Kingdom
d. The Algerian War ended, and Algeria became independent from France

34. Why was U.S. industrialization confined to the Northeast until after the Civil War?

a. Because the Civil War delayed the development of water-powered manufacturing
b. Because the Northeast had faster-running rivers than the rivers found in the South
c. Because Slater's first cotton mill with horse-drawn production lost so much money
d. Because the technical innovations for milling textiles had not as yet been invented

35. Which of the following statements is *not* an accurate statement about the Puritans in England?

a. The Puritans unconditionally gave all their support to the English Reformation
b. The Puritans saw the Church of England as too much like the Catholic Church
c. The Puritans became a chief political power because of the English Civil War
d. The Puritans' clergy mainly departed from the Church of England after 1662

36. Which of the following statements is *not* true about the Gilded Age in America?

a. The Gilded Age was the era of the "robber barons" in the business world
b. The Gilded Age got its name from the excesses of the wealthy upper class
c. The Gilded Age had philanthropy Carnegie called the "Gospel of Wealth"
d. The Gilded Age is a term whose origins have not been identified clearly

Copyright © Mometrix Media. You have been licensed one copy of this document for personal use only. Any other reproduction or redistribution is strictly prohibited. All rights reserved.

37. Which of the following is *not* true about Democracy and the formation of the United States?

 a. The founding fathers stated in the Constitution that the USA would be a democracy
 b. The Declaration of Independence did not dictate democracy but stated its principles
 c. The United States Constitution stipulated that government be elected by the people
 d. The United States Constitution had terms to protect some, but not all, of the people

38. Which of the following statements does *not* describe the average European diet BEFORE the expansion of trade routes?

 a. Europeans ate for survival, not enjoyment.
 b. They had an abundance of preservatives such as salt that could make food last longer.
 c. Grain-based foods such as porridge and bread were staple meals.
 d. Spices were unavailable.

39. Which of these is true concerning the French Revolution, America, and Europe?

 a. When France's revolution spread and they went to war with other European countries, George Washington allied with the French.
 b. During the time period around 1792, American merchants were conducting trading with countries on both sides of the war.
 c. American traders conducted business with various countries, profiting the most from the British West Indies.
 d. The Spanish navy retaliated against America for trading with the French by capturing American trading ships.

40. Which group overtook Rome in the mid-600s BC and established much of its infrastructure, including sewers, roads, and fortifications, only to be driven out of the city in 509 BC?

 a. Latins.
 b. Etruscans.
 c. Greeks.
 d. Persians.

41. The writers of The Federalist Papers published under the pen name "Publius." Who were the authors?

 a. James Madison, John Jay, and Alexander Hamilton
 b. George Washington, Thomas Jefferson, and James Madison
 c. Alexander Hamilton, Benjamin Franklin, and Thomas Jefferson
 d. Benjamin Franklin, John Jay, and Thomas Jefferson

42. Social studies education has many practical applications. Which of the following is the most direct application of teaching high school seniors the structure of the U.S. government?

 a. Knowledge of the fundamentals of federalism
 b. Informed participation in school elections
 c. Knowledge of a system of checks and balances
 d. Informed participation in U.S. political processes

Copyright © Mometrix Media. You have been licensed one copy of this document for personal use only. Any other reproduction or redistribution is strictly prohibited. All rights reserved.

43. The U.S. government is best understood as a federalist government because:

    a. the legislative branch consists of two representative bodies.

    b. it is a representative democracy rather than a direct democracy.

    c. political power is divided between the federal government and the states.

    d. a national Constitution shapes national legislation.

44. One reason the Articles of Confederation created a weak government was because it limited Congress's ability to do what?

    a. Declare war

    b. Conduct a census

    c. Vote

    d. Tax

45. The philosophy of the late 17th-18th centuries that influenced the Constitution was from the Age of:

    a. Enlightenment

    b. Empire

    c. Discovery

    d. Industry

46. The votes of how many states were needed to ratify the Constitution?

    a. Five

    b. Ten

    c. Nine

    d. Seven

47. Virginian _____ advocated a stronger central government and was influential at the Constitutional Convention.

    a. Benjamin Franklin

    b. James Madison

    c. George Mason

    d. Robert Yates

48. Power divided between local and central branches of government is a definition of what term?

    a. Bicameralism

    b. Checks and balances

    c. Legislative oversight

    d. Federalism

49. The Senate and the House of Representatives are an example of:

    a. Bicameralism

    b. Checks and balances

    c. Legislative oversight

    d. Federalism

Copyright © Mometrix Media. You have been licensed one copy of this document for personal use only. Any other reproduction or redistribution is strictly prohibited. All rights reserved.

50. The vice president succeeds the president in case of death, illness or impeachment. What is the order of succession for the next three successors, according to the Presidential Succession Act of 1947?

    a. President pro tempore of the Senate, secretary of state, and secretary of defense
    b. Speaker of the House, president pro tempore of the Senate, and secretary of state
    c. President pro tempore of the Senate, Speaker of the House, and secretary of state
    d. Secretary of state, secretary of defense, and Speaker of the House

51. The President has the power to veto legislation. How is this power limited?

    I. Congress can override the veto
    II. The President cannot line veto
    III. The President cannot propose legislation

    a. I and III
    b. II only
    c. I and II
    d. I only

52. The civil rights act that outlawed segregation in schools and public places also:

    a. Gave minorities the right to vote
    b. Established women's right to vote
    c. Outlawed unequal voter registration
    d. Provided protection for children

53. Which of the following is a power held only by the federal government?

    a. The power to levy taxes, borrow money, and spend money
    b. The power to award copyrights and patents to people or groups
    c. The power to establish the criteria that qualify a person to vote
    d. The power to ratify proposed amendments to the Constitution

54. Of the following actions, which one requires a three-fourths majority?

    a. State approval of a proposed amendment to the Constitution
    b. Submitting a proposal for an amendment to the Constitution
    c. Ratification for appointments to the Presidency in the Senate
    d. The introduction of charges for an impeachment in the House

55. Which of the following statements is *not* correct about U.S. westward expansion and Manifest Destiny?

    a. The idea that U.S. freedom and values should be shared with, even forced upon, as many people as possible had existed for many years.
    b. The term "Manifest Destiny" and the idea it represented had been used for many years prior to the 1830s.
    c. Many Americans believed that America as a nation should ultimately be extended to include Canada and Mexico.
    d. Increased nationalism after the resolution of the War of 1812 and rapid population growth added to Manifest Destiny.

Copyright © Mometrix Media. You have been licensed one copy of this document for personal use only. Any other reproduction or redistribution is strictly prohibited. All rights reserved.

56. Presidential candidates are eligible for public funding if they raise $5,000 per state in how many states?
    a. Twenty
    b. Ten
    c. Twenty-five
    d. Seventeen

57. What judicial system did America borrow from England?
    a. Due process
    b. Federal law
    c. Commerce law
    d. Common law

58. Which of the following is a possible absolute location for New Orleans?
    a. 30° S, 90° E
    b. 30° N, 90° E
    c. 30° S, 90° W
    d. 30° N, 90° W

59. On which type of map are different countries represented in different colors, with no two adjacent countries sharing a color?
    a. Physical map
    b. Political map
    c. Climate map
    d. Contour map

60. Which of the following statements about the equator is true?
    a. It intersects four continents.
    b. It is to the north of both horse latitudes.
    c. It is located at 0° longitude.
    d. It is not very windy.

61. The apparent distance between Greenland and Norway is greatest on a(n)
    a. Mercator Map.
    b. Conic Projection Map.
    c. Contour Map.
    d. Equal-Area Projection Map.

62. Which of the following is *not* a method of representing relief on a physical map?
    a. Symbols
    b. Color
    c. Shading
    d. Contour Lines

Copyright © Mometrix Media. You have been licensed one copy of this document for personal use only. Any other reproduction or redistribution is strictly prohibited. All rights reserved.

63. **Which map describes the movement of people, trends, or materials across a physical area?**
    a. Political Map
    b. Cartogram
    c. Qualitative Map
    d. Flow-line Map

64. **What is the most common type of volcano on earth?**
    a. Lava dome
    b. Composite volcano
    c. Shield volcano
    d. Cinder cone

65. **Water is continuously recycled in the hydrosphere. By which process does water return to the atmosphere after precipitation?**
    a. Percolation
    b. Cohesion
    c. Evaporation
    d. Condensation

66. **Which type of rock is formed by extreme heat and pressure?**
    a. Limestone
    b. Metamorphic
    c. Sedimentary
    d. Igneous

67. **Which part of a hurricane features the strongest winds and greatest rainfall?**
    a. Eye wall
    b. Front
    c. Eye
    d. Outward spiral

68. **Which of the following are not included in a geographical definition of Southeast Asia?**
    a. Myanmar, Laos, Cambodia, and Thailand
    b. Vietnam, the Malay Peninsula, and Brunei
    c. East Malaysia, Indonesia, and the Philippines
    d. These are all geographical parts of Southeast Asia

69. **Which of the following exemplifies the multiplier effect of large cities?**
    a. The presence of specialized equipment for an industry attracts even more business.
    b. The large population lowers the price of goods.
    c. Public transportation means more people can commute to work.
    d. A local newspaper can afford to give away the Sunday edition.

Copyright © Mometrix Media. You have been licensed one copy of this document for personal use only. Any other reproduction or redistribution is strictly prohibited. All rights reserved.

70. For thousands of years, Africans have cultivated the grasslands south of the Sahara Desert, an area known as the
    a. Qattara Depression.
    b. Great Rift Valley.
    c. Congo Basin.
    d. Sahel.

71. Tracy needs to determine the shortest route between Lima and Lisbon. Which of the following maps should she use?
    a. Azimuthal projection with the North Pole at the center
    b. Azimuthal projection with Lisbon at the center
    c. Robinson projection of the Eastern Hemisphere
    d. Robinson projection of the Western Hemisphere

72. Which of the following countries are separated by a geometric border?
    a. Turkish Cyprus and Greek Cyprus
    b. North Korea and South Korea
    c. France and Spain
    d. England and Ireland

73. During one year in Grassley County, there are 750 births, 350 deaths, 80 immigrations, and 50 emigrations. What is the natural increase rate for this year?
    a. 400
    b. 830
    c. 430
    d. More information is required.

74. Which of the following is *not* one of the world's four major population agglomerations?
    a. North Africa
    b. Eastern North America
    c. South Asia
    d. Europe

75. Which of the following statements concerning choice theory are correct?

    I. Scarcity forces people, including producers, to make choices
    II. Producers make choices and, as a result, face trade-offs
    III. Opportunity cost is one way to measure the cost of a choice

    a. I only
    b. I and II only
    c. II and III only
    d. I, II, and III

76. John Maynard Keynes advocated what?
    a. Supply-side economics
    b. Demand-side economics
    c. Laissez faire economics
    d. The Laffer Curve

Copyright © Mometrix Media. You have been licensed one copy of this document for personal use only. Any other reproduction or redistribution is strictly prohibited. All rights reserved.

77. Proponents of legislating greater societal income equity, support which of the following:

      I. Impose a progressive income tax
      II. Impose high estate taxes
      III. Impose a gift tax

a. I only
b. II only
c. I, II, and III
d. II and III only

78. Which of the following best defines American GDP?

a. The value, in American dollars, of all goods and services produced within American borders during one calendar year
b. The value, in American dollars, of all goods and services produced by American companies during one calendar year
c. The total value, in American dollars, of all American household incomes during one calendar year
d. The value, in American dollars, of a "market basket" of goods and services in one year divided by the value of the same market basket in a previous year multiplied by 100

79. Ivy loses her job because her skills as a seamstress are no longer required due to a new piece of machinery that does the work of a seamstress more quickly and for less money. Which type of unemployment is this?

a. Frictional
b. Structural
c. Cyclical
d. Careless

80. Which is considered part of the natural rate of unemployment?

a. Frictional unemployment only
b. Cyclical unemployment and frictional unemployment
c. Structural unemployment and cyclical unemployment
d. Frictional unemployment and structural unemployment

81. Which of the following is a supply shock NOT likely to produce?

a. An increase in input prices
b. An increase in price levels
c. An increase in employment
d. A decrease in GDP

82. Which of the following are true of the demand curve?

      I. It is normally downward sloping
      II. It is normally upward sloping
      III. It is influenced by the law of diminishing marginal unity
      IV. It is unaffected by the law of diminishing marginal unity

a. I and III only
b. I and IV only
c. II and III only
d. II and IV only

Copyright © Mometrix Media. You have been licensed one copy of this document for personal use only. Any other reproduction or redistribution is strictly prohibited. All rights reserved.

83. The price of fleece blankets goes up from $10 to $11. At the same time, demand goes down from 1,000 blankets to 800 blankets. Which of the following statements is true?

a. Demand is elastic
b. Demand is inelastic
c. The price elasticity quotient, or E_d, is less than 1
d. The price elasticity quotient, or E_d, is equal to 1

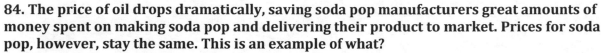

84. The price of oil drops dramatically, saving soda pop manufacturers great amounts of money spent on making soda pop and delivering their product to market. Prices for soda pop, however, stay the same. This is an example of what?

a. Sticky prices
b. Sticky wages
c. The multiplier effect
d. Aggregate expenditure

85. Which of the following will result if two nations use the theory of comparative advantage when making decisions of which goods to produce and trade?

a. Each nation will make all of their own goods
b. Both nations will specialize in the production of the same specific goods
c. Each nation will specialize in the production of different specific goods
d. Neither nation will trade with one another

86. Which of the following is most likely to benefit from inflation?

a. A bond investor who owns fixed-rate bonds
b. A retired widow with no income other than fixed Social Security payments
c. A person who has taken out a fixed-rate loan
d. A local bank who has loaned money out at fixed rate

87. What does the data in this table most directly describe?

Inputs	1	2	3	4
Output	20	50	80	100

a. The Law of Diminishing Marginal Returns
b. Law of Increasing Opportunity Cost
c. Law of Demand
d. Consumer surplus

88. How do banks create money?

a. By printing it
b. By taking it out of the Federal Reserve
c. By loaning it out
d. By putting it into the Federal Reserve

89. Which of the following correctly states the equation of exchange?

a. $MV = PQ$
b. $MP \times VQ$
c. MP/VQ
d. $VP = MQ$

Copyright © Mometrix Media. You have been licensed one copy of this document for personal use only. Any other reproduction or redistribution is strictly prohibited. All rights reserved.

90. Economics is best defined as the study of what?

a. Scarcity
b. Business
c. Trade
d. Supply and demand

Copyright © Mometrix Media. You have been licensed one copy of this document for personal use only. Any other reproduction or redistribution is strictly prohibited. All rights reserved.

Answer Key and Explanations

1. D: Of those countries listed here, the two countries whose respective indigenous populations are not as large as the populations of the other countries are Argentina and Uruguay. Argentina's population is approximately 86.4% of European descent, roughly 8% of mestizo (of mixed European and Amerindian heritage), and an estimated 4% of Arab or East Asian ancestry. Uruguay's population is estimated to be 88% of European descent, 4% of African, and 2% of Asian, with 6% of mestizo ancestry in its rural northwest region. Guatemala and Peru (a) have larger indigenous populations. Guatemala, in Central America, has approximately over 40% of its population as indigenous peoples. Peru, in South America, is estimated to have 45% indigenous peoples and 37% partly indigenous peoples for a total of 82%. Ecuador and Bolivia (b) in South America still have indigenous peoples. The population of Ecuador has an estimated 25% indigenous and 65% partly indigenous peoples, for a total of 90%. Paraguay in South America and Mexico in North America (c) both have sizeable indigenous populations. Paraguay's population is estimated to include 95% partly indigenous peoples. Mexico is estimated to have 30% indigenous and 60% partly indigenous peoples in its population for a total of 90%.

2. A: It is not true that England's defeat of the Spanish Armada in 1588 ended their war with Spain. It did establish England's naval dominance and strengthened England's future colonization of the New World, but the actual war between England and Spain did not end until 1604. It is true that Henry VIII's desire to divorce Catherine of Aragon strengthened English expansionism (b). Catherine was Spanish, and Henry split from the Catholic Church because it prohibited divorce. Henry's rejection of his Spanish wife and his subsequent support of the Protestant movement angered King Philip II of Spain and destroyed the formerly close ties between the two countries. When Elizabeth became Queen of England, she supported the Reformation as a Protestant, which also contributed to English colonization (c). Sir Francis Drake, one of the best known English sea captains during this time period, would attack and plunder Spanish ships that had plundered Native Americans (d), adding to the enmity between Spain and England. Queen Elizabeth invested in Drake's voyages and gave him her support in claiming territories for England.

3. B: The Virginia Company of London was based in London, not Massachusetts. It had a charter to colonize American land between the Hudson and Cape Fear rivers (c). The other Virginia Company was the Virginia Company of Plymouth, which was based in the American colony of Plymouth, Massachusetts (a). It had a charter to colonize North America between the Potomac River and the northern boundary of Maine (d).

4. C: Hernando Cortes conquered the Mexican Aztecs in 1519. He had several advantages over the indigenous peoples, including horses, armor for his soldiers, and guns. In addition, Cortes' troops unknowingly transmitted smallpox to the Aztecs, which devastated their population as they had no immunity to this foreign illness. Vasco Nunez de Balboa (a) was the first European explorer to view the Pacific Ocean when he crossed the Isthmus of Panama in 1513. Juan Ponce de Leon (b) also visited and claimed Florida in Spain's name in 1513. Cabeza de Vaca (d) was one of only four men out of 400 to return from an expedition led by Panfilio de Narvaez in 1528, and was responsible for spreading the story of the Seven Cities of Cibola (the "cities of gold").

5. B: Peter Zenger was an 18th century journalist in New York who was charged with seditious libel after he published articles critical of New York governor William Cosby. His subsequent acquittal in 1735 established a precedent for American freedom of the press. Options A, C, and D can all be rejected because they do not accurately describe the historical significance of Peter Zenger's trial.

179

Copyright © Mometrix Media. You have been licensed one copy of this document for personal use only. Any other reproduction or redistribution is strictly prohibited. All rights reserved.

Although these options name other important freedoms or rights in American history, these rights or freedoms were not central to Peter Zenger's trial. In particular, note that while answers B, C, and D all list rights contained in the First Amendment to the United States Constitution, only B contains the particular right at issue in the Zenger case.

6. A: The attitudes of American colonists after the 1763 Treaty of Paris ended the French and Indian War were not a direct contributor to the American Revolution. American colonists had a supportive attitude toward Great Britain then, and were proud of the part they played in winning the war. Their good will was not returned by British leaders (b), who looked down on American colonials and sought to increase their imperial power over them. Even in 1761, a sign of Americans' objections to having their liberty curtailed by the British was seen when Boston attorney James Otis argued in court against the Writs of Assistance (c), search warrants to enforce England's mercantilist trade restrictions, as violating the kinds of natural laws espoused during the Enlightenment. Lord George Grenville's aggressive program to defend the North American frontier in the wake of Chief Pontiac's attacks included stricter enforcement of the Navigation Acts, the Proclamation of 1763, the Sugar Act (or Revenue Act), the Currency Act, and most of all the Stamp Act (d). Colonists objected to these as taxation without representation. Other events followed in this taxation dispute, which further eroded Americans' relationship with British government, including the Townshend Acts, the Massachusetts Circular Letter, the Boston Massacre, the Tea Act, and the resulting Boston Tea Party. Finally, with Britain's passage of the Intolerable Acts and the Americans' First Continental Congress, which was followed by Britain's military aggression against American resistance, actual warfare began in 1775. While not all of the colonies wanted war or independence by then, things changed by 1776, and Jefferson's Declaration of Independence was formalized.

7. C: Colonists did find that tea shipped directly by the British East India Company cost less than smuggled Dutch tea, even with tax. The colonists, however, did not buy it. They refused, despite its lower cost, on the principle that the British were taxing colonists without representation (d). It is true that the British East India Company lost money as a result of colonists buying tea smuggled from Holland (a). They sought to remedy this problem by getting concessions from Parliament to ship tea directly to the colonies instead of going through England (b) as the Navigation Acts normally required. Boston Governor Thomas Hutchinson, who sided with Britain, stopped tea ships from leaving the harbor, which after 20 days would cause the tea to be sold at auction. At that time, British taxes on the tea would be paid. On the 19th night after Hutchinson's action, American protestors held the Boston Tea Party, dressing as Native Americans and dumping all the tea into the harbor to destroy it so it could not be taxed and sold. Many American colonists disagreed with the Boston Tea Party because it involved destroying private property.

8. C: Massachusetts did set a valuable example for other states by stipulating that its constitution should be created via a special convention rather than via the legislature. This way, the constitution would take precedence over the legislature, which would be subject to the rules of the constitution. It is not true that twelve states had new constitutions by the end of 1777 (a). By this time, ten of the states had new constitutions. It is not true that Connecticut and Massachusetts retained their colonial charters minus the British parts (b). Connecticut and Rhode Island were the states that preserved their colonial charters. They simply removed any parts referring to British rule. Massachusetts did not formalize its new constitution in 1778 (d). This state did not actually finish the process of adopting its new constitution until 1780.

9. D: The Louisiana Purchase actually increased the U.S.'s territory by 100% overnight, not 50%. The Louisiana territory doubled the size of the nation. It is true that Jefferson initially sent a delegation to Paris to see if Napoleon would agree to sell only New Orleans to the United States (a).

Copyright © Mometrix Media. You have been licensed one copy of this document for personal use only. Any other reproduction or redistribution is strictly prohibited. All rights reserved.

It is also true that Napoleon, who expected America to encroach on Louisiana, decided to avoid this by offering to sell the entire territory to the U.S. (b). It is likewise true that America only had authority to buy New Orleans. Nevertheless, the delegation accepted Napoleon's offer of all of Louisiana (c).

10. B: Hamilton did not object to U.S. western expansionism, and Burr did not support it. There were certain Federalists other than Hamilton who opposed expansion to the west as a threat to their position within the Union, and these opponents did attempt to organize a movement to secede (a). To get Aaron Burr to champion their cause, they offered to help him run for Governor of New York (c). Hamilton did lead the opposition against Burr's campaign (d).

11. A: The U.S. did carry out a three-pronged invasion of Canada early in the war, but they did not succeed on two fronts. Instead, they lost on all three. Americans did win sea battles against the British early in the war, but were soon beaten back to their homeports and then blockaded by powerful British warships (b). Admiral Perry did defeat the British on Lake Erie on September 10, 1813 (c). Perry's victory allowed William Henry Harrison to invade Canada (d) in October of 1813, where he defeated British and Native Americans in the Battle of the Thames.

12. D: Political corruption was not an immediate effect of the rapid urban growth during this time. The accelerated growth of cities in America did soon result in services being unable to keep up with that growth. The results of this included deficiencies in clean water delivery and garbage collection, causing poor sanitation (a). That poor sanitation led to outbreaks of cholera and typhus, as well as typhoid fever epidemics (b). Police and fire fighting services could not keep up with the population increases, and were often inadequate (c).

13. D: All the laws (d) named were instrumental in spurring westward migration to the Great Plains. The Homestead Act (a), passed in 1862, gave settlers 160 acres of land at no monetary cost in exchange for a commitment to cultivating the land for five years. The Timber Culture Act (b), passed in 1873, gave the settlers 160 acres more of land in exchange for planting trees on one quarter of the acreage. The Desert Land Act (c), passed in 1877, allowed buyers who would irrigate the land to buy 640 acres for only 25 cents an acre. Thus, (d), all of these laws were instrumental in spurring westward migration to the Great Plains during that period, is correct.

14. B: Germany's declaration of war on Russia in 1914, following the assassination of Archduke Ferdinand (b), did not contribute to ending American neutrality in World War I. Once Germany declared war, England, France, Italy, Russia, and Japan joined as the Allied Powers against the Central Powers of Germany and Austria-Hungary, and US President Woodrow Wilson declared America's neutrality. When Germany designated the area surrounding the British Isles as a war zone in February 1913 (a), and warned all ships from neutral countries to stay out of the zone, an end to American neutrality was prompted. President Wilson's responded to Germany's declaration by proclaiming that America would hold Germany responsible for any American losses of life or property. When Germany sank the British passenger vessel *Lusitania,* 128 American passengers were killed (c). This further eroded Wilson's resolve to remain neutral. In February 1917, Germany declared unrestricted submarine warfare on any ship in the war zone (d); this signified that ships from any country would face German attack.

15. A: The postwar conference that brought US-Soviet differences to light was (a) the Potsdam conference in July of 1945. The conference at Yalta (b), in February of 1945, resulted in the division of Germany into Allied-controlled zones. The Dumbarton Oaks conference (c) (1944) established a Security Council, on which with the US, England, Soviet Union, France, and China served as the five permanent members. Each of the permanent members had veto power, and a General Assembly,

Copyright © Mometrix Media. You have been licensed one copy of this document for personal use only. Any other reproduction or redistribution is strictly prohibited. All rights reserved.

with limited power, was also established. The Tehran conference (d) included FDR's proposal for a new international organization to take the place of the League of Nations. This idea would later be realized in the form of the United Nations.

16. D: In 1956, Egypt did not attack Israel. On October 29, 1956, Israel attacked Egypt. England and France did join this war within two days. It is true that Egyptian President Gamal Abdul Nasser refused to take America's side in the Cold War (a). In reaction to his refusal, President Eisenhower's administration pulled its funding from the Aswan Dam project in Egypt (b). Nasser then nationalized the British-owned Suez Canal (c).

17. C: The person or group not instrumental in advancing civil rights and desegregation immediately after WWII was (c), Congress. As African American soldiers came home from the war, racial discord increased. President Harry Truman (a) appointed a Presidential Committee on Civil Rights in 1946. This committee published a report recommending that segregation and lynching be outlawed by the federal government. However, Congress ignored this report and took no action. Truman then used his presidential powers to enforce desegregation of the military and policies of "fair employment" in federal civil service jobs. The National Association for the Advancement of Colored People (NAACP) (d) brought lawsuits against racist and discriminatory practices, and in resolving these suits, the Supreme Court (b) further eroded segregation. For example, the Supreme Court ruled that primaries allowing only whites would be illegal, and it ended the segregation of interstate bus lines. The landmark civil rights laws were not passed by Congress until the 1960s.

18. B: Of the programs enacted by Johnson, the one most closely related to JFK's legacy was (b), the Civil Rights Act, which Johnson pushed through Congress using allusions to Kennedy and his goals. While Kennedy received congressional backing for a raise in minimum wage and public housing improvements, his efforts regarding civil rights were thwarted by conservative Republicans and Southern Democrats in Congress. However, as the Civil Rights movement progressed through the campaigns of the Freedom Riders, Kennedy developed a strong commitment to the cause.

The Economic Opportunity Act gave almost $1 billion to wage Johnson's War on Poverty. The Great Society (c) was Johnson's name for his comprehensive reform program which included a variety of legislation (see also question #102).

19. B: The GATT countries did agree to abolish or decrease many of their tariffs, but this agreement did not include only 57 countries. It was much larger, including a total of 117 countries. The GATT was approved by Congress in 1994 (a). In addition to having 117 countries agree to increase free trade, the GATT also set up the World Trade Organization (WTO) for the purpose of settling any differences among nations related to trade (c). Another instance of free trade policy established in the 1990s was the Senate's ratification of NAFTA. The negotiation of this agreement was originally made by the first Bush administration, with President Bush and the leaders of Canada and Mexico signing it in 1992 (d), but it still needed to be ratified.

20. B: There was not a reduction in military spending after the war. Although the manufacturing demand for war supplies and the size of the military decreased, the government had increased military spending from $10 billion in 1947 to more than $50 billion by 1953—a more than fivefold increase. This increase strengthened the American economy. Other factors contributing to the strengthened economy included the significantly higher birth rates during the Baby Boom (a) from 1946 to 1957, which stimulated the growth of the building and automotive industries by increased demand. Government programs, such as the GI Bill (the Servicemen's Readjustment Act of 1944), other veterans' benefits, and the National Defense Education Act all encouraged college enrollments, which increased by nearly four times (c). Additionally, larger families, increased

Copyright © Mometrix Media. You have been licensed one copy of this document for personal use only. Any other reproduction or redistribution is strictly prohibited. All rights reserved.

mobility and low-interest loans offered to veterans led to suburban development and growth (d) as well as an increased home construction.

21. D: The statement that the 1986 Immigration Reform and Control Act reduced illegal Mexican immigration is not true. This legislation punished employers with sanctions for hiring undocumented employees, but despite this the illegal immigration of Mexicans to America was largely unaffected by the law. It is true that twice as many people immigrated to America in the 1980s than in the 1970s (a): the number reached over nine million in the 80s. It is true that the majority of immigrants were Latin American (b). In addition to Latin Americans, other large groups of immigrants in the 1980s were Asians and Caribbean inhabitants (c).

22. C: The Mississippi Freedom Democratic Party did attend the 1964 Democratic convention; however, they were unable garner Johnson's support to unseat the regular delegation from Mississippi. A riot did break out in Watts in 1965 (a), and in the following three years, more riots occurred in Newark, N.J. (b) and in Detroit, Michigan (d). These riots were manifestations of the frustrations experienced by blacks regarding racial inequities in American society.

23. A: The earliest written language in Mesopotamia was Sumerian. Ancient Sumerians began writing this language around 3500 BC. Elamite, from Iran, was the language spoken by the ancient Elamites and was the official language of the Persian Empire from the 6th to 4th centuries BC. Written Linear Elamite was used for a very short time in the late 3rd century BC. The written Elamite cuneiform, used from about 2500 to 331 BC, was an adaptation of the Akkadian cuneiform. Akkadian is the earliest found Semitic language. Written Akkadian cuneiform first appeared in texts by circa 2800 BC, and full Akkadian texts appeared by circa 2500 BC. The Akkadian cuneiform writing system is ultimately a derivative of the ancient Sumerian cuneiform writing system, although these two spoken languages were not related linguistically. Aramaic is another Semitic language, but unlike Akkadian, Aramaic is not now extinct. Old Aramaic, the written language of the Old Testament and the spoken language used by Jesus Christ, was current from 1100 BC-200 AD Middle Aramaic, used from 200-1200 AD, included literary Syriac (Christian groups developed the writing system of Syriac in order to be able to write spoken Aramaic) and was the written language of the Jewish books of Biblical commentary (Namely, the Talmud, the Targum, and the Midrash). Modern Aramaic has been used from 1200 to the present.

24. C: The New Kingdom was the period during which no more pyramids were built in Egypt. The Pyramids were built between the years of 2630 and 1814 BC, and the New Kingdom spanned from circa 1550-1070 BC. As a result, the last pyramid was built approximately 264 years before the New Kingdom began. 2630 BC marked the beginning of the reign of the first Pharaoh, Djoser, who had the first pyramid built at Saqqara. 1814 BC marked the end of the reign of the last Pharaoh, Amenemhat III, who had the last pyramid built at Hawara. In between these years, a succession of pharaohs built many pyramids. The Old Kingdom encompasses both the Third and Fourth Dynasties; therefore, all three of these choices encompass pyramid-building periods. Djoser's had his first pyramid built during the Third Dynasty. The Pharaohs Kufu, Khafre, and Menkaure, respectively, build the famous Pyramids of Giza during the Fourth Dynasty during their reigns at different times between circa 2575 and 2467 BC, the period of the Fourth Dynasty. The Middle Kingdom encompassed the 11th through 14th Dynasties, from circa. 2080 to 1640 BC—also within the time period (2630-1814 BC) when pyramids were built by the Pharaohs.

25. B: It is not true that the Crusades succeeded at Christians' reclaiming the "holy land" (the Middle East) from Muslims. Despite their number (nine not counting the Northern Crusades) and longevity (1095-1291 not counting later similar campaigns), the Crusades never accomplished this purpose (a). While they did not take back the Middle East, the Crusades did succeed in exacerbating

Copyright © Mometrix Media. You have been licensed one copy of this document for personal use only. Any other reproduction or redistribution is strictly prohibited. All rights reserved.

the decline of the Byzantine Empire (c), which lost more and more territory to the Ottoman Turks during this period. In addition, the Crusades resulted in Egypt's rise once again to become a major power (d) of the Middle East as it had been in the past.

26. D: After the Black Death killed a third of Europe's population (a), the survivors were mainly upper classes with more money to spend on art, architecture, and other luxuries. The plague deaths also resulted in a labor shortage, thereby creating more work opportunities for the surviving people in lower classes (b). As a result, these survivors' positions in society appreciated. Once plague deaths subsided and population growth in Europe began to reassert itself, a greater demand existed for products and services. At the same time, the number of people available to provide these products and services was still smaller than in the past. Consequently, more merchants, artisans, and bankers emerged in order to provide the services and products people wanted, thereby creating a class of citizens between the lower-class laborers and the upper-class elite (c). After the two major Italian banks collapsed, wealthy investors who would normally have reinvested their disposable income did not do this, since the economy did not favor it. Instead, they invested their money in artistic and cultural products.

27. B: In order to prosper, a nation should not try to increase its imports. Mercantilism is an economic theory including the idea that prosperity comes from a positive balance of international trade. For any one nation to prosper, that nation should increase its exports (c) but decrease its imports. Exporting more to other countries while importing less from them will give a country a positive trade balance. This theory assumes that money and wealth are identical (a) assets of a nation. Mercantilism dictates that a nation's government should apply a policy of economic protectionism (d) by stimulating more exports and suppressing imports. Some ways to accomplish this task have included granting subsidies for exports and imposing tariffs on imports. Mercantilism can be regarded as essentially the opposite of the free trade policies that have been encouraged in more recent years.

28. C: It is not true that the English Civil Wars between 1641 and 1651 legalized Parliament's consent as a requirement for a monarch to rule England. These wars did establish this idea as a precedent, but the later Glorious Revolution of 1688 actually made it legal that a monarch could not rule without Parliamentary consent. The wars from 1641-1651 were all fought between Royalists who supported an absolute monarchy and Parliamentarians who supported the joint government of a parliamentary monarchy (a). Parliament was the victor (b) in 1651 at the Battle of Worcester. As a result of this battle, King Charles I was executed, and King Charles II was exiled. In the first of these civil wars, from 1642-1646, and the second, from 1648-1649, supporters of King Charles I (d) fought against supporters of the Long Parliament.

29. D: Resentment against the Protestant Reformation was not a cause given for the French Revolution. Choices (a), (b), and (c) are just a few among many causes cited for the war. Famines caused malnutrition and even starvation among the poorest people (a). Escalating bread prices contributed greatly to the hunger. Louis XV had amassed a great amount of debt from spending money on many wars in addition to the American Revolution. Military failures as well as a lack of social services for veterans exacerbated these debts. In addition, the Court of Louis XVI and Marie Antoinette spent excessively and obviously on luxuries even while people in the country were starving, and France's monetary system was outdated, inefficient, and thus unable to manage the national debt (b). Much of the populace greatly resented the Catholic Church's control of the country (c). However, there was not great resentment against the Protestant Reformation (d); there were large minorities of Protestants in France, who not only exerted their influence on government institutions, but undoubtedly also contributed to the resentment of the Catholic Church.

Copyright © Mometrix Media. You have been licensed one copy of this document for personal use only. Any other reproduction or redistribution is strictly prohibited. All rights reserved.

30. A: In the 1780s, the French national debt was very high. The French nobility adamantly resisted attempts by King Louis XVI to reform tax laws, which led to a high tax burden on the French peasantry. The French government spent almost 50% of its national expenditures on debt-related payments during the 1780s; thus it could not and did not spend almost 60% to finance luxuries for the French nobility. This eliminates choice B. King Louis XVI temporarily banned the guild system to bolster, rather than stifle, free trade. Because this system gave skilled craftsmen economic advantages, journeymen opposed ending the system. This eliminates choice D. Regardless of the status of guilds before the French Revolution, French society did not offer many opportunities for upward social mobility. Few peasants were able to advance. This eliminates choice C.

31. C: The only accurate statement about the end of WWI is that President Wilson had proposed that the nations of the world form a coalition to prevent future world wars. While he did not give the coalition a name, he clearly expressed his proposal that such a group form in the fourteenth of his Fourteen Points. The Treaty of Versailles (1919) did not bring peace among all countries involved in the war (a); Germany and the United States arrived at a separate peace in 1921. Furthermore, the Treaty of Versailles did not contain a clause for establishing the United Nations (b); it contained a clause for establishing the League of Nations. The League of Nations was created as dictated by the treaty, but when the Second World War proved that this group had failed to prevent future world wars, it was replaced by the United Nations after World War II. President Wilson did not succeed in getting the USA to ratify the League of Nations (d).

32. A: Russian's involvement in World War I brought social tension in Russia to a head. Contributing factors included military defeats and civilian suffering. Prior to Russia entering the war, Russian factory workers could legally strike, but during the war, it was illegal for them to act collectively. This eliminates answer C. Protests continued during World War I, and the Russian government was overthrown in 1917. This eliminates answer D. Answer B can be rejected because World War I did not go well for the Russian Army; Nicholas III, therefore, had no successes upon which to capitalize.

33. A: The latest occurring decolonization event was the Eastern Bloc and Soviet Satellite states of Armenia, Azerbaijan, Estonia, Georgia, Kazakhstan, Kyrgyzstan, Latvia, Lithuania, Moldova, Russia, Tajikistan, Turkmenistan, Ukraine, and Uzbekistan, which all became independent from the Soviet Union in 1991. (Note: This was the last decolonization of the Cold War years, as the end of the Soviet Union marked the end of the Cold War.) Canada completed its independence from British Parliament via the Canada Act (b) in 1982. In the Caribbean, the Bahamas gained independence from the United Kingdom (c) in 1973. Algeria won its independence from France when the Algerian War of Independence, begun in 1954, ended in 1962 (d).

34. B: U.S. industrialization was confined to the Northeast until after the Civil War because the Northeast had faster-running rivers than the South. The earliest American factories used horse-drawn machines. When waterpower was developed and proved superior, the Northeast's faster rivers were more suited to water-powered mills than the South's slower rivers. The war did not delay the development of water power (a). Waterpower was developed before the Civil War in the late 1790s. Steam power, a more efficient alternative to water power, was developed after the Civil War and eventually replaced waterpower. With steam-powered engines, industry could spread to the South, since steam engines did not depend on rapidly running water like water-powered engines. While British emigré Samuel Slater's first cotton mill using horse-drawn production did lose a lot of money (c), this was not a reason for industrial delay. In fact, Slater's Beverly Cotton Manufactory in Massachusetts, the first American cotton mill, in spite of its financial problems, was successful in both its volume of cotton production and in developing the water-powered technology that ultimately would succeed the horse-drawn method. Slater's second cotton mill in Pawtucket,

185

Copyright © Mometrix Media. You have been licensed one copy of this document for personal use only. Any other reproduction or redistribution is strictly prohibited. All rights reserved.

Rhode Island, was water-powered. Industrial delay was not because milling technology had not yet been invented (d). Slater learned of new textile manufacturing techniques as a youth in England, and he brought this knowledge to America in 1789. Resistance of Southern owners of plantations and slaves did not slow the spread of industrialism. Rather, as seen in (b) above, the South did not have the geographic capability to sustain waterpower. Once steam power was developed, the South joined in industrialization.

35. A: The inaccurate statement is the Puritans unconditionally supported the English Reformation. While they agreed with the Reformation in principle, they felt that it had not pursued those principles far enough and should make greater reforms. Similarly, they felt that the Church of England (or Anglican Church), though it had separated from the Catholic Church in the Protestant Reformation, still allowed many practices they found too much like Catholicism (b). The Puritans did become a chief political power in England because of the first English Civil War (c) between Royalists and Parliamentarians. The Royalists had a profound suspicion of the radical Puritans. Among the Parliament's elements of resistance, the strongest was that of the Puritans. They joined in the battle initially for ostensibly political reasons as others had, but soon they brought more attention to religious issues. Following the Restoration in 1660 and the Uniformity Act of 1662, thereby restoring the Church of England to its pre-English Civil War status, the great majority of Puritan clergy defected from the Church of England (d).

36. D: It is not true that the Gilded Age is a term whose origins have not been identified clearly. In 1873, Mark Twain and Charles Dudley Warner co-authored a book entitled The Gilded Age: A Tale of Today. Twain and Warner first coined this term to describe the extravagance and excesses of America's wealthy upper class (b), who became richer than ever due to industrialization. Furthermore, the Gilded Age was the era of the "robber barons" (a) such as John D. Rockefeller, Cornelius Vanderbilt, J.P. Morgan, and others. Because they accumulated enormous wealth through extremely aggressive and occasionally unethical monetary manipulations, critics dubbed them "robber barons" because they seemed to be elite lords of robbery. While these business tycoons grasped huge fortunes, some of them—such as Andrew Carnegie and Andrew Mellon—were also philanthropists, using their wealth to support and further worthy causes such as literacy, education, health care, charities, and the arts. They donated millions of dollars to fund social improvements. Carnegie himself dubbed this large philanthropic movement the "Gospel of Wealth" (c).

37. A: It is not true that the founding fathers specifically stated in the Constitution that the USA would be a democracy. The founding fathers wanted the new United States to be founded on principles of liberty and equality, but they did not specifically describe these principles with the term "Democracy." Thus, the Declaration of Independence, like the Constitution after it, did not stipulate a democracy, although both did state the principles of equality and freedom (b). The Constitution also provided for the election of the new government (c), and for protection of the rights of some, but not all, of the people (d). Notable exceptions at the time were black people and women. Only later were laws passed to protect their rights over the years.

38. B: Preservatives such as salt were only introduced to the European diet after trade routes opened and these goods could be brought to Europe.

39. B: In 1792, when the French Revolution turned into European war, American traders conducted business with both sides. It is not true that Washington allied with the French (a) at this time. Washington issued a Proclamation of Neutrality in 1792 when the French went to war with European countries. While they did trade with both sides, American merchants profited the most from the French West Indies, not the British West Indies (c). The Spanish navy did not retaliate

Copyright © Mometrix Media. You have been licensed one copy of this document for personal use only. Any other reproduction or redistribution is strictly prohibited. All rights reserved.

against America for trading with the French (d). Though Spain was an ally of Britain, it was the British who most often seized American ships and forced their crews to serve the British navy.

40. B: The Etruscans were from a kingdom to the north that seized control of Rome from the Latins in the mid-600s BC. They began urbanizing the settlement, improving roads, adding drainage systems, etc. They were driven out of the region in 509 BC during an uprising of the Latins.

41. A: James Madison, John Jay, and Alexander Hamilton published The Federalist in the Independent Journal in New York. It was a response to the Anti-Federalists in New York, who were slow to ratify the Constitution because they feared it gave the central government too much authority.

42. D: A practical application of content learned involves action, not merely knowledge. Options A and C, although they describe content that students would reasonably learn in a class or unit on the structure of the U.S. government, do not describe applications of content, or applications of a social studies education. Therefore options A and C can both be rejected. Option B does involve action and not merely the acquisition of knowledge. However, it is not as directly tied to learning the structure of the U.S. government as option D, informed participation in U.S. political processes. This is because informed participation in school elections is quite possible without knowing the structure of the U.S. government. Informed participation in U.S. political processes requires knowledge of the structure of the U.S. government (i.e., voting on an issue requires an understanding of where a given candidate stands on that issue).

43. C: A federalist system of government is a government under which power is shared by a central authority and sub-components of the federation. In the United States in particular, power is shared by the federal government and the individual states. Option A, that the legislative branch consists of two representative bodies (the House of Representatives and the Senate) is true, of course, but does not describe a uniquely federalist structure. Rather, it describes the concept of bicameralism. Option A may thus be eliminated. Option B, likewise, describes different types of democracy but not federalism. B can thus be eliminated. Regarding option D, this statement is also true (the U.S. Constitution shapes national legislation) but it is not a descriptive statement of the federalist system because the statement makes no mention that power is shared by the states.

44. D: Congress did not have the authority to levy taxes under the Articles of Confederation. Without the ability to levy taxes, there was no way to finance programs, which weakened the government.

45. A: The Age of Enlightenment was a time of scientific and philosophical achievement. Also called the Age of Reason, human thought and reason were prized.

46. C: The Constitution was not ratified immediately. Only five states accepted it in early 1788; Massachusetts, New York, Rhode Island, and Virginia were originally opposed to the Constitution. Rhode Island reluctantly accepted it in 1790.

47. B: James Madison was a close friend of Thomas Jefferson and supported a stronger central government. George Mason and Robert Yates were both against expanding federal authority over the states. Benjamin Franklin was a proponent of a strong federal government, but he was from Massachusetts.

48. D: Some of the men who helped frame the Constitution believed the central government needed to be stronger than what was established under the Articles of Confederation. Others were against this and feared a strong federal government. A system of checks and balances was established to

Copyright © Mometrix Media. You have been licensed one copy of this document for personal use only. Any other reproduction or redistribution is strictly prohibited. All rights reserved.

prevent the central government from taking too much power. This arrangement is known as federalism.

49. A: The Senate and House of Representatives make up a bicameral legislature. The Great Compromise awarded seats in the Senate equally to each state, while the seats in the House of Representatives were based on population.

50. B: The Presidential Succession Act lists the Speaker of the House, president pro tempore of the Senate, and secretary of state next in succession after the vice president. However, anyone who succeeds as president must meet all of the legal qualifications.

51. C: The President has the power to veto legislation directly or use a pocket veto by not signing a bill within ten days after receiving it. Congress adjourns during this time period. A veto can be overridden if two-thirds of the House and the two-thirds of the Senate both agree. The President must veto a complete bill and does not have the authority to veto sections or lines.

52. C: The Civil Rights Act of 1964 affected the Jim Crow laws in the Southern states. Many minorities suffered under unfair voting laws and segregation. President Lyndon Johnson signed the Civil Rights Act of 1964 into law after the 1963 assassination of President Kennedy, who championed the reform.

53. B: Only the federal government has the power to give copyrights and patents to individuals or companies. The power to levy taxes, borrow money, and spend money (a) is a power shared by federal and state governments. The power to set the criteria that qualify individuals to vote (c) is a power given to state governments only. The power to ratify amendments proposed to the Constitution (d) is a power of only the state governments.

54. A: The action that needs a three-fourths majority vote is state approval of a proposed constitutional amendment. Proposing a constitutional amendment (b) requires a two-thirds majority vote. Ratifying presidential appointments in the Senate (c) also requires a two-thirds majority vote. Introducing charges for impeachment in the House of Representatives (d) requires a simple majority vote.

55. B: The term "Manifest Destiny" had not been used for many years before the 1830s. This term was coined in 1844. However, it is true that the idea this term expressed had been around for many years before that (a). It is also true that many Americans believed Manifest Destiny would mean America would ultimately encompass Canada and Mexico (c). Factors contributing to Manifest Destiny included the rise in nationalism that followed the War of 1812 and the population growth that increased that nationalism (d).

56. A: Presidential candidates are eligible for a match from the federal government (with a $250 per contribution limit) if they can privately raise $5,000 per state in twenty states. Candidates who accept public money agree to limit spending. Candidates who do not accept matching funds are free to use the money they raise privately.

57. D: America is a common law country because English common law was adopted in all states except Louisiana. Common law is based on precedent and changes over time. Each state develops its own common laws.

58. D: The only answer choice that represents a possible absolute location for New Orleans is 30° N, 90° W. When a location is described in terms of its placement on the global grid, it is customary to put the latitude before the longitude. New Orleans is north of the equator, so it has to be in the

Copyright © Mometrix Media. You have been licensed one copy of this document for personal use only. Any other reproduction or redistribution is strictly prohibited. All rights reserved.

Northern Hemisphere. In addition, it is west of the prime meridian, which runs through Greenwich, England, among other places. So, New Orleans must be in the Western Hemisphere. It is possible, then, to deduce that 30° N, 90° W is the only possible absolute location for New Orleans.

59. B: On a political map, countries are represented in different colors, and countries that share a border are not given the same color. This is so that the borders between countries will be distinct. Political maps are used to illustrate those aspects of a country that have been determined by people: the capital, the provincial and national borders, and the large cities. Political maps sometimes include major physical features like rivers and mountains, but they are not intended to display all such information. On a physical, climate, or contour map, however, the borders between nations are more incidental. Colors are used on these maps to represent physical features, areas with similar climate, etc. It is possible that colors will overrun the borders and be shared by adjacent countries.

60. D: Around the world, the area around the equator is known for a relative lack of wind. Indeed, the equatorial belt is sometimes called the doldrums because the constant warm water encourages the air to rise gently. To the north and south, however, there are trade winds that can become quite violent. The equator only intersects three continents: Asia, Africa, and South America. It is in between the north and south horse latitudes, which are belts known for calm winds. Finally, the equator is located at 0° latitude, not longitude, though the 0° line of longitude does intersect the equator.

61. A: The apparent distance between Greenland and Norway will be greatest on a Mercator map. The Mercator map is a type of cylindrical projection map in which lines of latitude and longitude are transferred onto a cylindrical shape, which is then cut vertically and laid flat. For this reason, distances around the poles will appear increasingly great. The Mercator map is excellent for navigation because a straight line drawn on it represents a single compass reading. In a conic projection map, on the other hand, a hemisphere of the globe is transposed onto a cone, which is then cut vertically (that is, from rim to tip) and laid flat. The apparent distances on a conic projection will be smallest at the 45th parallel. A contour map uses lines to illustrate the features of a geographic area. For example, the lines on an elevation contour map connect areas that have the same altitude. An equal-area projection map represents landmasses in their actual sizes. To make this possible, the shapes of the landmasses are manipulated slightly, and the map is interrupted (divided into more than one part).

62. A: Symbols are not used to represent relief on a physical map. A physical map is dedicated to illustrating the landmasses and bodies of water in a specific region, so symbols do not provide enough detail. Color, shading, and contour lines, on the other hand, are able to create a much more complicated picture of changes in elevation, precipitation, etc. Changes in elevation are known in geography as relief.

63. D: A flow-line map describes the movement of people, trends, or materials across a physical area. The movements depicted on a flow-line map are typically represented by arrows. In more advanced flow-line maps, the width of the arrow corresponds to the quantity of the motion. Flow-line maps usually declare the span of time that is being represented. A political map depicts the man-made aspects of geography, such as borders and cities. A cartogram adjusts the size of the areas represented according to some variable. For instance, a cartogram of wheat production would depict Iowa as being much larger than Alaska. A qualitative map uses lines, dots, and other symbols to illustrate a particular point. For example, a qualitative map might be used to demonstrate the greatest expansion of the Persian Empire.

Copyright © Mometrix Media. You have been licensed one copy of this document for personal use only. Any other reproduction or redistribution is strictly prohibited. All rights reserved.

64. B: The composite volcano, sometimes called the stratovolcano, is the most common type of volcano on earth. A composite volcano has steep sides, so the explosions of ash, pumice, and silica are often accompanied by treacherous mudslides. Indeed, it is these mudslides that cause most of the damage associated with composite volcano eruptions. Krakatoa and Mount Saint Helens are examples of composite volcanoes. A lava dome is a round volcano that emits thick lava very slowly. A shield volcano, one example of which is Mt. Kilauea in Hawaii, emits a small amount of lava over an extended period of time. Shield volcanoes are not known for violent eruptions. A cinder cone has steep sides made of fallen cinders, which themselves are made of the lava that intermittently shoots into the air.

65. C: After precipitation, the heat of the sun causes evaporation, a process by which water molecules change from a liquid to a gas, ultimately returning to the atmosphere. The other options describe processes that pertain to properties of water, but not to water's return to the atmosphere. Percolation is the process by which water moves down through soil. Cohesion (specifically, structural cohesion) is the property of matter by which the molecules in a single substance stay together. Condensation is the process by which matter changes from a gas to a liquid; after evaporation, molecules of water form rain droplets through condensation.

66. B: Metamorphic rock is formed by extreme heat and pressure. This type of rock is created when other rocks are somehow buried within the earth, where they are subject to a dramatic rise in pressure and temperature. Slate and marble are both metamorphic rocks. Metamorphic rocks are created by the other two main types of rock: sedimentary and igneous. Sedimentary rock is formed when dirt and other sediment is washed into a bed, covered over by subsequent sediment, and compacted into rock. Depending on how they are formed, sedimentary rocks are classified as organic, clastic, or chemical. Igneous rocks are composed of cooled magma, the molten rock that emerges from volcanoes. Basalt and granite are two common varieties of igneous rock.

67. A: The eye wall of a hurricane has the strongest winds and the greatest rainfall. The eye wall is the tower-like rim of the eye. It is from this wall that clouds extend out, which are seen from above as the classic outward spiral pattern. A hurricane front is the outermost edge of its influence; although there will be heavy winds and rain in this area, the intensity will be relatively small. The eye of a hurricane is actually a place of surprising peace. In this area, dry and cool air rushes down to the ground or sea. Once there, the air is caught up in the winds of the eye wall and is driven outward at a furious pace.

68. D: These are all geographically parts of Southeast Asia. The countries of Myanmar (Burma), Laos, Cambodia, and Thailand are considered Mainland Southeast Asia, as are Vietnam and the Malay Peninsula. Brunei, East Malaysia, Indonesia, and the Philippines are considered Maritime Southeast Asia, as are Singapore and Timor-Leste. The Seven Sister States of India are also considered to be part of Southeast Asia, geographically and culturally. (The Seven Sister States of India are Arunachal Pradesh, Assam, Nagaland, Meghalaya, Manipur, Tripura, and Mizoram, which all have contiguous borders in northeastern India.)

69. A: One example of the multiplier effect of large cities would be if the presence of specialized equipment for an industry attracted even more business. Large cities tend to grow even larger for a number of reasons: they have more skilled workers, they have greater concentrations of specialized equipment, and they have already-functioning markets. These factors all make it easier for a business to begin operations in a large city than elsewhere. Thus, the populations and economic productivity of large cities tend to grow quickly. Some governments have sought to mitigate this trend by clustering groups of similar industries in smaller cities.

Copyright © Mometrix Media. You have been licensed one copy of this document for personal use only. Any other reproduction or redistribution is strictly prohibited. All rights reserved.

70. D: The Sahel, a belt of grasslands just south of the Sahara Desert, has long been a focus of agricultural efforts in Africa. This semiarid region has provided sustenance to people and animals for thousands of years. In the last thousand years, stores of salt and gold were found there, giving rise to empires in Ghana and Mali. Changes in climate have expanded the Sahara, however, and pushed the Sahel farther south. The Qattara Depression is a low-lying desert in Egypt. The Great Rift Valley is a region of faults and rocky hills that extends along the southeastern coast of Africa. The Congo Basin is a repository of sediment from the Ubangi and Congo rivers. It is in the northern half of what is now called the Democratic Republic of the Congo.

71. B: To determine the shortest route between Lima and Lisbon, Tracy should use an azimuthal projection with Lisbon at the center. An azimuthal projection depicts one hemisphere of the globe as a circle. A straight line drawn from the center of the map to any point represents the shortest possible distance between those two points. Tracy could obtain her objective, then, with an azimuthal projection in which either Lisbon or Lima were at the center. If the North Pole were at the center, the map would not include Lima because this city is in the Southern Hemisphere. A Robinson projection approximates the sizes and shapes of landmasses but does distort in some ways, particularly near the poles.

72. B: North Korea and South Korea are separated by a geometric border, meaning that the boundary between the two nations is a straight line drawn on a map, without respect to landforms. Specifically, the boundary between the Koreas is the 38th parallel. Another example of a geometric border lies between the continental United States and Canada. The Turkish Cyprus–Greek Cyprus border is anthropogeographic, or drawn according to cultural reasons. The border between France and Spain is physiographic-political, a combination of the Pyrenees Mountains and European history. The Irish Sea separates England from Ireland.

73. D: More information is required to calculate the natural increase rate for Grassley County during this year. Natural increase rate is the growth in population measured as the surplus of live births over deaths for every thousand people. The calculation of natural increase rate does not take account of immigration or emigration. The natural increase rate for Grassley County cannot be calculated because the original population of the county is not given. As an example, if the beginning population of the county had been 10,000, the natural increase rate would be 40;

$$\frac{400 \times 1,000}{10,000} = 40$$

74. A: North Africa is not one of the world's four major population agglomerations. These are eastern North America, South Asia, East Asia, and Europe. The largest of these is East Asia, which encompasses Korea, Japan, and the major cities of China. The second-largest population agglomeration is South Asia, which includes India and Pakistan. Most of the population in this area is near the coasts. The European agglomeration is spread across the largest piece of land, while the much smaller agglomeration in eastern North America is primarily focused on the string of cities from Boston to Washington, DC.

75. D: It is true that scarcity causes producers (and other people) to make choices. Producers must choose what to produce with limited resources. It is also true that the choices a producer makes when faced with scarcity come with trade-offs. There are advantages and disadvantages to different production decisions. And, finally, calculating the opportunity cost of a choice provides a manner with which to measure the consequence of a choice and compare that against the consequence of other choices.

Copyright © Mometrix Media. You have been licensed one copy of this document for personal use only. Any other reproduction or redistribution is strictly prohibited. All rights reserved.

76. B: John Maynard Keynes argued that government could help revitalize a recessionary economy by increasing government spending and therefore increasing aggregate demand. This is known as demand-side economics.

77. C: If a society wants greater income equity, it will impose a progressive income tax, which taxes the wealthy at a higher rate; an inheritance tax, which prevents the wealthy from passing all their wealth on to the next generation; and a gift tax, which prevents the wealthy from simply giving their wealth away.

78. A: GDP (Gross Domestic Product) is restricted to value produced within borders, whereas GNP (Gross National Product) is focused on value produced by companies regardless of borders.

79. B: Structural unemployment is unemployment that results from a mismatch of job skills or location. In this case, Ivy's job skill—her ability to work as a seamstress—is no longer desired by employers. Frictional and cyclical are other forms of unemployment; economists do not use the term careless unemployment.

80. D: It is believed that some level of frictional and structural unemployment will always exist, and that the best economists (and politicians) can hope for is to reduce cyclical unemployment to zero. Therefore, frictional and structural unemployment are sometimes referred to as natural unemployment, meaning unemployment that naturally exists within an economy.

81. C: A supply shock is caused when there is a dramatic increase in input prices. This causes an increase in price levels and decreases in employment and GDP. A supply shock causes the AS curve to move to the left (in).

82. A: As people have more and more of something, they value it less and less. This is the law of diminishing marginal utility, and it is what causes the downward slope of the demand curve.

83. A: The change in demand is 20% ($1,000 - 800 = 200$), and the change in price is 10% ($\$11 - \$10 = \$1$). Because the change in demand is greater than the change in price, the demand is considered elastic. In this case, the price elasticity quotient is greater than 1.

84. A: The phenomenon of "sticky prices" refers to prices that stay the same even though it seems they should change (either increasing or decreasing).

85. C: When a nation follows the theory of comparative advantage, it specializes in producing the goods and services it can make at a lower opportunity cost and then engages in trade to obtain other goods.

86. C: A person who has taken out a fixed-rate loan can benefit from inflation by paying back the loan with dollars that are less valuable than they were when the loan was taken out. In the other examples, inflation harms the individual or entity.

87. A: The input and output data illustrate the Law of Diminishing Marginal Returns, which states that as inputs are added during production, there eventually comes a time when increased inputs coincide with a decrease in marginal return.

88. C: Banks create money by giving out loans. For example, assume a person puts $100 into a bank. The bank will keep a percentage of that money in reserves because of the reserve requirement. If the reserve requirement is 10% then the bank will put $10 in reserves and then loan out $90 of it to

Copyright © Mometrix Media. You have been licensed one copy of this document for personal use only. Any other reproduction or redistribution is strictly prohibited. All rights reserved.

a second person. The money total, which started at $100, now includes the original $100 plus the $90, or a total of $190. The bank creates $90 by loaning it.

89. A: The equation of exchange is MV = PQ. This means that M (a measure of the supply of money) multiplied by the velocity of money, V, (the average number of times a typical dollar is spent on final goods and services a year) = P, the average price level of final goods and services in GDP × real output, Q (the quantity of goods and services in GDP).

90. A: Economics is defined as the study of scarcity, the situation in which resources are limited and wants are unlimited.

Copyright © Mometrix Media. You have been licensed one copy of this document for personal use only. Any other reproduction or redistribution is strictly prohibited. All rights reserved.

How to Overcome Test Anxiety

Just the thought of taking a test is enough to make most people a little nervous. A test is an important event that can have a long-term impact on your future, so it's important to take it seriously and it's natural to feel anxious about performing well. But just because anxiety is normal, that doesn't mean that it's helpful in test taking, or that you should simply accept it as part of your life. Anxiety can have a variety of effects. These effects can be mild, like making you feel slightly nervous, or severe, like blocking your ability to focus or remember even a simple detail.

If you experience test anxiety—whether severe or mild—it's important to know how to beat it. To discover this, first you need to understand what causes test anxiety.

Causes of Test Anxiety

While we often think of anxiety as an uncontrollable emotional state, it can actually be caused by simple, practical things. One of the most common causes of test anxiety is that a person does not feel adequately prepared for their test. This feeling can be the result of many different issues such as poor study habits or lack of organization, but the most common culprit is time management. Starting to study too late, failing to organize your study time to cover all of the material, or being distracted while you study will mean that you're not well prepared for the test. This may lead to cramming the night before, which will cause you to be physically and mentally exhausted for the test. Poor time management also contributes to feelings of stress, fear, and hopelessness as you realize you are not well prepared but don't know what to do about it.

Other times, test anxiety is not related to your preparation for the test but comes from unresolved fear. This may be a past failure on a test, or poor performance on tests in general. It may come from comparing yourself to others who seem to be performing better or from the stress of living up to expectations. Anxiety may be driven by fears of the future—how failure on this test would affect your educational and career goals. These fears are often completely irrational, but they can still negatively impact your test performance.

> **Review Video: 3 Reasons You Have Test Anxiety**
> Visit mometrix.com/academy and enter code: 428468

Copyright © Mometrix Media. You have been licensed one copy of this document for personal use only. Any other reproduction or redistribution is strictly prohibited. All rights reserved.

Elements of Test Anxiety

As mentioned earlier, test anxiety is considered to be an emotional state, but it has physical and mental components as well. Sometimes you may not even realize that you are suffering from test anxiety until you notice the physical symptoms. These can include trembling hands, rapid heartbeat, sweating, nausea, and tense muscles. Extreme anxiety may lead to fainting or vomiting. Obviously, any of these symptoms can have a negative impact on testing. It is important to recognize them as soon as they begin to occur so that you can address the problem before it damages your performance.

> **Review Video: 3 Ways to Tell You Have Test Anxiety**
> Visit mometrix.com/academy and enter code: 927847

The mental components of test anxiety include trouble focusing and inability to remember learned information. During a test, your mind is on high alert, which can help you recall information and stay focused for an extended period of time. However, anxiety interferes with your mind's natural processes, causing you to blank out, even on the questions you know well. The strain of testing during anxiety makes it difficult to stay focused, especially on a test that may take several hours. Extreme anxiety can take a huge mental toll, making it difficult not only to recall test information but even to understand the test questions or pull your thoughts together.

> **Review Video: How Test Anxiety Affects Memory**
> Visit mometrix.com/academy and enter code: 609003

Effects of Test Anxiety

Test anxiety is like a disease—if left untreated, it will get progressively worse. Anxiety leads to poor performance, and this reinforces the feelings of fear and failure, which in turn lead to poor performances on subsequent tests. It can grow from a mild nervousness to a crippling condition. If allowed to progress, test anxiety can have a big impact on your schooling, and consequently on your future.

Test anxiety can spread to other parts of your life. Anxiety on tests can become anxiety in any stressful situation, and blanking on a test can turn into panicking in a job situation. But fortunately, you don't have to let anxiety rule your testing and determine your grades. There are a number of relatively simple steps you can take to move past anxiety and function normally on a test and in the rest of life.

> **Review Video: How Test Anxiety Impacts Your Grades**
> Visit mometrix.com/academy and enter code: 939819

Copyright © Mometrix Media. You have been licensed one copy of this document for personal use only. Any other reproduction or redistribution is strictly prohibited. All rights reserved.

Physical Steps for Beating Test Anxiety

While test anxiety is a serious problem, the good news is that it can be overcome. It doesn't have to control your ability to think and remember information. While it may take time, you can begin taking steps today to beat anxiety.

Just as your first hint that you may be struggling with anxiety comes from the physical symptoms, the first step to treating it is also physical. Rest is crucial for having a clear, strong mind. If you are tired, it is much easier to give in to anxiety. But if you establish good sleep habits, your body and mind will be ready to perform optimally, without the strain of exhaustion. Additionally, sleeping well helps you to retain information better, so you're more likely to recall the answers when you see the test questions.

Getting good sleep means more than going to bed on time. It's important to allow your brain time to relax. Take study breaks from time to time so it doesn't get overworked, and don't study right before bed. Take time to rest your mind before trying to rest your body, or you may find it difficult to fall asleep.

> **Review Video: The Importance of Sleep for Your Brain**
> Visit mometrix.com/academy and enter code: 319338

Along with sleep, other aspects of physical health are important in preparing for a test. Good nutrition is vital for good brain function. Sugary foods and drinks may give a burst of energy but this burst is followed by a crash, both physically and emotionally. Instead, fuel your body with protein and vitamin-rich foods.

Also, drink plenty of water. Dehydration can lead to headaches and exhaustion, especially if your brain is already under stress from the rigors of the test. Particularly if your test is a long one, drink water during the breaks. And if possible, take an energy-boosting snack to eat between sections.

> **Review Video: How Diet Can Affect your Mood**
> Visit mometrix.com/academy and enter code: 624317

Along with sleep and diet, a third important part of physical health is exercise. Maintaining a steady workout schedule is helpful, but even taking 5-minute study breaks to walk can help get your blood pumping faster and clear your head. Exercise also releases endorphins, which contribute to a positive feeling and can help combat test anxiety.

When you nurture your physical health, you are also contributing to your mental health. If your body is healthy, your mind is much more likely to be healthy as well. So take time to rest, nourish your body with healthy food and water, and get moving as much as possible. Taking these physical steps will make you stronger and more able to take the mental steps necessary to overcome test anxiety.

Copyright © Mometrix Media. You have been licensed one copy of this document for personal use only. Any other reproduction or redistribution is strictly prohibited. All rights reserved.

Mental Steps for Beating Test Anxiety

Working on the mental side of test anxiety can be more challenging, but as with the physical side, there are clear steps you can take to overcome it. As mentioned earlier, test anxiety often stems from lack of preparation, so the obvious solution is to prepare for the test. Effective studying may be the most important weapon you have for beating test anxiety, but you can and should employ several other mental tools to combat fear.

First, boost your confidence by reminding yourself of past success—tests or projects that you aced. If you're putting as much effort into preparing for this test as you did for those, there's no reason you should expect to fail here. Work hard to prepare; then trust your preparation.

Second, surround yourself with encouraging people. It can be helpful to find a study group, but be sure that the people you're around will encourage a positive attitude. If you spend time with others who are anxious or cynical, this will only contribute to your own anxiety. Look for others who are motivated to study hard from a desire to succeed, not from a fear of failure.

Third, reward yourself. A test is physically and mentally tiring, even without anxiety, and it can be helpful to have something to look forward to. Plan an activity following the test, regardless of the outcome, such as going to a movie or getting ice cream.

When you are taking the test, if you find yourself beginning to feel anxious, remind yourself that you know the material. Visualize successfully completing the test. Then take a few deep, relaxing breaths and return to it. Work through the questions carefully but with confidence, knowing that you are capable of succeeding.

Developing a healthy mental approach to test taking will also aid in other areas of life. Test anxiety affects more than just the actual test—it can be damaging to your mental health and even contribute to depression. It's important to beat test anxiety before it becomes a problem for more than testing.

> **Review Video: Test Anxiety and Depression**
> Visit mometrix.com/academy and enter code: 904704

Copyright © Mometrix Media. You have been licensed one copy of this document for personal use only. Any other reproduction or redistribution is strictly prohibited. All rights reserved.

Study Strategy

Being prepared for the test is necessary to combat anxiety, but what does being prepared look like? You may study for hours on end and still not feel prepared. What you need is a strategy for test prep. The next few pages outline our recommended steps to help you plan out and conquer the challenge of preparation.

STEP 1: SCOPE OUT THE TEST

Learn everything you can about the format (multiple choice, essay, etc.) and what will be on the test. Gather any study materials, course outlines, or sample exams that may be available. Not only will this help you to prepare, but knowing what to expect can help to alleviate test anxiety.

STEP 2: MAP OUT THE MATERIAL

Look through the textbook or study guide and make note of how many chapters or sections it has. Then divide these over the time you have. For example, if a book has 15 chapters and you have five days to study, you need to cover three chapters each day. Even better, if you have the time, leave an extra day at the end for overall review after you have gone through the material in depth.

If time is limited, you may need to prioritize the material. Look through it and make note of which sections you think you already have a good grasp on, and which need review. While you are studying, skim quickly through the familiar sections and take more time on the challenging parts. Write out your plan so you don't get lost as you go. Having a written plan also helps you feel more in control of the study, so anxiety is less likely to arise from feeling overwhelmed at the amount to cover.

STEP 3: GATHER YOUR TOOLS

Decide what study method works best for you. Do you prefer to highlight in the book as you study and then go back over the highlighted portions? Or do you type out notes of the important information? Or is it helpful to make flashcards that you can carry with you? Assemble the pens, index cards, highlighters, post-it notes, and any other materials you may need so you won't be distracted by getting up to find things while you study.

If you're having a hard time retaining the information or organizing your notes, experiment with different methods. For example, try color-coding by subject with colored pens, highlighters, or post-it notes. If you learn better by hearing, try recording yourself reading your notes so you can listen while in the car, working out, or simply sitting at your desk. Ask a friend to quiz you from your flashcards, or try teaching someone the material to solidify it in your mind.

STEP 4: CREATE YOUR ENVIRONMENT

It's important to avoid distractions while you study. This includes both the obvious distractions like visitors and the subtle distractions like an uncomfortable chair (or a too-comfortable couch that makes you want to fall asleep). Set up the best study environment possible: good lighting and a comfortable work area. If background music helps you focus, you may want to turn it on, but otherwise keep the room quiet. If you are using a computer to take notes, be sure you don't have any other windows open, especially applications like social media, games, or anything else that could distract you. Silence your phone and turn off notifications. Be sure to keep water close by so you stay hydrated while you study (but avoid unhealthy drinks and snacks).

Also, take into account the best time of day to study. Are you freshest first thing in the morning? Try to set aside some time then to work through the material. Is your mind clearer in the afternoon or evening? Schedule your study session then. Another method is to study at the same time of day that

Copyright © Mometrix Media. You have been licensed one copy of this document for personal use only. Any other reproduction or redistribution is strictly prohibited. All rights reserved.

you will take the test, so that your brain gets used to working on the material at that time and will be ready to focus at test time.

STEP 5: STUDY!

Once you have done all the study preparation, it's time to settle into the actual studying. Sit down, take a few moments to settle your mind so you can focus, and begin to follow your study plan. Don't give in to distractions or let yourself procrastinate. This is your time to prepare so you'll be ready to fearlessly approach the test. Make the most of the time and stay focused.

Of course, you don't want to burn out. If you study too long you may find that you're not retaining the information very well. Take regular study breaks. For example, taking five minutes out of every hour to walk briskly, breathing deeply and swinging your arms, can help your mind stay fresh.

As you get to the end of each chapter or section, it's a good idea to do a quick review. Remind yourself of what you learned and work on any difficult parts. When you feel that you've mastered the material, move on to the next part. At the end of your study session, briefly skim through your notes again.

But while review is helpful, cramming last minute is NOT. If at all possible, work ahead so that you won't need to fit all your study into the last day. Cramming overloads your brain with more information than it can process and retain, and your tired mind may struggle to recall even previously learned information when it is overwhelmed with last-minute study. Also, the urgent nature of cramming and the stress placed on your brain contribute to anxiety. You'll be more likely to go to the test feeling unprepared and having trouble thinking clearly.

So don't cram, and don't stay up late before the test, even just to review your notes at a leisurely pace. Your brain needs rest more than it needs to go over the information again. In fact, plan to finish your studies by noon or early afternoon the day before the test. Give your brain the rest of the day to relax or focus on other things, and get a good night's sleep. Then you will be fresh for the test and better able to recall what you've studied.

STEP 6: TAKE A PRACTICE TEST

Many courses offer sample tests, either online or in the study materials. This is an excellent resource to check whether you have mastered the material, as well as to prepare for the test format and environment.

Check the test format ahead of time: the number of questions, the type (multiple choice, free response, etc.), and the time limit. Then create a plan for working through them. For example, if you have 30 minutes to take a 60-question test, your limit is 30 seconds per question. Spend less time on the questions you know well so that you can take more time on the difficult ones.

If you have time to take several practice tests, take the first one open book, with no time limit. Work through the questions at your own pace and make sure you fully understand them. Gradually work up to taking a test under test conditions: sit at a desk with all study materials put away and set a timer. Pace yourself to make sure you finish the test with time to spare and go back to check your answers if you have time.

After each test, check your answers. On the questions you missed, be sure you understand why you missed them. Did you misread the question (tests can use tricky wording)? Did you forget the information? Or was it something you hadn't learned? Go back and study any shaky areas that the practice tests reveal.

Copyright © Mometrix Media. You have been licensed one copy of this document for personal use only. Any other reproduction or redistribution is strictly prohibited. All rights reserved.

Taking these tests not only helps with your grade, but also aids in combating test anxiety. If you're already used to the test conditions, you're less likely to worry about it, and working through tests until you're scoring well gives you a confidence boost. Go through the practice tests until you feel comfortable, and then you can go into the test knowing that you're ready for it.

Test Tips

On test day, you should be confident, knowing that you've prepared well and are ready to answer the questions. But aside from preparation, there are several test day strategies you can employ to maximize your performance.

First, as stated before, get a good night's sleep the night before the test (and for several nights before that, if possible). Go into the test with a fresh, alert mind rather than staying up late to study.

Try not to change too much about your normal routine on the day of the test. It's important to eat a nutritious breakfast, but if you normally don't eat breakfast at all, consider eating just a protein bar. If you're a coffee drinker, go ahead and have your normal coffee. Just make sure you time it so that the caffeine doesn't wear off right in the middle of your test. Avoid sugary beverages, and drink enough water to stay hydrated but not so much that you need a restroom break 10 minutes into the test. If your test isn't first thing in the morning, consider going for a walk or doing a light workout before the test to get your blood flowing.

Allow yourself enough time to get ready, and leave for the test with plenty of time to spare so you won't have the anxiety of scrambling to arrive in time. Another reason to be early is to select a good seat. It's helpful to sit away from doors and windows, which can be distracting. Find a good seat, get out your supplies, and settle your mind before the test begins.

When the test begins, start by going over the instructions carefully, even if you already know what to expect. Make sure you avoid any careless mistakes by following the directions.

Then begin working through the questions, pacing yourself as you've practiced. If you're not sure on an answer, don't spend too much time on it, and don't let it shake your confidence. Either skip it and come back later, or eliminate as many wrong answers as possible and guess among the remaining ones. Don't dwell on these questions as you continue—put them out of your mind and focus on what lies ahead.

Be sure to read all of the answer choices, even if you're sure the first one is the right answer. Sometimes you'll find a better one if you keep reading. But don't second-guess yourself if you do immediately know the answer. Your gut instinct is usually right. Don't let test anxiety rob you of the information you know.

If you have time at the end of the test (and if the test format allows), go back and review your answers. Be cautious about changing any, since your first instinct tends to be correct, but make sure you didn't misread any of the questions or accidentally mark the wrong answer choice. Look over any you skipped and make an educated guess.

At the end, leave the test feeling confident. You've done your best, so don't waste time worrying about your performance or wishing you could change anything. Instead, celebrate the successful

Copyright © Mometrix Media. You have been licensed one copy of this document for personal use only. Any other reproduction or redistribution is strictly prohibited. All rights reserved.

completion of this test. And finally, use this test to learn how to deal with anxiety even better next time.

Review Video: 5 Tips to Beat Test Anxiety
Visit mometrix.com/academy and enter code: 570656

Important Qualification

Not all anxiety is created equal. If your test anxiety is causing major issues in your life beyond the classroom or testing center, or if you are experiencing troubling physical symptoms related to your anxiety, it may be a sign of a serious physiological or psychological condition. If this sounds like your situation, we strongly encourage you to seek professional help.

Copyright © Mometrix Media. You have been licensed one copy of this document for personal use only. Any other reproduction or redistribution is strictly prohibited. All rights reserved.

Thank You

We at Mometrix would like to extend our heartfelt thanks to you, our friend and patron, for allowing us to play a part in your journey. It is a privilege to serve people from all walks of life who are unified in their commitment to building the best future they can for themselves.

The preparation you devote to these important testing milestones may be the most valuable educational opportunity you have for making a real difference in your life. We encourage you to put your heart into it—that feeling of succeeding, overcoming, and yes, conquering will be well worth the hours you've invested.

We want to hear your story, your struggles and your successes, and if you see any opportunities for us to improve our materials so we can help others even more effectively in the future, please share that with us as well. **The team at Mometrix would be absolutely thrilled to hear from you!** So please, send us an email (support@mometrix.com) and let's stay in touch.

If you'd like some additional help, check out these other resources we offer for your exam:

http://MometrixFlashcards.com/ILTS

Copyright © Mometrix Media. You have been licensed one copy of this document for personal use only. Any other reproduction or redistribution is strictly prohibited. All rights reserved.